Kosovo Divided

Kosovo Divided

Ethnicity, Nationalism and the Struggle for a State

Marius-Ionut Calu

I.B. TAURIS
LONDON • NEW YORK • OXFORD • NEW DELHI • SYDNEY

I.B. TAURIS
Bloomsbury Publishing Plc
50 Bedford Square, London, WC1B 3DP, UK
1385 Broadway, New York, NY 10018, USA
29 Earlsfort Terrace, Dublin 2, Ireland

BLOOMSBURY, I.B. TAURIS and the I.B. Tauris logo are trademarks of Bloomsbury Publishing Plc

First published in Great Britain 2020
This paperback edition published in 2021

Copyright © Marius-Ionut Calu, 2020

Marius-Ionut Calu has asserted his right under the Copyright, Designs and Patents Act, 1988, to be identified as Author of this work.

For legal purposes the Acknowledgements on p. vii constitute an extension of this copyright page.

Cover design by Adriana Brioso

All rights reserved. No part of this publication may be reproduced or transmitted in any form or by any means, electronic or mechanical, including photocopying, recording, or any information storage or retrieval system, without prior permission in writing from the publishers.

Bloomsbury Publishing Plc does not have any control over, or responsibility for, any third-party websites referred to or in this book. All internet addresses given in this book were correct at the time of going to press. The author and publisher regret any inconvenience caused if addresses have changed or sites have ceased to exist, but can accept no responsibility for any such changes.

A catalogue record for this book is available from the British Library.

A catalogue record for this book is available from the Library of Congress.

ISBN: HB: 978-1-7883-1501-2
PB: 978-0-7556-3724-9
ePDF: 978-1-8386-0660-2
eBook: 978-1-8386-0661-9

Typeset by Integra Software Services Pvt. Ltd.

To find out more about our authors and books visit www.bloomsbury.com and sign up for our newsletters.

Contents

List of Illustrations	vi
Acknowledgements	vii
List of Abbreviations	viii
Political Parties in Kosovo	x
Introduction	1
1 Statebuilding and Multiethnic Governance	15
2 Post-conflict and Post-independence Statebuilding in Kosovo	51
3 The Integration, Accommodation and Protection of Kosovo Serbs	81
4 Non-dominant Minorities in Kosovo	107
5 Managing Diversity through Decentralization	145
Conclusion: The Struggle Continues	187
Notes	199
Bibliography	237
Index	250

List of Illustrations

Figure

1 State responses to group (ethnocultural) diversity   31

Tables

1 A typology of state-, nation- and democracy-building strategies in multinational polities   32
2 Municipalities with minority communities in majority (excluding North of Kosovo)   160

Acknowledgements

This book is the result of the advice, encouragement and support from many who deserve my thanks and appreciation. I owe a great deal to my PhD supervisor, Adam Fagan. He constantly guided, encouraged, revised and critiqued my work and helped me to remain focused on achieving my goals. His insightful comments and suggestions helped me to establish the overall direction of my research and to identify and express the most valuable ideas and contribution of my work.

My first book is the culmination of a long academic journey and I would like to thank those who, either by directly reviewing my thesis or by commenting during seminar and conference presentations, have advised me or assisted me to clarify and refine my research.

With regards to my fieldwork in Kosovo, I am grateful for the time given by the respondents to my in-depth interviews and I am particularly indebted to Venera Hajrullahu, Taulant Hoxha, Fatmir Curri and Besnike Kocani from Kosovo Civil Society Foundation (KCSF).

Thank you to all my friends and close ones for always being there for me and to my family for their long-distance, continuous support, patience and understanding.

Dedicated to my dearly missed mother, who has never stopped inspiring and guiding my life, my dreams and my ambitions.

List of Abbreviations

CCC	Consultative Council for Communities
CEC	Central Electoral Commission
CoE	Council of Europe
CRIC	Committee on the Rights and Interests of Communities and Returns
CSO	Civil Society Organisations
DCC	Deputy Chairperson for Communities
DMC	Deputy Mayor for Communities
EC	European Commission
ECMI	European Centre for Minority Issues
ECRML	European Charter for Regional or Minority Languages
EU	European Union
EULEX	European Union Rule of Law Mission in Kosovo
FCNM	Framework Convention for the Protection of National Minorities
ICG	International Crisis Group
ICR	International Civil Representative
IPOL	Balkan Policy Institute
HLC	Humanitarian Law Centre
IKS .	Kosovo Stability Initiative
KAS	Kosovo Agency of Statistics
KFOS	Kosovo Foundation for Open Society
KIPRED	Kosovo Institute for Policy Research and Development
KJC	Kosovo Judicial Council
KLGI	Kosovo Local Government Institute
KPC	Kosovo Prosecutorial Council
MCR	Ministry of Communities and Returns
MEST	Ministry of Education, Science and Technology
MHRU	Municipal Human Rights Unit
MRG	Minority Rights Group International
MLGA	Ministry of Local Government Administration
MOCR	Municipal Office for Communities and Returns
NATO	North Atlantic Treaty Organisation

NDI	National Democratic Institute
NHC	Norwegian Helsinki Committee
OCA	Office for Community Affairs
OLC	Office of the Language Commissioner
OSCE	Organization for Security and Co-operation in Europe
PER	Project on Ethnic Relations
POE	Publicly Owned Enterprise
RAE	Roma, Ashkali and Egyptians
RTK	Radio Television of Kosovo
UDHR	Universal Declaration of Human Rights
UN	United Nations
UNDP	United Nations Development Programme
UNMIK	United Nations Interim Administration Mission in Kosovo
USAID	United States Agency for International Development
WB	World Bank

Political Parties in Kosovo

AAK	Alliance for the Future of Kosovo
BSDAK	Bosniak Party of Democratic Action of Kosovo
CDS	Montenegrin Democratic Party
CLS	Montenegrin Liberal Party
CNS	Montenegrin People's Party
GIG	Gora Citizen's Initiative
GIS	Civic Initiative 'Srpska'/G.I. Srpska
GIZ	Citizens Initiative Zavičaj
GIZO	Citizens Initiative Together for Survival
IRDK	New Democratic Initiative for Kosovo
JLS	United Serb List
KDTP	Turkish Democratic Party of Kosovo
KG	Coalition Gora
KNPR	New Kosovo Roma Party
KTAP	Kosovo Turkish Justice Party
KTB	Kosova Türk Birligi
LDK	Democratic League of Kosovo
NDS	New Democratic Party
NI	People's initiative
PAI	Ashkali Party for Integration
PDAK	Democratic Ashkali Party of Kosovo
PDK	Democratic Party of Kosovo
PLE	Liberal Egyptian Party
PREBBK	United Roma Party of Kosovo
SDA	Party of Democratic Action
SKMS	Serbian Party of Kosovo and Metohija
SL	Serbian List
SLS	Independent Liberal Party
SSDS	Serbian Social Democratic Party
VV	Self-determination Movement

Introduction

The presence of minority groups with different ethnic, national, cultural, religious or linguistic identities within almost all contemporary societies has gradually gained more significance for both long-established and new states, particularly in post-conflict, post-communist and postcolonial contexts. Consequently, contemporary processes of state formation have included the *management of diversity* as a highly prioritized task in response to the historical changes in the practice and understanding of the relationship between state and society. In other words, the modern state has become more preoccupied with finding solutions for the integration, accommodation and protection of all its constituent peoples.

Nonetheless, this preoccupation of Western-centric modern statebuilding has been historically shaped by an oxymoronic perception of diversity as an *asset* and as a *burden* at the same time.[1] In this sense, the troubled relations between the nation state model, liberal values, democratic governance, migration, multiculturalism and various processes of globalization continue to dominate some of the key challenges of current international relations. This is evidenced by recent general trends of resurging politics of nationalism, populism, far right, isolationism and inequality, as well as by specific issues like extremism, migrant crisis and spread of civil wars and state fragility. In light of these problems, it is important to continue discussing how the international efforts to export the modern liberal democratic state have founded precarious political environments, hybrid governance and, broadly speaking, 'delusory efficacy and hallucinatory legitimacy'.[2]

This book analyses and measures the impact of adopting a liberal democratic state model that aims to secure unity at the same time with accommodating diversity by looking at the process of statebuilding in post-conflict and post-independence Kosovo. The main research question of this book is: *Why, how and to what extent has Kosovo been able to manage diversity as part of statebuilding by adopting a multiethnic legal and institutional framework designed to integrate, accommodate and protect the ethnic minority groups within its territory?*

Methodologically, the approach is explicitly analytical and interdisciplinary and driven by a set of key questions that are addressed through formal models and theoretical frameworks. The investigation of the contemporary and highly complex situation in Kosovo has made use of detailed case studies and qualitative data analysis consisting, for instance, of the evaluation of the constitution, laws, policy briefs, official local and international documents, treaties, reports, political debates, conferences. The information collected as a result of document-based research is complemented by the original empirical content and rich primary data gathered through fieldwork. More precisely, I triangulated the preliminary research findings as regards post-conflict and post-independence statebuilding in Kosovo by conducting semi-structured and elite interviews, ethnographic work and participant observation. Overall, the research design and methods employed in this book allowed me to reflect on the central elements of nation-building/statebuilding in Kosovo and the particularities of this complex case study, while also discussing its relevance for the general study of the symbiotic relationship between processes of state formation and the management of diversity.

The statebuilding dilemmas discussed throughout this book also apply to the wider global context, as similar solutions have been adopted in neighbouring statebuilding cases like Bosnia-Herzegovina and North Macedonia and in longstanding post-conflict state formation processes in Iraq and Afghanistan. What they all have in common is the perpetual struggle to synchronize liberal democratic norms with conditions of ethno-national, cultural, religious and social diversity. The promise of liberal democratic governance has been the sine qua non of contemporary international interventions, peacebuilding and statebuilding, as evidences by practices designed and conducted by the UN, the EU or the OSCE. The promotion of democracy, good governance, the rule of law, economic development and social equality are typical for these interventions and are intended to ease the local needs while also supporting these societies in creating legitimate and stable governance. But the reality of international interventions can be far apart from their proclaimed intentions in meeting local requirements. To the contrary, the promotion of liberal democracy by the state-centric ideological and institutional framework of interventionism can produce unintended consequences for local societies. In the case of Kosovo, the management of ethnic diversity has been a fundamental challenge after its break-up from

Serbia in the post-conflict and post-independence contexts as reflected by the interplay of three core statebuilding tasks:

1. Developing institutions, implementing the legal framework (institution-building/setting up the constitution, legal framework, democratization) and enshrining core liberal-democratic values
2. Post-ethnic conflict reconciliation through legislative and institutional power-sharing arrangements designed to foster interethnic cooperation and accommodation of minorities (mainly minority Serbs and majority Albanians)
3. The 'generic' integration and protection of all other ethnic minorities (Bosniak, Turkish, Roma, Ashkali, Egyptian, Gorani, Montenegrin and Croat communities).

Kosovo has been the topic of many international controversies and academic debates over the politics of interventionism, international law, ethnic cleansing, peacebuilding and statebuilding, the role of international administrators in post-conflict states, secessionism and the right to self-determination and, most recently, the problems around the 2008 unilateral declaration of independence. Kosovo therefore declared itself an independent state nine years after the 1999 conflict, but the lack of unanimous international recognition[3] continues to divide the international community on the status and future of the province. Although not the focus of this study, this situation is particularly important given that the international community has been involved in all stages of Kosovo's development from intervention (the role of the North Atlantic Treaty Organization (NATO)), peacebuilding/statebuilding (the administration of Kosovo by UNMIK and by the European Union, but also the involvement of OSCE and international donors) and post-independence (the continuing primary role of the EU by including Kosovo within the Europeanization process and also, more specifically, through its EULEX mission). In the meantime, Kosovo has been aiming to foster its international recognition and defend its status[4] while also building up its domestic sovereignty and continuing its transition to a sustainable liberal democracy. In other words, in its post-2008 quest to meet international/EU standards and construct stable, functional and legitimate democratic governance, Kosovo has also continued to have a highly contested statehood, including five EU countries withholding recognition of the entity as an independent state.

Given that the liberal-democratic (nation state) model has become the dominant form of modern political organization of states, it is essential to understand how the mutual relationship between state and society, between rulers and subject, between institutions and people has transformed over time. For instance, the civic homogenizing identity of the nation state model has proven to be more fragile than initially thought, and even in old plural democracies like the UK and Spain, the overarching multinational civic identity has been gradually more contested by its constituent nations. Furthermore, while most Western and other long-established states 'are the result of centuries of context-specific social conflict, historically contingent processes and institutional learning and adaptation',[5] contemporary new states are limited by their little experience of building and consolidating their sovereignty, legitimacy and capacity to offer security, socioeconomic development and justice within its territory and in relation to the other states on international arena. As a result, the ability to manage diversity and the solutions adopted for this purpose are also very different from what more mature states have been practising. In this sense, the recognition, integration and protection of minorities have become essential features of modern liberal-democratic state formation and even more so for contemporary post-ethnic conflict statebuilding cases where political authority needs to be legitimized by all the constituent peoples.

Drawing on Joel Migdal's 'state in society' approach,[6] this book adopts a view of the state as intrinsically embedded in society, thus reflecting the symbiotic state-society relationship confirmed by the mutual capacity to transform each other. From this perspective, the state is both the 'image' of a unitary and clearly bounded political body in control of a given territory and the 'practices' of its different social actors and agencies.[7] The state is not a fixed political entity and it can be seen as a process, as a changing form of political organization responding to the impact of society. Therefore, the analysis of the statebuilding process in Kosovo and of the impact of adopting a multiethnic liberal-democratic state model will be focused on the character of the state-society link. The levels of state strength and legitimacy are tested through an assessment of Kosovo's efforts and capacity to manage diversity and gain the obedience of its population by particularly attempting to integrate, accommodate and protect the rights of its minority communities. Given the important role of minorities in legitimizing a post-conflict state, the promotion and protection of minority rights is a key indicator of Kosovo's willingness and capacity to deliver essential political goods. This becomes a vital responsibility if the state has also experienced major discrimination of a certain ethnic group and a history of ethnic conflict, similar to the case of Kosovo.

Furthermore, this will also help to study Kosovo's efforts to develop domestic sovereignty, which for Stephen Krasner refers to the actual strength of a state's authority, as well as its capacity to use it effectively and secure legitimacy.[8] Therefore, building legitimate domestic sovereignty depends on repairing or preventing social division and a broken state-society link, which is why the integration and protection of ethnic minorities have become fundamental statebuilding objectives. Political consensus and social cohesion are considered to be essential factors that work in favour of building a steady democracy, while political disagreement and deep social division are made responsible for the instability and potential breakdown. When trying to understand what kind of state the international community has attempted to build in Kosovo, a useful model is that of the *democratic legal authority*, which according to Richard Ponzio is 'based on a belief, by the people in a geographically defined polity, in the legality of democratically enacted rules and the right of democratic authorities to issue commands under such rules'.[9] If this is the objective of post-conflict statebuilding missions, then the understanding of authority will impact on the functionality of statebuilding processes. However, the 'gap in conceptions of authority'[10] between international officials and the local population could represent the key challenge to all contemporary attempts to implement democratic legal authority in post-conflict societies. This is related to the concerns over the character of the under-construction domestic sovereignty and the risks of destabilizing democratization and reactivating latent tensions. These are just some of the reasons why dealing with diversity in post-conflict societies is more challenging than the situation of a plural society that has not experienced a recent violent conflict.

The critique of contemporary statebuilding needs to look more carefully at fundamental differences between mature-plural-democratic states without any recent conflicts and young-plural post-conflict democracies that are importing external models of democratic governance. Therefore, the management of diversity has been a problem for the development and proliferation of liberal-democratic norms of governance, it has been the source of external and domestic violent conflicts in the peoples' quest for self-determination and it has then become a fundamental task for contemporary statebuilding. In the contexts of decolonization and then of the collapse of communism, a large number of ethno-national groups within multinational states and of minority groups have asked for full recognition of their rights to political participation, equality and protection of their identities, which has meant either autonomy on ethnic lines or self-determination. Contemporary new 'polities' have experienced the challenge of internal disputes over establishing what the identity of the political community and their members should be. This state legitimacy issue has been described by Linz and Stepan as the *stateness problem*,[11] originating in the relationship between the state, the nation and democracy and the difficulties in establishing territorial boundaries and the conditions of citizenship.

While nationalism offers the possibility of defining the demos, this may not include the entire population or all the constituent peoples of the state. When 'stateness' and 'nationness' overlap, building democracy and legitimate governance is expected to occur more easily, while when they are not in congruity, the process is likely to be more challenging and unstable. For instance, democratization in post-communist countries like Poland, Czech Republic or Hungary is relevant example of the first situation, whereas the conflicts and instability of states from former Yugoslavia illustrate 'the severe consequences for states beset by contentious multinationalism and weak citizen-institutional loyalties'.[12] Therefore, given that popular sovereignty requires the democratic legitimization of political authority and embodies the interdependency between state and society, *social cohesion* has become an essential element for building stable and legitimate liberal democratic governance. But securing unity and social cohesion has proven to be more complicated for contemporary young democratic states, in contrast not only with long-established democracies, but also with the previous regimes that used to govern these transitional societies. Furthermore, the absence of a strong political authority has also been an issue for the most recent examples of statebuilding in post-conflict societies that have been under the administration of external/international actors. In a similar fashion to former colonies and former communist societies, post-conflict societies have had to accept an external form of authority that did not need (direct) popular legitimization while having to develop non-coercive means of governance. The common problem of all these three contexts of contemporary statebuilding is that they have produced states with little capacity to monopolize violence and secure social cohesion. Therefore, the understanding and practice of state sovereignty in new plural liberal democracies has been challenged by the absence of a bond between state and society.

The *management of diversity* has become both a challenge and an objective for contemporary processes of state formation. On the one hand, it has been a challenge primarily because it complicates the task to secure unity for the liberal-democratic nation state model built around the norms of popular sovereignty, social solidarity and reliance on a dominant nation. On the other hand, it has become a key objective for statebuilding not only because of the social-demographic and political changes of the twentieth century, but also because of the increasing number of internal (ethnic) divisions, conflicts and civil wars. These issues have characterized the ex-colonial and ex-communist societies aiming to adopt the liberal state model but struggling to synchronize the (proposed) state-society relationship with the ground realities. Challenges for contemporary post-conflict statebuilding practices have been generally studied within the critique of liberal interventionism.[13] This literature has been focused on the imposing character of international involvement in peacekeeping and post-conflict administration such as the United Nations-led missions in Bosnia-Herzegovina, Kosovo, East Timor, Iraq, South Sudan or Afghanistan.

From this perspective, the international involvement in Kosovo has started with a controversial humanitarian intervention, followed by the imposition of a multiethnic state model and the administration of post-conflict reconstruction. This suggests that the international community has become responsible for the flaws of statebuilding in Kosovo and for creating a certain degree of external dependency in the detriment of democratization, local ownership and domestic legitimacy. International administration has thus been identified as the key problem because it installs an exogenous source of legitimacy and undermines domestic sovereignty. The post-conflict statebuilding literature underlines the non-democratic and illiberal character of liberal interventionism in its paradoxical quest to spread liberal-democratic ideals through statebuilding missions. At the same time, this criticism also questions the self-proclaimed universality of an externally generated political model. The identification of the flaws of international statebuilding is not, however, always supported by endogenous, case-specific and convincing explanations for the multifaceted causes of why states fail to develop sustainable democratic governance or to achieve long-term reconciliation and inter-ethnic cooperation.

Moreover, in the case of Kosovo its unresolved status is often overemphasized and used to explain almost all deficiencies of the statebuilding process, despite the fact that scholars[14] have observed that processes of democratic transition and institution-building are not unique to established states and can occur outside the state system as confirmed by the post-1999 *standards before status* approach in Kosovo. This highlights the dynamic character of the state under the impact of a multitude of external and internal processes. Furthermore, Krasner's taxonomy of sovereignty is also relevant here because despite the absence of international/legal sovereignty, Kosovo has developed domestic sovereignty. This is extremely important for my book's aim to contribute to these debates by analysing the capacity and willingness of Kosovo to integrate and accommodate its minorities as potential indicators of the legitimacy and strength of domestic sovereignty.

The encouragement of local autonomy for self-governing capacity can be one of the solutions for progress and the development of internal popular legitimacy.

However, in practice this may not work given that the problem of post-conflict societies to develop a democratic legal authority has more significant and complex origins. Furthermore, liberal-democratic measures and standards that define contemporary statebuilding are implemented improperly not necessarily because they are imposed and given a different character, but because they are in conflict with the internal fracture between the state and its population and because of the incompatibility between institutional/legal solutions and case-specific circumstances. The literature that this book puts forth includes therefore the critique of liberal interventionism, which emphasizes the changing character of sovereignty and the society-state rift so as to explain why contemporary statebuilding has a paradoxical effect of state weakening and state failure. I highlight that a competing literature[15] has been emerging with the aim of stimulating more consistent explanations of state weakness. This can be done by also focusing on the legacy of the past in relation to the absence of social cohesion and a strong state-society relationship. The aim of this theoretical comparison will be to show the importance of identifying valid causes for malfunctions in statebuilding by complementing exogenous explanations with endogenous factors.

Indeed, Kosovo represents a unique endeavour and a very ambitious case of statebuilding not just because of its internationally contested statehood,[16] the circumstances of the 1999 war and the subsequent international administration, but also because of the impact of the dual legacy of communism and conflict. My research thus also explores why the literature on statebuilding in Kosovo has generally overlooked the role of endogenous factors[17] that may obstruct the aims of building a multiethnic liberal-democratic state capable of securing unity and managing a plural society. In this sense, 'the twin and deeply intertwined dynamics of post-Communist and post-conflict transition'[18] have simultaneously complicated the state-society relationship in Kosovo and the externally led efforts to establish a multiethnic polity. This dual legacy has been characterized by illiberal practices and understanding of governance, substate forms of authority, ethnic, social and political fragmentation, the absence of national cohesion, economic dependency, institutional weakness and security issues. The combination of exogenous and endogenous factors indicates why a particular type of statebuilding has been developed in the contemporary context of post-conflict societies, which in the case of Kosovo has a multiethnic political-institutional model at the forefront of the process. Nevertheless, this interplay also helps to analyse the difference between theory and practice, between legislation and implementation and between intended and unintended consequences of adopting and implementing a particular state model.

Post-conflict statebuilding in Kosovo has been an externally driven multifaceted process aiming to build peace, stabilize and reconcile ethnic tensions and to develop at the same time a functional liberal-democratic form of governance. Therefore, the immediate goal was to pacify the relations between Albanians and Serbs while keeping the province under the administration of the international community (UNMIK mission) until its future legal status would be resolved. Maintaining peace and achieving sustainable reconciliation has become part of the liberal statebuilding process. In Kosovo, this has consisted of adopting and implementing of a multiethnic liberal state model aiming to develop the capacity to secure unity, perform the main tasks of a functional state and also manage ethnic diversity through a set of far-reaching legal and institutional framework for the integration, accommodation and protection of minorities.

For the purpose of this book, a minority is a group or a community that identifies itself as different by virtue of a shared ethnic, national, religious, cultural, linguistic or communal identity and has historically been marginalized by policies and practices of a state, and normally also constitutes a numerical minority within a state with a majority group. It is therefore crucial for the study of the management of plurality during statebuilding to establish the official position of the state as regards ethnic diversity and the relationship between majority and minority groups. A state may therefore recognize the dominance of an ethnic majority, it may associate the national identity with that of the majority group, it may disregard ethnic identities by promoting an overreaching civic identity or it may actually declare itself multiethnic/multinational/multicultural with a non-partisan national identity despite the existence of a majority group. Furthermore, this book will analyse the extent to which this intersection of pro-communality and pro-distinctiveness rationales of state formation may result in an oxymoronic form of statebuilding in Kosovo. By looking at post-conflict power-sharing models of governance for diverse societies, I will also explore different ways in which minority rights can be institutionalized within constitutional and legal frameworks and how this is reflected by the implementation of territorial and non-territorial mechanisms. The suitability of different models and solutions for ethnic conflict regulation and management of plurality in Kosovo is assessed by taking up a number of issues such as the following:

- Is the multiethnic political and institutional setup of Kosovo an accurate representation of its actual social configuration?
- Do all minorities benefit equally and proportionally from the complex set of provisions and rights?
- How practical and beneficial are these measures?

Through an exploration of these dilemmas, this study aims to highlight that the understanding and practice of measures adopted to manage diversity in Kosovo vary among different minority communities depending on many endogenous factors and on their will and capacity to assume their rights. The single focus of this study on post-independence Kosovo and the evidence presented limit its scope to the particular analysis of the adoption and implementation of rights and provisions for the integration, accommodation and protection of minority communities in Kosovo. However, this case study can also be used to illustrate the complexity of contemporary post-conflict statebuilding and the changing character of the practices and understanding of state formation under the impact of case-specific circumstances. Contemporary statebuilding processes have included the acceptance and respect for diversity as an indispensable element within their rationale of how to construct a functional, all-inclusive liberal-democratic polity. The character of statebuilding in Kosovo reflects the intersection of the traditional liberal democratic (nation-) state model requiring some form of national cohesion (civic identity), with the contemporary focus on distinctiveness and, more specifically, on the accommodation of different ethnic communities coexisting within the same state.

With the purpose of arguing my case that local particularities need much more consideration by both policymakers and scholars of post-ethnic conflict statebuilding, this study identifies both intended and unintended consequences of implementing the multilayered institutional and legal framework for managing multiethnicity in Kosovo. The asymmetrical impact of the top-down measures among different communities and the risk of further political, linguistic, social and territorial segregation and marginalization may have a fundamental role in the long-term effects of statebuilding. Overall, this book aims to explain why regardless of how far reaching the rights and institutional provisions for ethnic minorities may be, they cannot compensate for a sustainable de facto integration and accommodation of these communities. By the same token, Kosovo's de jure identity and image as a multiethnic liberal-democratic state is not necessarily an accurate reflection of the complexities of ground realities and actual societal practices.

Outline of the book

This book takes up the central questions and arguments raised so far through a dissemination of the particular model of integrating, accommodating and protecting ethnic minorities in post-conflict and post-independence Kosovo and of its relevance for the general study of why and how statebuilding includes the management of diversity within its key tasks.

Chapter 1 will examine the conceptual framework that investigates why the management of diversity has become a vital part of modern liberal democratic state formation. In other words, it will discuss the contemporary statebuilding dilemma of securing unity and managing diversity at the same time. For this purpose, I look at different definitions and dimensions of the concepts of state sovereignty and legitimacy and identify the state-society relationship as the core element of modern liberal-democratic governance. At the same time, this chapter examines the different models of governance in plural societies that aim to integrate, accommodate or protect groups with different identities. I consider the distinctions between integrationists and accommodationist strategies and the different power-sharing models of democratic governance that have also inspired statebuilding in Kosovo.

The empirical component of this book starts with **Chapter 2**, which provides a historical account of the political context before and after the 1999 conflict and an overview of the post-independence complex far-reaching legislation and measures taken for adopting a multiethnic framework. Firstly, it introduces the post-conflict role of the international administration and the fundamental problems determined by the unsettled status of the province. Secondly, it investigates the extent to which the necessary democratic link between state and society was undermined by the top-down character of international administration. And thirdly, this chapter discusses how the post-independence legal framework provides extensive minority rights at central and local levels of governance.

Chapter 3 analyses the situation of the Serb community in Kosovo. As the largest minority community, and politically the most difficult ethnic group to integrate within the new state, it seems appropriate to begin an assessment of the efforts, solutions and framework to manage diversity in Kosovo from this empirical perspective. While emphasizing that under the guidance of the international community Serbs have been the main target of designing the multiethnic model of governance, this chapter also examines the interplay of progress and problems characterizing the Serb community after independence.

I discuss how the implementation process reveals the persistence of important shortcomings as regards the sustainable integration of Kosovo Serbs. For this purpose, this chapter looks at their political participation and representation and then examines the socioeconomic challenges that influence the effectiveness of the de jure provisions. Given the research findings presented here, I argue that while there have been some concrete results with the integration of Kosovo Serbs, the legislative framework and the formal provisions for protecting minority rights cannot fully compensate for practical needs.

Chapter 4 examines the situation of non-dominant minority communities in Kosovo and illustrates how promoting and protecting minority rights in Kosovo through legal and political provisions intersects with the complexity of needs and requirements coming from different minority groups. This chapter presents the situation of each of the non-dominant minorities in Kosovo starting with the Bosniaks and the Turks and ending with the smallest, Montenegrins and Croats. Overall, the circumstances revealed in this chapter expose how the implementation of minority rights has been creating a hierarchy among the different ethnic groups. Moreover, this chapter argues that the inconsistency regarding minority rights protection towards the smaller communities in Kosovo indicates a potential discrepancy between unfitting measures that could become counterproductive and cause segregation instead of integration.

Finally, **Chapter 5** looks at decentralization as a main mechanism adopted to integrate, accommodate and protect minorities at the local level of governance in Kosovo. In continuation of the argument that the multiethnic legislative and institutional framework in Kosovo has largely been put in place to address the Serb minority, this chapter discusses arguments that show both positive and negative aspects of combining decentralization with integration and accommodation of minorities. By considering the demographic, economic, administrative and political situations of different municipalities, this chapter will explore post-decentralization benefits and challenges related to the management of diversity.

The **Conclusion** will link the case-specific elements with the relevant literature and will discuss some implications for current and future work in this area of study. Firstly, it will evaluate the interplay of intended and unintended consequences of implementing the legal-institutional framework for managing minorities in post-independence Kosovo. Secondly, it will measure the concrete impact on the situation of all communities and on the cohesion of the state and society. Thirdly, the conclusion will aim to explain how, why and to what extent the multiethnic liberal-democratic model imported by Kosovo has been transformed and limited by local idiosyncrasies. Lastly, the conclusion will also discuss the relevance of the case study to the current literature on the symbiotic relationship between processes of state formation and the management of diversity, and the links of these phenomena with similar studies of the region of the Western Balkans, but also in relation to the perennial problems of statebuilding in the Middle East and Africa.

1

Statebuilding and Multiethnic Governance

This chapter will set out the theoretical framework employed in the analysis of Kosovo's liberal democratic state model of governing its multiethnic society in the post-conflict and post-independence context. At the same time, it will complement the empirical study of my book focused on the gap between de facto and de jure integration of Serb and non-Serb minorities and the protection of their rights at both central and local levels of governance. One of the overall tasks of this book is to analyse the difference between the ideal type of contemporary states (which focuses, among others, on the integration and protection of ethnic minorities) and the actual character of the under-construction state in Kosovo as revealed by the mixture of intended and unintended consequences of adopting and implementing a multiethnic institutional and legal framework (actual level of integration and the risk of reversing or causing segregation).

Therefore, reviewing the principles of sovereignty, political authority and legitimacy is crucial for starting a valid assessment of the functionality of statebuilding. The character of sovereignty being built in Kosovo under the influence of the international community, the source and legitimacy of state authority and the effectiveness of governance are all indispensable elements that will help me to examine Kosovo's determination and capacity to perform its key state functions and manage diversity at the same time.

The modern liberal democratic state

The conceptualization and practice of state formation or statebuilding has changed over history but the origins of the modern liberal state can be traced back to the ideas found in the social contract theory, the Weberian view of the state as a 'corporate group'[1] and the political theory that focuses on the juridical statehood of a state.[2] The modern state as a solution for the issue of political order was famously explained by Charles Tilly's representation of 'war-making and state-making as organized crime', based on the idea that security is essentially offered in return for extraction.[3] Altogether, these different conceptions on the modern state formation indicate three core functions and responsibilities of the state as a provider of security, representation and welfare.[4] Hence, the capacity and will of states to perform these main functions of governance have permanently been vital elements of modern state formation.

> State formations is defined as the extension of the effective powers of this state over a population within an identifiable geographical area on the one hand, and progressive political integration of the population into the exercise of state powers on the other.[5]

Most significant, however, is the idea developed by the liberal tradition of political thought that state formation depends on establishing a social contract between rulers and subjects. This has subsequently made legitimacy a vital element of modern statebuilding. The key elements of modern statebuilding that this first section has already introduced are state's functions/responsibilities and state's legitimacy authorized by its subjects. In order to evaluate the state model for contemporary statebuilding, it is thus essential to examine not only why the state encompasses public institutions for extraction, security or representation but also why it is more extensive than government and it is subject to the relationship with its citizens.[6] Given the modern argument for a contractual-based state formation, it is important to highlight that the self-perpetuating, inalienable, indivisible and absolute idea of sovereignty is, in this way, established by an authority awarded by the people. The relationship between rulers and subjects, between institutions and people, between state and society is at the heart of understanding the origins of the modern state.

On the one hand, *external* sovereignty relates to a state's position in the international order and its right and capacity to act as an independent and autonomous entity. This is used by international law and it is echoed by the concepts of 'national sovereignty' and 'sovereign state' when discussing the relationship between states and the idea of non-interference in the domestic affairs of sovereign governance.[7] On the other hand, the *internal* dimension of sovereignty refers to the highest authority within a state that, as Max Weber famously described it, possesses the monopoly over the legitimate use of physical force within a defined territory. Therefore, in opposition to the state of nature (anarchy), a sovereign state has an internal political framework characterized by centralization and hierarchy.[8] Nonetheless, internal sovereignty 'is exercised within the borders of the state and refers to the relationship between sovereign power and the subjects of that power,[9] from which arises the question of (popular) legitimacy to exercise authority. The idea of *domestic sovereignty*[10] confirms the exclusive right of a state to exercise its supreme political authority (executive, legislative and judiciary) over a defined territory and a group of people (nation) and the effectiveness of these authority structures. Domestic sovereignty is a key concept for this book in trying to examine how the accommodation of diversity has become a key element of statebuilding so that all its constituent peoples legitimize the political authority of the state.

The state-in-society approach

> The state should not be taken as a free-standing entity, whether and agent, instrument, organization or structure, located apart from and opposed to another entity called society.[11]

In his *State in Society: Studying How States and Societies Transform and Constitute One Another*, Joel S. Migdal[12] offered a thorough analysis of the relationship between state and society and argued that it is imperative to avoid analysing the state as a separate entity from society. He considered that the main problem with theorizing the state as a stand-alone organization is that it can exaggerate its capabilities, while 'an approach that focuses on the state in society, on the process of state engagement with other social forces highlights the mutual transformation of the state and other social groups, as well as limitation of the state'.[13] Migdal looks at the patterns of domination and change as explained, on the one hand, by the *social-system* approach[14] and, on the other hand, by *state-oriented* theorists who have followed on Weber's interpretation of the state. While the first approach puts emphasis on the set of social values and norms that connects elites and institutions from the social, political, religious and economic realms (normative solidarity of the West), the second approach portrays the state as an autonomous organization with extraordinary means to dominate: 'Through law, bureaucracy, violence, and other means, the argument goes, the modern state has reshaped people's behaviour and, by extension, their sense of who they are.'[15]

Moreover, Weber described the rational, goal-oriented character of the state symbolizing a relation of domination regulated by the principle of legitimate violence: 'the modern state is a compulsory association which organizes domination'.[16] As Migdal highlights in his analysis of the definition of the state, Weber was very careful to include the quality of 'successfully' monopolizing violence so as to show that this is not a feature of every state. In matter of fact, Weber noted 'how limited the experience of states *successfully* centralizing and monopolizing violent means actually was'.[17] From this perspective, in comparison with the ideal version of the Weberian state, in practice there can only be one type of state: *the limited state*. In response, Migdal puts forward a state-in-society approach that offers an alternative definition of the state as: 'a field of power marked by the use and threat of violence and shaped by (1) the image of a coherent, controlling organization in a territory, which is a representation of the people bounded by that territory, and (2) the actual practice of its multiple parts'.[18] As a result, states are in practice determined by two elements, image and practice. *Image* refers to the internal and external perception of states as the chief and suitable rule maker within its territory and *practices* represent 'the routine performance of state actors and agencies'.[19] The latter may reinforce or weaken the *image* of the state and at the same time it may bolster or neutralize what Migdal describes as territorial and social boundaries. Given the key aim of this book is to evaluate the process of building state-society cohesion (securing unity) while also accommodating diversity through a multiethnic model of governance, I intend to adopt this view of the Kosovo's dual character shaped by the interplay of state *image* and *practices*.[20]

The nation state

> The nation-state, in the form in which we know it, is a rather recent phenomenon. It represents the coincidence in space of a number of principles of social and economic organization. It is the primary focus of collective identity, reinforced and transmitted through culture and socialization. This collective identity in turn provides the basis for social solidarity.[21]

The relationship between the state and its subjects was at the core of the development of the modern state as the political idea of *nation* became more significant concomitantly with the emergence of the sovereign state. The people living inside the borders of the same state were becoming more aware of the fact that they belonged to a national (political) community, that they shared a common history and most importantly that they had common interests that they could defend better as part of a state.[22] A nation can be defined as 'a human group conscious of forming a community, sharing a common culture, attached to a clearly demarcated territory, having a common past and a common project for the future, and claiming the right to self-rule'.[23] Therefore, the key attribute of the nation as a political community has been its claim to self-determination, the right to decide its political fate based on a common will resulted from a sense of unity among members of the same nation. Consequently, in the eighteenth century took place the significant transition from monarch sovereignty to nation or peoples' sovereignty.

The issue of legitimacy has therefore been introduced in political theory in relation to the transition from direct rule to representative government, which introduces the separation between the 'real' holders of legitimacy (the governed) and the formal holders (the elected). Nevertheless, since the French Revolution the civic/ethnic dichotomy has been attached to the idea of 'nation', which has come to mean either *political community* or *cultural community*.[24] The issue of legitimacy has since been used to make the distinction between a *civic nation* (political community) legitimized by the principle of *equality* and an *ethnic nation* (cultural community) legitimized by *cultural distinctness*. It has been however more difficult to clearly separate these principles in the practice of statebuilding as the political and cultural types of nation 'cannot be empirically dissociated in concrete cases, since, [...] at the heart of every nationalism lies a "profound dualism"'.[25] With the rise of the nation state and the modern model of liberal democracy, the people (the nation) were empowered to decide the fate of the state (form of governance, institutions, laws and rulers), which also meant that it became more important to remain or develop as a cohesive/undivided nation with a common, general will. Therefore, the liberal doctrine of popular sovereignty developed the argument that 'the authority of the final word resides in the political will or consent of the people of an independent state'.[26]

However, it is essential to say that the idea of nation was interpreted as a 'homogeneous people'. In other words, the origins of the modern liberal democratic state vested power in the hands of a dominant people or nation, which meant that the (homogeneous) nation state had to face the immediate challenge of securing a unitary national identity. In this sense, the nation state was developed as a 'modern institution, characterized by the formation of a kind of state that has the monopoly of what it claims is the legitimate use of force within a demarcated territory and that seeks to unite the people subject to its rule by means of cultural homogenization'.[27] By contrast, the ethnocultural complexity of many modern societies has been constantly modifying and growing since the second part of the twentieth century when new states started emerging in the postcolonial, post-communist and post-conflict contexts. This has complicated the claim that states and nations are and should be congruent and has further challenged the task of nation states to maintain and develop national unity based on an overriding collective identity.

The main question that I want to raise here is concerning the modern liberal democratic states' increasing determination to manage and accommodate diversity. Statebuilding has had a complex task of merging and securing the unity of the psychological, cultural, territorial, political and historical dimensions of a nation,[28] while also having to consider the role of *minority peoples*, which are 'culturally distinct groups in plural societies who seek equal rights, opportunities, and access to power within existing political communities'.[29] Diversity has become over time an increasingly important challenge and the solutions for this have also evolved in reply to different contexts and objectives of statebuilding practices. In other words, different answers have been given to the question of how to deal effectively with diversity, of which assimilation and accommodation have been two dominant policies.

Externally led statebuilding and sovereignty from above

The common feature of contemporary statebuilding has become its externally driven nature, be that as part of decolonization, post-communist transition to liberal democracy or as part of liberal interventionism and peacebuilding missions. In the context of decolonization, the Western/Eurocentric origins of state formation were immediately challenged by the mission to align people and territory: 'It is often problematic, both politically and morally, either to redraw territorial borders or to relocate populations in an effort to achieve alignment. The first raises the questions of partition or secession, the second questions of forced population transfers or what has come to be called ethnic cleansing.'[30] International/external statebuilders have shown great incapacity to avoid either internal or external contestation of new states. Thus, it should come as a no surprise that after two decades since the 1999 NATO intervention, the emergence of discussions about territorial swap and 'correction of border' are once again threatening the stability of Kosovo and the entire Western Balkans.[31]

The link between the people and the state, between the nation and the political authority, required reinterpretation, leading to the transformation of the character of both territorial sovereignty and popular sovereignty. It is thus essential to indicate that the consensus within international relations regarding the universality of the sovereignty of the nation state and the inviolability of borders has actually been a factor of perennial division and conflict between different ethnic, racial, cultural or linguistic groups. Consequently, the mobilization, sometimes violent, of groups based on their different identities has not been as much of a challenge or an obstacle for contemporary statebuilding as it has been its direct consequence. While state formation in the Western world took centuries, 'western state forms were "delivered" like products to many parts of the Global South in a relatively short time span during the era of decolonisation'.[32] However, the sovereignty of these new states was instantly undermined not only by the perpetual dependency on external guidance but also by the divided character of these societies.[33]

Without a link between society and state, the character of domestic sovereignty in liberal democratic nation states (legitimized and developed out of collective will) had to be reconstructed. The postcolonial critique[34] emphasizes here that the Western-centric norms of sovereignty must have predicted the difficulties for political self-creation in the absence of positive sovereignty: 'This idea that states can fail is obviously the precursor to the idea that states need to be rebuilt.'[35] Postcolonial statebuilding was an externally driven top-down process that prioritized the construction of the state as an institution designed to govern the people within its borders under the umbrella of an artificial (civic) identity. These 'people(s)' were however detached from the identity and authority of these new *state-nations* as they represented a complex mixture of different ethnic and cultural groups.[36]

In the absence of self-government and local ownership capacity, the ex-colonial states became *quasi-states*: 'Their populations do not enjoy many of the advantages traditionally associated with independent statehood. Their governments are often deficient in the political will, institutional authority, and organised power to protect human rights or provide socio-economic welfare. [...] empirical statehood in large measure still remains to be built.'[37] The formal declaration of independence was associated with the formation of states by both political elites and the international community, disregarding the many challenges that statebuilding still faced.

In this context, the accommodation of diversity becomes more than a task of statebuilding meant to secure social cohesion and popular legitimacy. It also represents a critical condition for the aim of new states to obtain the endorsement of the international community and to be recognized as strong states capable of monopolizing violence within their borders despite the diverse character of their societies. Quasi-states struggle to guarantee the control over their societies and develop a form of political authority deriving from 'collective consciousness',[38] which means that sovereignty as control is prioritized over sovereignty as responsibility.

> In so far as sovereignty is the exercise of the general will, the idea of sovereigns being responsible for their citizens is merely tautologous. Insofar as sovereignty is accountable to external power, it means that the sovereign is evidently not supreme, and therefore, logically speaking, not sovereign.[39]

With the end of the Cold War the external restraints of the United States and of the Soviet Union were lifted, but in return the new situation revealed even more the fragile domestic structure of ex-colonial and ex-socialist states. Various factors like resurgent identity politics, the weakening of intergroup linkages, the determination to stop state repressiveness, and the flow of refugees across borders have contributed to a revised view of the legitimate claims of the state upon society.[40] In the new international context, the profound administrative weaknesses in many developing countries could not be obscured anymore by the legal form of state sovereignty.[41]

Contemporary statebuilding outside the Western world has thus distanced itself from the traditional model and has developed different objectives, different mechanisms, different structures, different distribution of power and different state-society relationships. Unlike the world in which the European states came of age, postcolonial and post-communist states emerged within a context 'characterised by external superpowers with both incentives and capabilities to maintain a stable international order and by international norms that discouraged both territorial conquest and secession'.[42] As a result, in contrast to the traditional model that required resources and capacity to survive external competition while building up their strength, contemporary statebuilding has been dealing with states that have weak institutions and limited resources, vulnerable to internal threats and unable to contain internal violence.[43]

The case of Kosovo too falls into the paradigm of contemporary liberal statebuilding, where the absence of a strong state-society link is a constant challenge for the processes of democratization, institution-building and the development of domestic sovereignty. In this context, the task of building an inclusive state is very much dependent on the central governments' capacity and will to put together a political regime that can promote, respect and assure an effective participation of minorities in the exercise of power.

Post-conflict statebuilding: The exogenous perspective

Contemporary international liberal post-conflict statebuilding missions have been heavily criticized[44] not only for their externally imposed character but also for not achieving their *liberal peace* goals and, paradoxically, perpetuating or even producing *state failure* or *state weakness*. Given the paramount role of managing diversity in post-(ethnic)conflict reconciliation and statebuilding contexts such as Kosovo, it is helpful to see why the success or failure of this task can also be indicative of how strong or weak a state is and, consequently, to study the impact of *externally driven* contemporary statebuilding missions. The purpose is not only to see why contemporary statebuilding produces weak states, but also to try to understand how and why post-conflict states are, in Migdal's words, 'limited' by their inability to secure unity, develop political authority and build popular legitimacy by accommodating all its constituent peoples.

While peacekeeping missions started during the Cold War with the purpose of resolving conflicts between states, the concepts of *peacebuilding* and *statebuilding* have become central for discussing international intervention in post-conflict countries in the last three decades. Peacebuilding has many definitions and can have different meanings for different actors. For example, Lederach considered:

> The process of building peace must rely on and operate within a framework and a time frame defined by sustainable transformation ... a sustainable transformative approach suggests that the key lies in the relationship of the involved parties, with all that the term encompasses at the psychological, spiritual, social, economic, political and military levels.[45]

This suggests that peacebuilding must not look only at the immediate post-conflict problems, but instead to try to adopt a long-term strategy without neglecting factors of transformation. Peacebuilding in this sense must be able to predict and permanently ready to adapt to new challenges that may occur at different societal levels. Lederach's definition is good starting point for the discussion of post-conflict societies as it underlines that peacebuilding depends on the evolution of the relationship between the parties involved in the process and helps differentiate between imposing and cooperating logics of peacebuilding.

Liberal peacebuilding

In the broader context where the international community has tried to eliminate the root causes of conflict, to promote human security and to create a stable peace,[46] liberal peacebuilding supports various processes like democratization, establishing a legislative framework, equal rights, free elections and the development of civil society. The overarching aim has been to spread *liberal peace* by creating states organized around these liberal principles designed to maintain domestic and external stability. Therefore, peacebuilding missions have attempted to transplant and nurture these features, but by 'exhibiting their own brand of shock therapy, international peacebuilders attempt to transform nearly all features of the state and society, accomplishing in a matter of months what took decades in the West'.[47]

The normative model of liberal peace highlights the role of the decision-making process within states to explain the absence of violent conflicts between democracies. If decision-makers support liberal democratic norms, then in resolving conflicts they prioritize 'compromise, respecting the rights and continued existence of opponents'.[48] In addition, given the reciprocal trust between democracies that they follow the same norms, incertitude can derive from the lower level of political stability in *young democracies*.[49] Some of the problems that young democracies have to face are the role played by the elites who had had access to power in the previous regime (autocracy, for instance), imperfect and immature institutions,[50] or in general a political system with a democratic structure that lacks the experience and knowledge to implement the required norms.

These ideas have been materialized during post–Cold War peacebuilding operations like those in Bosnia, Kosovo, Afghanistan, Iraq, Panama or East Timor. The emphasis has constantly been on exporting liberal norms: central role of liberty, representation, constitutions, progress, development, rights. However, the implementation of these principles has been troublesome as indicated by three key dimensions of peacebuilding: (a) creating *stability* (focus on the security/military factors – eliminate sources of conflict), (b) the restoration of state *institutions* and (c) the *socioeconomic* dimension (develop the socioeconomic infrastructure and underpin economic development).[51]

Not only Peacebuilding scholars like Michael Barnett,[52] who focuses on improving the liberal model, but also critical scholars such as Thomas Carothers[53] and Roland Paris[54] have concluded that, in general, the second dimension referring to *building state institutions* has been neglected by peacebuilding activities in comparison with the other two dimensions. For this reason, the literature on post-conflict peacebuilding has underlined that peacebuilders are more concerned about the kind of state that they try to construct, thus the preference for a 'liberal state, which respects human rights; protects the rule of law; constrained by representative institutions, a vigilant media, and periodic elections; and protects markets'.[55] However, as critics[56] of externally driven statebuilding have observed, even though these kinds of peacebuilding projects aim to establish liberal peace, they often end up by regenerating the conditions for conflict.

Also in search of a new type of peacebuilding is the 'institutionalization before liberalization' (IBL) strategy developed by Roland Paris. While he agrees with the Wilsonian argument that market democracies tend to consolidate peace both domestically and internationally, he opposes the methods generally employed by peacebuilding missions of the 1990s to reach this goal.[57] More precisely, the aim of quickly building liberal market democracies has often increased the likelihood of renewed violence in post-conflict societies as result of stimulating the level of societal competition while lacking institutions capable of containing tensions within peaceful bounds. Paris suggests that the focus should be on building effective institutions prior to economic and political liberalization. This strategy would be more complex and less democratic, but it would be a necessary effort so as to consolidate peace and avoid the cost of lives and material resources produced by a potential escalation of violence.

The high instability of the post-conflict societies justifies from this perspective why political and economic freedoms should be limited in the short run.[58] For instance, quick elections may jeopardize the goal of establishing a liberal democracy because the winners may actually use their power to control institutions, undermine democratic principles of governance and possibly foster populist and nationalist sentiments to gain electoral support. This argument has also been clearly put forward by Susan Woorward, who has written extensively on statebuilding and democratization in the Balkans:

> Not only is democracy promoted to satisfy the foreign policy and international security goals of outside powers and interests rather than what democracy is supposed to accomplish [...]. But also, democratic elections have become the primary vehicle of state-building and the obstacle themselves of further democratization.[59]

Consequently, this may reiterate division and spark conflict again. In the case of Kosovo, the post-conflict popularity of the ex-warring group Kosovo Liberation Army (KLA) as the representatives of the Albanian majority community posed a great risk of undermining democracy and perpetuating ethnic politics. In the absence of stability and compliance, this could have placed all political power into the hands of one ethnic group. In order to avoid such situations, Paris argued it is better to wait for ethnic tensions to fade away over time and suggests different methods to promote moderation of politics (appropriate electoral systems and constitutional rules, penalizing extremism),[60] to develop a 'good' civil society (cross-factional social groups), to control hate speech (thus limit freedom of speech through codes of conduct),[61] to adopt economic policies that reduce the risk of conflict and, most importantly, to build effective and strong state institutions. However, what needs to be highlighted is that this approach also relies heavily on the role of the international administrators. Peacebuilding missions following this strategy would need to remain in place for as long as it takes to establish well-functioning central institutions and make sure that democratization and marketization are evolving in the right direction.[62]

EU post-liberal statebuilding: Discourse and impact

The principal exogenous factors that have been shaping contemporary statebuilding factors can also be taken into consideration when analysing the role of the European Union in Kosovo, acting both as a statebuilder and as an agent of Europeanization in the Balkans. As regards the responsibility of the EU in Southeastern Europe, Chandler[63] highlighted the dual character of the intervention: reinforcing the EU's projection of its power as a civilizing mission while trying to minimize its direct political responsibility derived from this power by developing, what he names, a *post-liberal discourse*:

> Rather than legitimize policy-making on the basis of representative legitimacy, post-liberal frameworks of governance problematize autonomy and self-government, inverting the liberal paradigm through establishing administrative and regulative frameworks as necessarily prior to democratic choices.[64]

The immediate risk of this model of governance is to undermine democratic accountability and the legitimacy of governing institutions in states that 'have international legal sovereignty but lack genuine mechanisms for politically integrating society'.[65] For this reason, Kosovo's contested statehood (including by five EU members) creates an even more complex challenge for the EU's involvement in the process of statebuilding. According to this critique of EU's statebuilding practices, an inverted logic of liberal statebuilding that prioritizes institution-building rather than democratization faces the downside of lacking popular legitimacy. By trying to diminish the imposing character of external administration during statebuilding, the EU statebuilding has been focusing on developing local ownership and setting up the administrative/bureaucratic apparatus prior to fully implementing liberal democratic principles of governance.

As this book's discussion of Kosovo's internal conditions will illustrate, these arguments regarding the EU's model of governance highlight the negative effect on the relationship between state and society and thus encourage criticisms of the post-liberal state model, but overall, they discount the endogenous roots of state weakness. Nevertheless, the focus on investigating the problems of prioritization (liberal vs. post-liberal institutionalist) should include the question of whether the two approaches can actually be clearly separated in practice. While domestic sovereignty is at stake in the absence of representative accountability and the state-society fracture that these states including Kosovo are facing, the fundamental problem might not actually be the absence of mechanisms of integration and social cohesion, but their functionality. The functionality argument could provide a more consistent response to understanding the relationship between state and society because it also focuses on endogenous factors like the inherited distrust for central government that have determined over time the lack of social cohesion. These elements of distrust in combination with the influence of post-1990 parallel structures incorporated later as both state and non-state agents have severally jeopardized the independence of the statebuilding process and the development of a pluralist civil society.

Even though state mechanisms are in place, they may not be fully functional because of the pre-established decentralized illiberal non-state notions of authority rooted in ethnic, national, economic or religious ties: 'Can a post-communist, post-conflict, contested entity such as Kosovo, [...] develop such a political system without reverting to ethnic exclusion, with all the inconsistencies, nuance and idiosyncrasies that have been long compensated for by the local processes of donor states?'[66] Given the detrimental legacy of communism and conflict, state weakness became visible with 'malfunctions in terms of provision of national cohesion and public goods'.[67] The risk of permanent state weakness has thus both structural and political roots. Consequences of this dual weakness are corruption and unofficial economy, hindered structural economic reform and development, and inability to establish proper market institutions. It is therefore essential to reiterate not only that (1) Kosovo remains a post-conflict, post-communist multiethnic political entity with contested statehood but also that (2) it represents a particular example of EU statebuilding, combining efforts in support of democratization and institutional capacity while highlighting its role to advise and develop sustainable local ownership.

State failure and state weakness

In a systematic analysis of the contemporary world states, Robert Rotberg[68] has categorized them in the following order: strong, weak, failing and collapsed.

The criteria for such classification are mainly derived from the states' ability or inability to deliver high qualities and quantities of *'essential political goods – the critical ingredients of good governance'.*[69] The essential political goods that Rotberg highlights are security, good governance, effective rule of law, freedom and rights, functional economy and infrastructure.

Indirectly, the management of plurality has become one of the essential political goods that the modern state should be able to deliver, be that understood as the accommodation of different ethno-national groups or the integration and protection of minorities through specific measures and a set of collective rights and privileges. Furthermore, the focus is on domestic sovereignty when evaluating whether 'the state has the capacity to govern and is able to exercise its powers and use its resources for the benefit of its people'.[70] Security is the ultimate responsibility of the state, thus the need to maintain the monopoly on the use of force within its borders and reduce or eliminate external and internal threats. Security is about the needs of individuals who make up states, and states cannot be secure if the individuals comprising them are insecure. These are necessary conditions for a state to maintain its authority and avoid state failure or civil wars, which often originate in ethnic, religious, linguistic or other intercommunal enmities.[71]

There are both immediate and mediate causes for state weakness included in analyses of global insecurity and underdevelopment[72] that underline the challenge of good governance: 'While, in the West, it is understood that the state provides the institutional framework enabling its citizens to pursue their personal and economic interests within a framework of order and security, the failing state is seen to lack this institutional framework.'[73] Furthermore, a statist approach to explain governance failure focuses on top-down factors (poor design or policies, incompetence of officials, lack of resources) and may neglect more complex circumstances of the problem. Hence, state weakness can be provoked by the domestic environment of conflict over the control of society.[74] The role of society was also used in another study of the weak/strong states paradigm by Barry Buzan, who looked at the degree of sociopolitical cohesion to emphasize a fundamental particularity of weak states in 'their high level of concern with domestically generated threats to the security of the government; in other words, weak states either do not have, or have failed to create, a domestic political and societal consensus'.[75] When security threats occur, strong political fragmentation and socioeconomic discrepancies make weak states extremely vulnerable not only to domestic disintegration but also to external intervention and control. In the context of high levels of social division, the state might be perceived as representing the interests of a particular group or more precisely ethnic groups in the case of multiethnic states. Given the state's internal insecurity, it becomes necessary to strengthen its coercive power, thus the correlation between post-conflict statebuilding and the prioritization of capacity/institution-building.

Contemporary statebuilding, be that in the postcolonial, post-communist or post-conflict contexts, has imported a modern West-centric liberal democratic model of governance but it has also inevitably adapted to the local understanding and practices of authority and to the particular necessity to manage plurality and accept the heterogeneous character of these societies. This analysis of the combination of formal and informal actors, institutions and societal relations helps to understand why post-conflict states like Kosovo might have limited capacities to control means of violence via legitimacy, but this does not mean they are inevitably heading towards state failure. Nonetheless, the key aim here remains to discuss to what extent and in what ways the state model proposed to be constructed in Kosovo has been 'limited' and transformed by the conditions of diversity and the task to manage this issue by pledging to the integration and protection of its minority communities.

It will thus be useful to further discuss these challenges in relation to particular models of democratic governance in plural (post-conflict) societies, which the next section of this chapter focuses on. The interplay between developing liberal/democratic norms of governance and the focus on managing diversity (the integration, accommodation and protection of minority rights) is the constant challenge that this book analyses in trying to reveal the intended and unintended consequences of statebuilding. This will result in a comprehensive study of the actual outcomes of multiethnic statebuilding and of the fragility of Kosovo in its dual task to secure unity at the same time while enshrining minority rights and accommodating diversity.

Models of democratic governance in plural societies

> The state's self-definition as a unitary, a federal or even a multinational political institution holds significant consequences for the peoples living within its boundaries [...] This is particularly evident in the case of a state that declares itself to be multinational, thus assuming the coexistence of more than one nation within its territory. Such a position entails an automatic distinction between nation and state that challenges the commonly accepted coincidence between the two.[76]

This section expands the theoretical framework of this research by focusing on the challenges faced by deeply divided societies that must remedy longstanding conflicting identities and learn to co-exist peacefully and by interrogating various models and approaches for managing plural systems and considering their relevance for post-conflict Kosovo. In the context of Kosovo's liberal democratic statebuilding, the new state's sovereignty and legitimacy could not have been built if it had denied the existence and importance of ethnocultural diversity within its territory. However, integrationist and accommodationist solutions can produce very different outcomes and an active accommodation and/or integration of minorities will impact on the immediate and long-term relations between state, society and its constituent ethno-national groups. Similarly, the integrative vs. consociational approaches to power-sharing in divided post-conflict states have been creating different mechanisms and tools for statebuilding, reconciliation and the ultimate management of diversity.

Inclusionary and exclusionary state responses to diversity

The first part of this chapter explained how the growing social diversity and ethnocultural complexity of modern states have become a problem for the development and preservation of authority and legitimacy of liberal democracies, very much dependent on sociopolitical cohesion. In response, the modern state has become responsible for securing sociopolitical stability and unity while also managing plurality, or more specifically, dealing with the existence of different ethnic, racial, national, cultural, religious or linguistic communities within its territory. The various policies that have been adopted by states vis-à-vis diversity can be generally differentiated by looking at the level of acceptance of the presence of different ethnocultural groups in combination with the state's inclination towards a more civic or ethnic understanding of national identity (nationalism).

The spread of the nation state model has confirmed cultural homogenization through *assimilation* as one of the most popular answers/policies to the challenge of diversity. Assimilation means the absorption of all different ethnocultural identities by one dominant 'national' identity, generally that of the majority ethnic (national) group, and it can be achieved through either *fusion* or *acculturation*. The alternative to assimilation has been the actual *acceptance* of diversity by states willing or having to integrate or accommodate different communities.

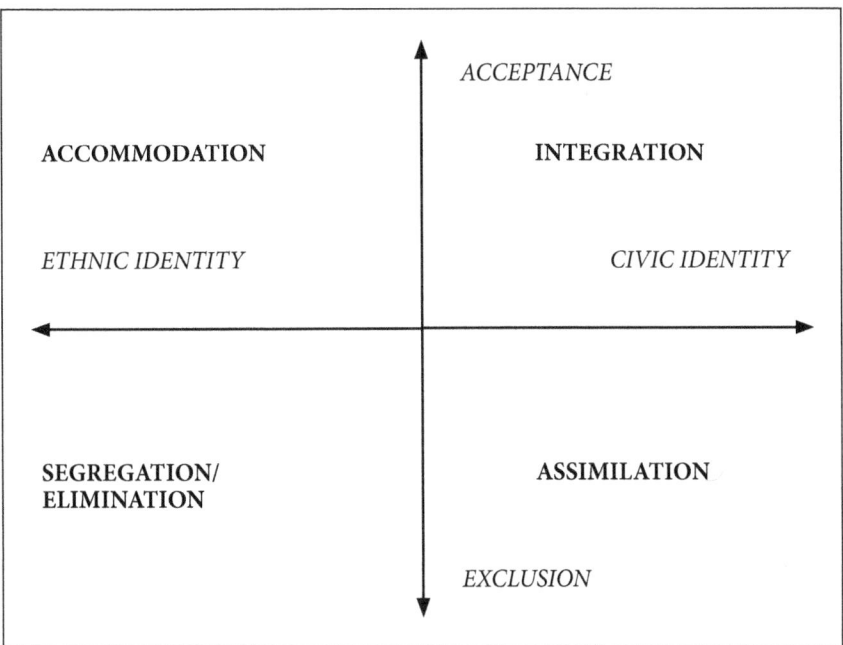

Figure 1 State responses to group (ethnocultural) diversity.

On the one hand, *integration* involves recognizing and respecting subnational identities (ethnocultural) in the private domain but, at the same time, it does not accept differences in the public sphere and promotes a single public identity (civic) within 'a common public space'.[77] Integration seeks the equality of individual citizens regardless of their ethnic/national/cultural identities and aims to create public unity and stability by creating laws and institutions that are neutral towards these non-civic differences. Cultural rights (collective) are separated from political rights (individual basis). Social cohesion through public homogenization is equally important to the respect for diversity. Legitimacy of the state is secured by the single public identity.

On the other hand, *accommodation* does not only tolerate diversity but also promotes public and private maintenance of cultural differences. Accommodation allows different communities to protect and manifest their identities both privately and publically through political participation and representation based on collective rights guaranteed by the state. Cultural rights are intersected with political rights (collective). Social cohesion is guaranteed by the coexistence of different groups, not by uniformity. The legitimacy of the state may be more fragmented. Therefore, statebuilding strategies that accept and are willing to manage diversity can aim to integrate or accommodate the constituent groups (peoples) of the society.

Moreover, the process of integration is multidimensional as it targets every level and sector of a society, which means that it needs to consider social, economic, political and cultural integration of minorities. Political integration is mainly focused on creating the necessary conditions for minorities to be able to exercise their rights as citizens and, at the same time, to stimulate political participation and representation. The socioeconomic dimension of the process of integration mainly addresses the social and economic equality between minorities and the rest of the society, while cultural integration looks at the way minorities are permitted to protect and manifest their cultural values within the private and public spheres. As a result of these different levels of acceptance or rejection of the idea of diversity and necessity to manage minorities, different nation- and statebuilding strategies have been developed. In this sense, Linz and Stepan[78] distinguished between unifying and differentiating types of nation-building, respectively, between inclusionary and exclusionary statebuilding. As Table 1 illustrates, by combining these categories the result is four types of possible ethno-political strategies that could be used to address the situation of minorities: rejection, isolation, assimilation or balance.

Table 1 A typology of state-, nation- and democracy-building strategies in multinational polities.

Nation-building strategies: Ideology towards demos/ nation relationship	Statebuilding strategies towards non-national minority or minorities	
	Exclusionary strategy	Inclusionary strategy
Demos and nation should be the same	Type I Expel or at least systematically encourage the 'exit' option	Type III Make major efforts to assimilate minorities into national culture and give no special recognition to minority political or cultural rights
Demos and nation can be different	Type II Isolate from political process by granting civil liberties but no political rights and thus discouraging 'voice' option	Type IV Make major efforts to accommodate minorities by crafting a series of political and civil arrangements that recognize minority rights

Source: Juan J. Linz and Alfred Stepan, *Problems of Democratic Transition and Consolidation: Southern Europe, South America, and Post-Communist Europe* (Baltimore: Johns Hopkins University Press, 1996).

Contemporary models of democracy

Another evaluation of different types of contemporary democratic states has been offered by Sammy Smooha,[79] who looked at the impact of global and domestic challenges on the liberal democratic nation state in relation to five possible models of democracies: individual-liberal democracy (ideal), republican liberal democracy, consociational democracy, multicultural democracy and ethnic democracy. The first two types derive from the democratic nation state as the dominant model for Western countries.

The *individual liberal democracy* places the individual citizen at the core of the society and the national identity of citizens is defined in relation to their respect for democratic principles, for the equality of rights for the individuals who belong to the society, for free competition and privatization of religion and ethnicity.[80] Nonetheless, the individual liberal democracy is only an ideal model, while in practice most of the Western states have developed as *republican liberal democracies*. As mentioned earlier in this chapter, the classical nation state required homogenization and imposed a single culture and a single language and denied ethnic groups the institutional mechanisms for separate existence. The members of this type of society do not define themselves only as individual citizens of the state but also as members of a national community sharing a common civic identity. For instance, contemporary liberal democracies like France and the United States treat all their citizens as equal members of a common civic nation, while 'ethnic cultures and identities are allowed but not recognised nor encouraged by the state'.[81] This is a key point as it highlights the difference between active and passive forms of accommodating diversity.

Smooha indicates that an important alternative to the republican liberal democracies has been the *consociational democracy*, which takes national and ethnic differences as given, grants official recognition of ethnic groups and aims to reduce or prevent ethnic conflict through a set of mechanisms.[82] The special mechanisms of this model, famously conceptualized by Arendt Lijphart,[83] include power-sharing, proportionality, veto power and politics of negotiation, compromise, consensus and indecision, which will be examined in detail in the last part of this chapter. The role of a state in dealing with its minority groups and supporting them can thus be expressed indirectly through the configuration of state institutions or indirectly through special policies. In the first situation, the key elements are the electoral system, the party system and the level of decentralization, while for a direct impact the state develops, for instance, policies for the use of minority languages. As regards the concrete application of these policies, while there have been several empirical variations and partially consociational arrangements, Belgium and Switzerland remain perhaps the best-known and long-standing examples.

In order to examine the next two types of democracies, it should be reiterated that the traditional type of liberal democracy has been influenced by different factors that activate either from 'above' or from 'below'. While the effects of regionalization and globalization dominate the first category, factors from 'below' include immigration and the emergence of indigenous minority nationalism, thus challenging 'the homogeneity of the nation state and its tolerance of ethnic and cultural diversity'.[84] In this context statebuilding has adjusted and has shifted away from full assimilation and towards multiculturalism by respecting 'the desire for separateness of small indigenous minorities, immigrants from former colonies or foreign workers'.[85] Therefore, another consequence has been the differentiation of the nation state and the promotion of multiculturalism as an alternative ideology. In this sense, the model of *multicultural democracy* involves recognition of ethnic differences without institutionalizing particular political mechanisms to promote them. Given the lack of ethnocultural homogeneity in states like those in Central and Eastern Europe, the nation state model was not fully compatible with the particular conditions for democratization or democratic consolidation after the fall of communism.[86] According to Smooha, post-Apartheid South Africa and Netherlands are prime examples of the nascent multicultural democracy, but many Western liberal democracies have also been leaning towards this model.[87]

Multicultural democracies, the same author argues, have combined features of the liberal and consociational democracies and have created a hybrid civic form of democracy that 'decouples state and nation, recognises cultural rights of minorities, but neither makes these rights official nor institutionalises the standard mechanisms of consociational democracy'.[88] Nevertheless, similar to the previously mentioned types of democracies, it values the interconnected principles of centrality of citizenship, equality of rights and civic nationalism. The management of diversity can thus differentiate between cultural (collective) and political (individual) rights and between ethnic and civic identities of citizens. From this perspective, citizens can have multiple identities, and, most importantly, the ethnocultural identity of people (or minorities) does not necessarily need to translate into a political one too. As specified before, under this model minorities are integrated rather than accommodated.

The last type of democracy from Smooha's classification is the *ethnic democracy*. This model is defined by the presence of a core ethnic nation, which is the owner of the state and which leads the state for its own benefit. There is a differentiation between national identity and citizenship while the groups that are not part of the dominant nation have incomplete individual and collective rights. The marginal groups are perceived as a threat for the survival and the integrity of the core national group and in response their members are permanently isolated from state institutions.

For this type of democracy, ethnic identity prevails over civic identity and the defining element of the state is the ethnic nation rather than citizenship. It can barely be considered a democratic state since there is a lack of equality of rights. The majority is privileged and the 'minority cannot fully identify itself with the state, cannot be completely equal to the majority and cannot confer full legitimacy of the state'.[89] This is a fundamental remark about this type of clearly exclusionary states as it underlines how in the absence of any kind of acceptance of diversity, a plural state that aims to be liberal democratic lacks legitimacy and cannot consolidate its domestic sovereignty by non-coercive means. The ethnic democracy typology is another example of sovereignty as control prioritized over sovereignty as responsibility, and consequently, of a state linking with only a part of its society. The state does not recognize all its constituent peoples, while the society remains divided between the nation (dominant majority) and the excluded minorities.

Conflict management and statebuilding in multiethnic divided societies

The discussion around different state models of dealing with ethno-national diversity in plural societies will now focus on the dilemma of how democracy can manage post-conflict divided societies efficiently. In other words, the biggest challenge yet for liberal democratic statebuilding has been developing functional and legitimate governance in societies where diversity is not just a challenge for constructing (national) unity but it represented the source of violent conflict in the past. Moreover, diversity in post-conflict societies represents a risk of perennial social (ethnic, racial) division, thus the task of contemporary statebuilding to reconcile divided groups and secure social cohesion. The legitimacy of the state in such cases is directly linked to the promotion and protection of group rights, and normally the key challenge is the integration and/or accommodation of minorities so as to avoid any potential discrimination by the majority community.

Similar to the different approaches to dealing with diversity in general, a taxonomy of methods of ethnic conflict regulation (covering both termination and management of conflict) can be used to distinguish between (1) *methods of eliminating differences* like genocide, forced mass-population transfers, partition and/or secession (self-determination) and integration and/or assimilation and (2) *methods for managing differences* such as hegemonic control, arbitration (third-party intervention), cantonization and/or federalization and consociationalism or power-sharing.[90] As already discussed, the most extreme responses to plurality have been attempts to eliminate differences by genocide or forced mass-population transfers, strategies which are incompatible with liberal democratic principles, have no moral justification and are an 'abhorrent'[91] response to the challenge of diversity.

The second strategy of ethnic cleansing was used in the 1990s wars in Bosnia and Herzegovina and in Kosovo. The illiberal practices and the violation of human rights provoked the intervention of the international community and the subsequent post-conflict statebuilding in Kosovo, the case study of this book. Therefore, the post-1999 internationally driven statebuilding mission in Kosovo with the UN and the EU as the leading actors is related to the method of arbitration, which involves the intervention of a neutral, bi-partisan or multi-partisan authority and it is therefore different from other strategies for stabilizing 'antagonistic societies because it involves conflict regulation by agents other than the directly contending parties'.[92] In this sense, peacebuilding and statebuilding practices of liberal interventionism have been the dominant externally led forms of arbitration of contemporary conflict and post-conflict societies.

The idea of hegemonic control for the aim of managing differences is also in contrast with liberal democratic norms. Hegemonic control involves the state's control of diversity within its territory 'through coercive domination and elite co-option'.[93] The example of former Yugoslavia is once again relevant, as the ethnic domination by Serbs in regions where they were not in majority (Kosovo too) established a system of minority hegemonic control. Nonetheless, hegemonic control can occur in multiethnic democratic regimes too (majority rule) if ethnic parties are in a zero-sum competition: 'a majoritarian system of liberal democratic government, designed to create strong powers for the governing party, is no guarantee of liberty for ethnic minorities'.[94]

From the list of exclusionary measures designed to eliminate differences, integration and/or assimilation has been in accordance with the norms of building unitary nation states with a common transcendent identity. Integration has been 'the dominant goal and embodies the received wisdom regarding conflict regulation and conflict resolution in the longer established democracies',[95] and it has been achieved either by creating a civic national identity and integrating all different ethnic or national groups under its umbrella or by seeking to assimilate differences under a common ethnic identity. While contemporary examples like the United States, Canada and Australia are considered to be cases of moderately successful integration/assimilation, and thus potential models of managing (potential) ethnic tensions or conflicts, what also needs to be highlighted is that they 'involved migrations to a "new" country, where the migrants, in principle, were willing to adapt their cultures to their new host country and accept a new civic identity'.[96] Moreover, these Western states' willingness to accept and even encourage diversity has been favoured by the fact that the presence of different ethnocultural communities within their borders has not been a serious security threat. Even if minority groups gain extensive autonomy and the right to self-determination and, consequently, may jeopardize the territorial integrity and social cohesion of the state, there is little risk of violent conflict.

New states that focus on consolidating national legitimacy are particularly prone to accentuating boundaries of exclusion. Well-established states, on the other hand, where the institutional infrastructure of the state is not under scrutiny, are more prepared to accommodate minorities on some levels, so long as the inherited national identity of the state is not questioned.[97] Therefore, in the context of post-conflict statebuilding, an integration/assimilation approach would be instantly challenged by the legacy of ethnic divisions and by the mere fact that it would not necessarily be complemented by a voluntary decision of different communities to integrate and/or be assimilated. The risks of inconsistent integration and maintenance of segregation and unequal opportunities for different communities will all be discussed in relation to the case of Kosovo.

The alternative to the idea of eliminating differences, supported by liberal integrationists, is offered by liberal multiculturalists who have considered ways of resolving conflicts by managing differences instead. By looking at how human rights are a response to the practical needs of minority groups, Will Kymlicka[98] criticizes the solution proposed for diminishing the source of conflict by separating the state from ethnicity following the model of secularization. Kymlicka[99] considers that classical liberal democracies are not neutrally from an ethno-political perspective because neutrality is nothing more than an illusion denied by all the symbols promoted by the state but at the same time associated most of the times with one of the ethnic groups: national language, anthem or culture. For multiculturalists, a separation of state from ethnicity is unrealistic because as regards the official languages, territorial boundaries and power-sharing, the state cannot avoid supporting one of the ethnocultural groups or make decisions regarding the majority (education, national holidays, symbols or immigration policies). In a democratic society the ethnic group in majority will always have protection of its own language and culture, as well as the legislative power to protect its interests. The task is nonetheless to understand to what extent minority groups can be granted similar benefits and opportunities. For a long period of time it has been considered that citizenship and granting equal rights are sufficient elements to respect the interests of different minorities within the territory of a state. However, the debates over minority rights from the last few decades, as Kymlicka argues, have shown that the human rights doctrine is not capable of addressing all the problems regarding minority groups. In different parts of the world, majorities and minorities have been in dispute over language rights, representation, education, autonomy, federalism, national symbols and thus have showed that some forms of diversity can only be accommodated through measures that reach beyond citizenship rights.

Other solutions that have been proposed to advance and encourage cooperation in ethnically divided societies are specifically targeting territorial reorganization. Different forms of territorial administration (based or not on ethnic identity) are very important for minorities. A common territorial principle of macro-political ethnic conflict regulation in multiethnic societies has been decentralization. Decentralization offers communities a chance to work out differences where elites fail and, consequently, build cooperation and moderation starting with the local level (bottom-up). Different degrees of decentralization, going as far as federalism, are designed to allow local ethnic communities decide on many aspects of their lives without threatening the integrity of the state. Federalism and autonomy do not only support preserving the identity and representation of minorities but also favour the active participation of minorities in the decision-making process, 'with obvious moral advantages over pure control'.[100] The role of territorial administrative reforms designed to manage diversity will be discussed in detail in the last chapter of this book, which looks at the decentralization process in Kosovo. The last section of this chapter will focus on the (ethnic) conflict management solution of *power-sharing*, which involves integrative and/or consociational strategies targeting the reform of political, electoral and institutional norms of democratic governance.

The Lijphart-Horowitz debate on power-sharing

The idea of power-sharing between different (ethnic) groups that form a society is the common point of the two key approaches as regards the management and (re)construction of ethnically divided states. These approaches were initiated by Arendt Lijphart and Donald Horowitz and they became known as (1) the *group building-block approach* or *consociational* and (2) the *integrative approach*. They both start from the assumption that 'a democracy in which crosscutting cleavages interact with the institutions of competitive politics to moderate political behaviour is a centripetal democracy; [and] a democracy in which the institutions of competitive politics interact with segmental cleavages is a centrifugal democracy that will literally fly apart'.[101] What separates the two theories are the arguments they give about whether ethnic cleavages should be officially recognized and used to build peace (accommodationist) or whether differences between groups should be diminished while aiming to integrate society along the line of division (more integrationist).

The consociational approach argues that ethnic division needs to be constitutionalized and become the basis of the political system and depends on the accommodation by ethnic group representatives at the political centre and guarantees for group autonomy and minority rights. One of the reasons consociational democracy is a better alternative in a divided society is that the leaders of rival groups 'can build institutions and foster policies to stabilize democracy by constraining certain forms of democratic competition'.[102] On the other hand, the integrative approach claims that the political system should not be constructed on the lines of ethnic division and it should try instead to integrate ethnic groups. Horowitz[103] argues that it is important to have an electoral system that is capable 'to create ongoing incentives for interethnic cooperation' and to promote federalism or regional autonomy, to implement 'policies that give regionally concentrated groups a strong stake in the center', thus avoiding separatism by supporting devolution.

Consociationalism

Lijphart's proposal for the challenges of democracy in ethnically divided societies is the concept of *consociational democracy*. This was presented as an alternative to the democratic system that has a majority government and a homogeneous and secular political culture or what Gabriel Almond named as the 'Anglo-

American' model. According to Lijphart, consociationalism 'means government by elite cartel designed to turn a democracy with a fragmented culture into a stable democracy'.[104] Lijphart highlights from the start of his analysis that it is not possible to eliminate the differences between ethnic groups once they appear. Consequently, if a conflict involved the use of the differences between the ethnicity of particular groups, it is better to accept these differences and to build a new state so that it includes, confirms and constitutes these ethnic distinctions. Otherwise, one would need to try to eliminate or ignore ethnic divergence, which Lijphart does not consider achievable.[105]

Given that the removal of the ethnic cleavages is not a realistic objective, Lijphart indicates two possible solutions for the management of a multiethnic state: (1) the partition of a state and secession or (2) a power-sharing approach. With regard to the first one he writes that both partition and secession are impractical, as a division of territory would unavoidably involve violence among the conflicting parties. He also suggests that violence is rather provoked by the efforts to prevent the partition than by the very fact of this partition. There is always a power centre tempted to fight for keeping the territory of a country together at any cost. This devotion to counteract the partition stimulates violence, which would be avoidable otherwise.

By considering different disadvantages of the partition of a territory, Lijphart puts forward the idea of accommodating most of the interests of all the ethnic groups within one state and the adjustment of the state structure so that those groups have equal influence on the decision-making process and the governing of the country. Furthermore, consociationalism reflects the experience of countries with a distinctive plural structure of the society. Their particularity is given by the grouping of political subcultures (political cleavages) in different and independent pillars (segments of the society) that interact and become institutionalized and organized in a hierarchal order. In 'pillarised' societies different communities have not only set up their 'own ideologically sensitive organisations (e.g., a political party, a youth movement, schools, a newspaper, libraries and a broadcasting company), they also established many organisations and institutions with purely secular social functions (e.g., hospitals, sport clubs, housing associations, insurance companies and even animal protection societies and associations of stamp collectors)'.[106]

The implementation and the functionality of consociational democracy depend mainly on the relationships that are established between subcultures, but also on the relationship between elites and their followers within each subculture. There are several conditions for the good functioning based on cooperation among elites: the absence of a majority that is not interested in power-sharing and which, contrariwise, is in favour of adopting a majoritarian model; similar socioeconomic levels of subcultures; reduced number of subcultures; balance between subcultures; reduced territory; existence of an external threat or danger; tradition of consensus. Based on the example of four consociational democracies – Netherlands, Switzerland, Belgium and Austria – Lijphart remarked that in plural societies, structural cleavages become over time cleavages of the party system. In cases of social segmentation, the result is segmental parties. In Belgium, for instance, the Flemish and the French communities have gradually created their own political parties. These have detached themselves from national parties so as to represent the interests of one linguistic community only.

The defining four elements of the consociational model are: (1) *grand coalition* (elites of each segment of the society come together to rule so as to avoid the risks of noncooperation), (2) *segmental autonomy* (protecting the plural character of the society), (3) *proportionality* (for the electoral system, for recruiting public servants and for distributing public funds) and (4) *mutual veto* (for the benefit of political minorities).

The *grand coalition* is the key feature of the consociational democracy as it brings together representatives of all communities to govern a country. It can take many different institutional forms. The simplest form is that of a grand coalition government within a parliamentary system, while in presidential democracies power-sharing can be accomplished by rotating presidency and other key executive roles between the different communities. The second consociational element of *segmental autonomy* aims to delegate powers directly to the communities, thus enabling self-governance for ethnic communities/ minorities in areas that are of exclusive interest for them.[107] Segmental autonomy can take the form of territorial and/or non-territorial autonomy depending on the geographic distribution of the ethnic communities.

Proportionality is also a significant consociational element that deviates from democracy based on majority rule as it aims to allocate political and public positions (civil service) proportionally to all communities and distribute public funds among different segments in proportion to their population size.[108] Therefore, whereas the grand coalition secures representation of all communities, proportionality is more specific by making groups represented proportionally within decision-making institutions and, thus, acting as a 'neutral and impartial standard of allocation'.[109] Moreover, proportionality models can vary and go further by either deliberately offering overrepresentation of small communities (minorities) or by parity of representation: 'The minority or minorities are overrepresented to such an extent that they reach a level of equality with the majority of the largest group.'[110] The aim is to protect minorities in situations where proportionality is not sufficient to manage the power of the majority community, especially when a diverse society is divided between two communities of unequal size. As the following chapters will reveal, this principle has been particularly important in relation to the management of minorities in post-conflict Kosovo.

The fourth element of consociational democracies is the *mutual veto* highlighted by Lijphart as a procedure that prevents the minority from being outvoted by the majority. The presence of minorities within a grand coalition does not guarantee their full protection as long as their political interests can be outvoted. The risk posed by the use of veto is that it can undermine political cooperation, but Lijphart does not see this as a big problem for three reasons. Firstly, the veto is *mutual*, which means that it will not be used very frequently because it can work both for and against minorities. Secondly, the veto represents a potential weapon for minorities and offers a sense of security even if it is not used. And, thirdly, each community will aim to cooperate and avoid the risk of political deadlock which can be provoked by unlimited use of the veto. In addition, Lijphart has revised the consociational model recently by classifying the mutual veto and proportionality as secondary elements designed to support the two key principles of grand coalition and segmental autonomy.[111]

The integrative approach

While the consociational solutions for power-sharing focus on the elite-level representation and participation of different groups in divided societies, the integrative approach developed by Horowitz, or centripetalism,[112] affirms that cross-ethnic links are necessary at all levels of society through sociopolitical and institutional integration. At the political level, for instance, instead of stimulating representation of groups by their own parties, integrative measures seek to encourage them to cooperate as part of multiethnic parties so as to reduce the significance of the ethnic cleavage. The two contrasting approaches to power-sharing in divided societies make therefore a fundamental contribution to the broader debate between accommodationist and integrationists.

With the purpose of facilitating reconciliation and the integration of all constituent groups of a society, the integrative approach sees interethnic cooperation as more important than the consociational emphasis on minority representation. In other words, adopting measures that stimulate cross-ethnic social, political and institutional cooperation does not mean that minorities are more vulnerable. Moreover, the idea of protecting and promoting minorities should not be understood as a right or as a necessity of communities to differentiate themselves from the others not only culturally but also socially, politically, institutionally, economically or territorially. Horowitz criticizes the fact that the success of consociational democracy relies exclusively on the willingness of different groups to work together. In his view this is not sufficient because the leaders of a majority group will not be interested in compromise and will want majority decisions while the elites of different groups are not necessarily less ethno-centric or more moderate than the people they represent. Moreover, by collaborating with representatives of other groups, leaders risk being accused by more radical rivals from their own community of betrayal and of not representing and defending their particular interests.

Consociationalism is therefore a constraining approach. Horowitz suggests instead that a positive strategy is necessary for building effective democratic governance in divided societies. This can be done by rewarding moderation and stimulating integration across communal divides so as to motivate politicians to reach beyond their own communal segments for support. Politicians are seen as rational actors by Horowitz, and given that their main purpose is to be re-elected, an effective solution would be to create a political and institutional setting where moderation increases the chances of leaders to be elected.[113] The key element of the integrative approach's aim to moderate elites is the electoral system. For this reason, Horowitz rejects the proportionality element of consociational democracy because, in his view, it stimulates the formation of parties reflecting the social segmentation and re-enforces communal cleavages.

For the integrative approach, a truly efficient electoral system for divided societies must stimulate coalitions of commitment, in which its members have the key objective of reconciliation and cooperation. Thus, the aim is to de-ethnicize politics by making politicians, as much as possible, mutually dependent on the voters of other groups other than their own: 'Since the parties must pool votes rather than pool merely seats, they must find ways before the election to communicate their ethnically and racially conciliatory intentions to the voters.'[114] Horowitz considers that there are at least three main methods that could help reducing political fragmentation on ethnic lines. The first one is related to presidential elections and relies on introducing additional conditions for victory besides securing the majority of the votes. One example he used in his studies was Nigeria, where between 1979 and 1983 the elected candidate had to win not only an absolute majority, but also at least 25 per cent of the votes in no less than two-thirds of the total then nineteen federal states.[115] The immediate advantage of this model is that it prevents the election of a candidate who could claim popular legitimacy but was actually supported by only one ethnic group.

A second solution for the de-ethnicization of politics is to make parties build ethnically mixed candidate lists (ethnically mixed slates). Horowitz gives the example of Malaysia, where even if this is not a prerequisite by law, in practice the coalition partners found the single slate to be more advantageous.[116] A more formal application of this idea was though found in Lebanon, where the electoral system between 1943 and 1976 consisted of reserved seats, mixed constituencies and communal rolls, which stimulated candidates 'to exchange with each other the votes of their supporters and thus to put up what were tantamount to mixed lists'.[117] The third solution that Horowitz put forward is alternative voting (AV), the preferential electoral system in which second and subsequent preferences of voters whose first preference is not one of the two top candidates are reallocated until a candidate attains a majority. Horowitz considers that by using AV in ethnically mixed constituencies, vote pooling between different groups is stimulated because candidates cannot be elected only with votes from their own community and have to moderate their attitude towards other groups and be interested in their problems and their interests.[118] A similar electoral system is the single transferable vote (STV), which is appropriate for constituencies with more than one member. The voters make a hierarchal list of the candidates based on their preferences (primary, secondary, third, etc.) and the candidates must overpass a certain quota to be elected. The advantage of SVT is argued to be the fact that it produces a result that is more proportional than alternative voting. All these electoral options put forward by Horowitz for democracies with divided societies promise to moderate candidates and to make them reach beyond their own communities to gain votes and support from other groups.

In addition to an electoral system that stimulates vote pooling, the integrative approach also recommends the adoption of a presidential regime and the federalization of divided states. As regards presidentialism, Horowitz supports it because the presence of two centres of power is more favourable for power-sharing by reducing the possibility of having one single group in control of the state. Moreover, the majoritarian character of presidentialism can be controlled by adopting an appropriate electoral system that, as discussed earlier, encourages vote pooling between divided groups. Horowitz also uses federalism as a method of conflict regulation. Democratic federations are compound sovereign states in which the power and constitutional competencies are distributed between at least two governmental units, the federal and the regional.[119] Horowitz highlights four functions of federation that make it a suitable political system for managing divided societies. Firstly, it can complement an accommodative electoral system. Secondly, federal units can offer politicians a first opportunity to work on crucial issues for a divided society before doing so at the national level of governance. Thirdly, territorial devolution of power can also help to dissolve conflict by proliferating the points of power vertically. Lastly, federal units can support a sustainable democratic governance by 'making hegemony more difficult to achieve'.[120]

Furthermore, while this approach is similar to the consociational focus on the devolution of power, the integrative strategy of managing conflict/division in multiethnic societies through federalism is not based along ethnically homogeneous lines. In contrast to Lijphart's approach, Horowitz supports strong national federations based on heterogeneous federal units that favour interethnic cooperation, prevents regional majoritarianism and can stabilize and unify the state. The ethno-national, cultural, linguistic or religious diversity of a state should not determine the territorial-administrative structure of a federation so as to avoid segregation. A federation with a plural society should seek to unite people who desire a common political unit that nonetheless respects and protects diverse ethnic identities, while heterogeneous regional units (local governance) stimulate interethnic cooperation at all levels. From Horowitz's perspective, federalism recognizes the plural character of the society and the coexistence of different groups but devolves power with the purpose managing their different (collective) interests at the local level. This is different from Lijphart's view of federalism as an opportunity not only to give autonomy to different groups but to institutionalize this through (ethno) territorial units.

As the chapter on decentralization in Kosovo will illustrate, a key dilemma dominates the discussion: is the geographic distribution of individuals belonging to different communities (homogeneously or heterogeneously) going to determine the actual demarcation of (federal, regional, municipal, local) borders or is a solely top-down territorial organization going to regulate the demographic composition of local units of governance? A top-down artificial division of regional boundaries that supports devolution on ethnic-territorial basis is seen by Horowitz as a stimulus for secession. However, this is not an argument in favour of centralization as the attempt to strengthen central authority in fear of separatism is more likely to discriminate minorities at the local level and provoke a reaction and mobilization against the (unitary) state in seek of autonomy and self-determination: 'Regional autonomy or federalism – on a territorial and not an ethnic or "homeland" basis – allows such minorities nationally to form majorities locally, the result is unlikely to be an aggravation of separatism.'[121] It is not therefore accurate to disregard federalism or decentralization as potential tools for conflict regulation in multiethnic societies because autonomy and self-rule for minorities can undermine the territorial integrity of a state. As Horowitz suggests, the problem may rather be with the character of federalization (federation model) that needs to be integrative and may encourage inter-ethnic cooperation at the local level (heterogeneous local units) instead of perpetuating or creating segregated homogeneous units.

Assessing power-sharing

> The inefficiency of externally-driven measures for power-sharing has highlighted that there is no universal solution to manage diversity and that consociational and/or integrative arrangements must be carefully adapted to the circumstances of each society and state.[122]

Proponents of 'imposed' power-sharing will not only have to look more closely at the best practices in power-sharing systems around the world but also will have to work in close conjunction with the 'bottom-up' approach of proponents of social transformations in order to achieve democratic and cohesive plural societies.[123] Moreover, as Snyder[124] highlights, the consociational arrangements alone with the institutionalized ethnic divisions may not be enough to stimulate permanent reconciliation of conflicting groups. This is a significant critique of the power-sharing strategies because, in the case of post-conflict liberal statebuilding for instance, the task is not only to stop a conflict but also to build and maintain sustainable peace. The management of diversity in this context is not only an immediate task (bring violence to an end and build peace through strong institutional/legal provision for all groups), but also a long-term commitment to develop necessary conditions where different communities (previously in conflict with each other in some cases) learn and accept to coexist within the post-conflict state. Thus, while consociational measures seem more appropriate for short-term peacebuilding, a long-term strategy is also more likely to use integrative tools for building an efficient and sustainable governance of diverse societies. However, making power-sharing a durable solution for divided societies is difficult to achieve as both approaches depend on volatile political, social and cultural factors.[125] Furthermore, the role of the international community is of fundamental importance in choosing between models of integration or accommodation for post-conflict states and needs to be addressed before summing up the power-sharing debate. In this sense, the first chapter discussed some of the key points of the critique of contemporary international statebuilding and underlined its top-down character. While this identified the imposition of a generalized version of the Western liberal democratic state model, it should be emphasized that post-conflict reconstruction has also promoted power-sharing as an essential structuring principle in divided societies.[126] Power-sharing arrangements have been included in the institution-building processes in cases like Northern Ireland, South Africa, Bosnia-Herzegovina, Cyprus, Kosovo, Macedonia, Burundi or Afghanistan. Therefore, the outcome of statebuilding is marked by the international actors' preference for integration or accommodation, for consociationalism or centripetalism in the design of post-conflict constitutional and institutional frameworks. Furthermore, this is sustained by the dependency of these states on the international community and its military, financial and technical assistance for ethnic conflict regulation: 'international organisations influence both the policy choices that states make regarding the diversity and the likelihood that the chosen policies will succeed'.[127] What is also noteworthy then is that, while Western states, the UN and other international organizations have generally favoured integration as the dominant approach to manage plurality and minority rights[128] (more appropriate with longer established states), in the actual practice of case-specific management of diversity in new states with deeply divided societies, the accommodationist approach has been endorsed as a necessary alternative.[129]

As already indicated by Horowitz's response to Lijphart, consociationalism has been criticized[130] for issues like the reliance on elites and the support of their communities for reconciling behaviour. Nonetheless, there are also significant implementation challenges for the integrative model of power-sharing for democratic management of divided societies. Firstly, the role of elites can also be problematic for the integrative approach, as they need to gain political support not only from their own community/ethnic group, but also from voters belonging to other groups. Therefore, a strong and sustainable support for political elites becomes even more difficult to achieve under these conditions. Furthermore, consociational democracy is also considered vulnerable because elites from the majority group will not easily accept institutional constrains and may decide to dissolve or reduce special collective rights of minorities when they get an opportunity to do so.[131] The volatility of elites is a key threat to the durability of power-sharing arrangements.

As regards the alternative voting favoured by the integrative approach, consociationalists point out[132] that it remains a majoritarian electoral system. As a result, if applied in a constituency where one of the ethnic groups has absolute majority, then the results will be similar to that of a purely majoritarian system. The effectiveness of the AV system in integrative models is thus preconditioned by the dominance of mixed, heterogeneous constituencies. Demarcation of constituencies in order to achieve this is, however, subject to the geographical spread of different communities/ethnic groups.[133] In the case of states with geographically concentrated groups (ethnically homogeneous regions), creating heterogeneous electoral districts would require a demarcation of constituencies that is not congruent and intersects with ethnic boundaries. The implementation of this measure would be inevitably contested as it would be very difficult for different groups (particularly minorities) not to see this as a disadvantage and a threat to their collective power and/or to their particular interests.

These multifaceted challenges highlight that power-sharing arrangements assume groups to be unitary entities and overlook the actual character and structure of each community by not taking into consideration intra-ethnic divisions or the wishes and interests of individuals. Furthermore, if the power-sharing toolbox used for the reconstruction of post-conflicts societies is going to be effective, 'it must complement its political and social environment'.[134] In this regard, Pildes[135] argues that, depending on the context, there can be a dynamic relationship between the design of democratic institutions and the ethnic identities expressed. Democratic institutions can be designed to accommodate ethnic differences for practical reasons but 'the aim should be to do this while also building in as much flexibility as possible to enable democratic institutions to be responsive to changes in ethnic identifications over time'.[136] As the case analysis of Kosovo will also show, besides the exogenous conditions, the effectiveness of power-sharing depends on the good will of the constituent groups that make up the society and is influenced by the volatility of the sociopolitical, cultural and demographic particularities of each state and of each community (endogenous factors).

Conclusion

The last part of this chapter has addressed the key concepts and debates around the state models, political solutions and institutional mechanisms for managing diverse societies in process of building or consolidating democratic governance. In general terms, the state has reacted to the challenge of plurality by either excluding or accepting the presence of different ethnic, national or cultural groups within its territory. Consequently, the liberal democratic state has adopted different policies and has remodelled its political and institutional structure, but at the same time, it has also changed the character of its society with an overarching aim of building or maintaining social cohesion and legitimacy by all its constituent peoples.

By presenting the different political/theoretical solutions for democracies with plural societies, I will now be able to evaluate better the multiethnic post-conflict model of democratic governance built in Kosovo. The departure from the Western liberal democratic state model, on the one hand, and the rift between ideal models of governance (promoted by the international community) and the actual practice of post-conflict statebuilding, on the other, are both relevant to the study of the case of Kosovo. In this respect, I will look at the design and activity of the main institutional components that confirm the efforts made to construct a multiethnic republic requiring both majority rule and minority protection and representation, both accommodation of minorities and their civic integration, both securing unity and accommodating diversity at the same time. Overall, the analytical framework developed in this chapter combines different literatures from the fields of comparative politics, nationalism studies, statebuilding and international relations. More precisely, it provides a useful overview of the obstacles and solutions for dealing with one of the most complex dilemmas of contemporary statebuilding: securing social, institutional and political unity of the state at the same time with enshrining ethnic diversity and minority representation in governance.

For the rest of this book, I will analyse the process of designing and implementing the multiethnic liberal democratic state model in Kosovo and I will discuss the motivation, the mechanisms and the de facto results of the complex aim to integrate, protect and accommodate minorities while building social cohesion in the post-conflict and post-independence context.

2

Post-conflict and Post-independence Statebuilding in Kosovo

Kosovo before and after the 1999 conflict

However, a Western Balkan state lacks cohesion in two ways. It is typically an ethnified state, for which the notion of national cohesion is elusive. It is also a state in which the privilege of majority nations is a fact of life, even though it may not be a fact of law. An equally important line of division runs along the position towards the responsibility for the crimes committed by members of one's nation, denialists vs. liberals calling for reckoning and ethnic reconciliation.[1]

This chapter will introduce the historical context before and after the 1999 conflict, the role of the international administration in Kosovo and the problems deriving from the unsettled status of the province. It is essential to understand the issue of diversity in Kosovo from a historical perspective too, as many of the present challenges faced by the post-war society are deeply rooted in the multifaceted sociopolitical legacies of the past. For instance, Kosovo Albanians and the leaders of the Kosovo Liberation Army (KLA) adjudicated the contest for political authority after 1999 in a peacebuilding framework that, at least under United Nations Interim Administration in Kosovo (UNMIK), ignored the historical, sociopolitical and cultural factors while imposing a liberal peace model.[2]

To this end, more attention should have been devoted to the post-1990 political context of the region, when in response to the drastic measures of the Milosevic regime, the Kosovo Albanian leadership declared the independence of the 'Republic of Kosova' in 1991 'and started to organize a parallel state, financed by taxes on Albanians in Kosovo and in the diaspora'.[3] This represented a peaceful resistance that even organized unofficial elections and designated Ibrahim Rugova as president, but could not eventually prevent the radical aggressiveness of the Serbian state in parallel with the 'increasing attacks by the Kosovo Liberation Army (KLA)'.[4] The violent contest over the autonomy of Kosovo reached its climax with the March 1999 NATO bombing campaign against Yugoslavia, which consequently established the international authority in Kosovo (UNMIK) through Resolution 1244 of the UN Security Council. The immediate problem with this resolution was the ambiguity of its aim to facilitate transitional administration while developing self-governing institutions, but with no reference to a potential final status of Kosovo.

Kosovo before 1999

Kosovo had been a troublesome region for a long time. For instance, under the impact of various sources of authority, the interethnic relations between Albanians and Serbs living in Kosovo changed constantly at the beginning of the twentieth century. That period was initially marked by the end of the First Balkan War in 1912 and the Treaty of London that recognized Serbia's control over Kosovo. Afterwards, the First World War brought Kosovo under the occupation of Austria-Hungary and Bulgaria, but in 1919 it became part of the new Kingdom of Serbs, Croats and Slovenes, eventually renamed as Yugoslavia in 1929.[5] During the Second World War the region was occupied by Italy, while the end of the war finally reincorporated Kosovo under the jurisdiction of Belgrade and the Federal People's Republic of Yugoslavia. It should be mentioned that, during this period, not only the territory of the region was constantly under different rule and modification but the population also suffered significant changes as both Albanians and Serbs migrated inside and outside Kosovo.[6]

The 1946 Yugoslav Constitution granted Kosovo and Metohija the status of an Autonomous Region within Serbia and demarcated the contemporary boundaries of the region. In the following decades, Kosovo Albanians demanded greater autonomy and ultimate recognition as a republic of federal Yugoslavia, alongside Serbia, Croatia, Bosnia and Herzegovina, Slovenia, Macedonia and Montenegro. Marshal Tito, the leader of Yugoslavia, did not accept these requirements and could not recognize Kosovo Albanians as a nation within Yugoslavia, but only as one of the minority 'nationalities'.[7] However, Yugoslavia adopted a new Constitution in 1974 that now called Kosovo an Autonomous Province, which elevated its status nearly equivalent to that of a republic and authorized Kosovo to adopt its own Constitution, assembly and awarded the province a seat on the federal council. Despite these concessions, Kosovo Albanians continued to aspire towards the recognition of Kosovo as a republic, and after Tito's death in 1980 a series of demonstrations by Albanian students highlighted the growing ethnic tensions in the region. Meanwhile, Serb nationalists were increasingly arguing that Kosovo Serbs lived under threat and were discriminated by Albanians. This context favoured the nationalist rhetoric and ascendance to power of Slobodan Milosevic, who in 1989 revoked Kosovo's autonomous status and replaced the local officials in order to re-establish the Serbian domination of the region.[8]

As already mentioned, in the context of the collapse of Yugoslavia in 1991 and the declaration of independence by Croatia and Slovenia, the Kosovo Albanian leaders part of the Democratic League of Kosovo (LDK) responded by organizing a referendum on independence. This was followed by the 1992 unofficial election of Ibrahim Rugova as president and the formation of parallel political, economic and social service institutions. At the same time, the war in Bosnia between 1992 and 1995 diverted the attention of the international community largely away from Kosovo. The exclusion of Kosovo's independence from the agenda of the Dayton peace talks further discredited Rugova's policy of non-violent resistance and favoured the emergence of KLA at the forefront of a more assertive approach.[9] The earlier sporadic violence became increasingly frequent and better organized, and the first planned attacks by the KLA took place in February 1996 against a police patrol. The intensifying attacks primarily aimed at Serb police forces, but also targeting Albanians loyal to the Serb administration and by late 1997 the KLA controlled many rural areas of Kosovo.

The Serbian government considered the KLA a terrorist organization, a viewpoint that was also famously confirmed by the US special envoy for the Balkans, Robert Gelbard.[10] In early 1998 Serb forces responded with a campaign of intimidation, followed by bolder attacks against Albanian civilians and supposed KLA enclaves. Paramilitary police led the attacks with support from army and regular Serbian forces. The members of the Contact Group, consisting of France, Germany, Italy, Russian Federation, the UK and the United States, confirmed Kosovo as a matter of high priority and established a working group to address the situation. Several resolutions of the UN Security Council have characterized Milosevic's actions as a threat to international peace and security especially that the Serbian leader ordered deportations and ethnic cleansing campaigns.[11] However, the lack of agreement and a persistent reluctance to take action beyond condemnation and appeals for dialogue hindered the development of a lasting political solution. It was not until the heightened level of violence and destruction endangered the fragile post-Dayton stability of the region that the international community began to take a more active role. More than 800,000 Kosovo Albanians[12] had to leave their homeland and about 13,000 people died during the period of conflict.[13]

After the failure of the negotiations at Rambouillet and in the absence of an explicit mandate from the UNSC, but not on contradiction with the purpose of its previous resolutions, NATO launched a strategic aerial bombardment campaign on the night of 24 March 1999. The war lasted for seventy-eight days and was used as a preventive measure against Milosevic so as to stop the abuse towards the Albanian civilians. The outcome of the campaign was the de facto withdrawal from Kosovo of the Serbs and the decision to place the province under the authority of the UN. The UN's actions were going to be secured by the NATO-led Kosovo Force (KFOR) in order to avoid recurrence of an ethnic conflict and to ensure public order and safety and 'to deter renewed hostilities, establish a secure environment and ensure public safety and order, demilitarize the Kosovo Liberation Army, support the international humanitarian effort and coordinate with the international civil presence'.[14]

Post-1999 UNMIK period: Minorities at risk during 'standards before status'

The previous chapter has already highlighted how a state could be considered *successful* from a Weberian point of view if it has control over the *legitimate* use of violence within its own borders. Thus, when this control is broken and central authority collapses, the existence of the state itself is at threat and a vulnerable regime can turn into a failed state. Furthermore, the state does not need legitimacy to potentially control the means of violence, but it would need legitimacy if it made use of these means. In any case, legitimate authority can be evaluated by looking at

> a) the credibility of the institutions invested by free elections. b) the capacity of political authority to fulfil its social tasks. c) the compatibility of power with the system of values proposed and accepted. d) the way in which those who govern have obtained power and the exercise of power itself.[15]

Legitimacy is thus linked not only with legality but also with the criteria of performance and certification: 'Transparency in governance and accountability in administration are important for sovereignty to become a meaningful exercise of power by the state and its apparatus.'[16] This means that in post-war Kosovo, the development of civil society, the level of political culture among people, the indifference or the incompetence of those who govern have all been additional yet fundamental elements of legitimacy and, implicitly, of strong statehood.

In general, the ideas around state weakness and state failure have been discussed by adopting two different variants, which Trutz von Trotha[17] identifies as (a) 'institutionalist' and (b) 'functionalist'. Furthermore, internationally driven liberal statebuilding (particularly in post-conflict societies) has generally attempted to put into practice one of these approaches and export a particular state model. The *institutionalist* variant reflects a view of the state which is narrowed beyond the Weberian conceptualization of the state, as it 'regards the OECD model of the strong state and democratic rule of law as the yardstick by which to measure statehood. Its criteria are specific institutions such as general and fair elections guaranteeing secrecy; parliaments; parties; independent judiciaries; and human rights'.[18] The state in this view is mainly a clear-cut set of institutions and rules reflecting a Western-centric model (Weberian/neoliberal), and consequently, statebuilding is limited to establishing institutions without seriously challenging their appropriateness and their changing character under the impact of endogenous factors.

By contrast, the *functionalist* account measures the degree of state failure by going beyond the presence and mechanisms of specific institutions and by analysing the fulfilment of functions that the modern western state typically delivers. However, 'state-centrism here is indirect, a kind of "second-order" state-centrism, because the achievements of non-state political orders are measured against (and research criteria are orientated towards) the functions of the modern state'.[19] By evaluating the functionality of the institutions, rules and mechanism put in place by processes/missions of liberal statebuilding, this variant tries to identify flaws of the model and find solutions like the refocus on legitimizing the state apparatus based on the efficiency of its functions. This does not represent however recognition of the fact that the Westphalian-Weberian state is not necessarily a suitable model. Moreover, the critique to these state-centric variants is re-enforced by the fact that scholars readily associate failed or anarchical states with the lack of a central government. As Hagmann and Hoehne[20] point out, life goes on with non-state actors performing many of the functions usually associated with the state, contrary to the state-centred approaches. This simultaneity of state, non-state and international actors claiming the monopoly of force over a territory also challenges the Weberian view of the state.

After 1999, Kosovo was under the administration of the UN in accordance with UNSC Resolution 1244, which established a status of autonomy. The Resolution established the UNMIK with the role to administer the province 'while establishing and overseeing the development of provisional democratic self-governing institutions to ensure conditions for a peaceful and normal life for all inhabitants in Kosovo'.[21] As a consequence, UNMIK set up an international presence in Kosovo and was tasked with

> undertaking a major reconstruction programme to establish democracy, stability and self-government [...] facilitating the process that would determine the future status of Kosovo, coordinating the international humanitarian agencies, supporting the reconstruction of key infrastructures, maintaining law and public order, promoting human rights, and guaranteeing security and safe return of displaced persons.[22]

As these key responsibilities indicate, UNMIK had a very difficult objective to govern the province and to secure peace while coordinating the local authorities to develop capacity for self-government without pre-settled future status. UNMIK's structure was divided into four pillars 'with a Special Representative of the UN Secretary-General (SRSG) to hold overall authority and coordinate the different international agencies involved'.[23] These were Pillar I: Police and justice, Pillar II: Civil administration, Pillar III: Democratization and institution building and Pillar IV: Reconstruction and economic development. While the first two pillars were to be led by the UN, Pillar III came under the administration of the Organization for Security and Co-operation in Europe (OSCE) and Pillar IV was in the hands of the European Union.

Even though 'these efforts led to a greater level of involvement of local actors in the process of Kosovo's governance, the balance of authority still lay clearly with UNMIK and the SRSG retained final executive and legislative authority'.[24] Giving the multiple responsibilities of the international community, it can be affirmed that UNMIK was a robust mission from the beginning 'especially at the levels of executive powers and the ability to intervene in all aspects of the province's political and socio-economic life'.[25] It is important to highlight here the official involvement of the EU under the fourth pillar as for the first time in history the EU was in charge of a full policy area of a UN mission.[26] The same report illustrates that the EU's contribution to statebuilding in Kosovo was already introducing crucial innovations to the 'traditional' approach of UN past activities as it 'pointed out the necessity to create viable, competitive economic institutions and the costs of non-action in terms of development and stability foregone ... [EU Pillar's policies] were driven by the goals of fostering the sustainable development of a market economy in Kosovo'.[27]

The EU thus became determined to promote Kosovo's regional integration (bilateral free trade agreements, energy policy, transport integration), which was also perceived as part of the EU's plans for integration of the Balkans area. The EU's participation also highlights the approach of *functional engagement* permitting a direct involvement of representatives of Kosovo's institutions in the negotiations of different agreements. Overall, as part of UNMIK, the EU played a significant role in the development of Kosovo's institutions and as the Report on the EU Pillar affirms, the innovative measures 'have proven that the institutional integration is the key to create long-term structures of cooperation and peaceful handling of disagreement'.[28]

Another essential part of EU's role in Kosovo has been reflected by the Stabilisation and Association Process (SAP), the framework for EU's engagement with the Western Balkans for guidance regarding the eventual accession of the states from this region. In 2001 a constitutional framework was adopted to prepare general elections and the creation of an assembly, a government and the presidency. This also 'gave the SRSG extensive powers, including the authority to dismiss the Assembly, control the budget, and appoint and remove judges and prosecutors'.[29] The Assembly had the duty to elect the president and the prime minister. In 2007 three sets of legislative elections were already organized having the Democratic League of Kosovo and the Democratic Party of Kosovo (PDK) as main contenders. And during 2002 and 2006 the two presidents elected by the Parliament were Ibrahim Rugova and Fatmir Sejdiu. An eloquent conclusion was that

> a coalition government is in place, and a vigorous opposition regularly questions government policy and action. The Constitutional Framework provides a legal foundation for the operation of government and specifies the competencies of the various branches of the political structure. While Kosovo lacks official recognition of statehood, and has an uncertain political future, it has nonetheless developed many of the core features of a democratic political regime.[30]

In order to understand the evolution of statebuilding during that period, it would be useful to briefly analyse the 2007 Communication from the European Commission on the subject of the Enlargement Strategy. This included a comprehensive evaluation of the progress of UNMIK under the UNSCR 1244 and described the progress that was made in as regards the political criteria. In the area of *Democracy and the rule of law*, the report said that 'Kosovo has made progress in addressing some key partnership priorities. The provisional institutions of self-government (PISG) have fulfilled their core roles in their areas of competence. However, the United Nations Interim Administration Mission in Kosovo (UNMIK) still bears ultimate legislative and executive responsibility'.[31] The Commission confirmed therefore that Kosovo institutions had made some progress as indicated by the overall stability, transfer of responsibilities, a more active assembly, stable coalition government and a more efficient public administration.

The report showed however that some of the key problems continued to be the 'weak and unstable' judicial system as well as the widespread corruption. As regards *Regional issues and international obligations*, the report was rather vague stating that 'Kosovo participates actively and constructively, to the extent its present status permits, in regional co-operation initiatives'.[32] This communication also talked about the economic development and suggested that there was still much to improve before fulfilling the EU standards (internal market, competition, employment and social policies, sectoral policies). Both the political and the economic criteria were clearly still affected by the Kosovo's ongoing status issue. Despite the fact that policy and legislation have been developed and approximated in line with European standards, the key problem remained the lack of an efficient and complete implementation process.[33] Just like in the case of peacebuilding and statebuilding in Bosnia and Herzegovina, implementation has been a key challenge for an approach that hurried to elaborate rules, laws, guiding principles, measures to be taken and so forth but without having the legitimacy, capacity and means to make all of these work in practice. The difficulty of transferring the authority to local actors is all the more highlighted by the fact that UNMIK's preliminary role was also to smooth the transition to local ownership. Even when structures such as UNMIK manage to put into practice some of its immediate objectives, prolonged external peacebuilding gradually reduces the chances of efficient and legitimate local ownership:

> Standards may have been set in terms of governance and human rights, but they cannot be imposed or are not readily accepted, when there is no agreement on the final status – on whom these rights will be applicable to and who will guarantee them.[34]

As regards *Human rights and the protection of minorities*, there was little progress concerning religious freedom, women's rights, children's rights and property rights, while minority rights are 'guaranteed by law but restricted in practice because of security concerns'.[35] In this regard, the 2004 riots were the most violent events in Kosovo after the 1999 war. As indicated before, KFOR was made responsible for the transition to peace in Kosovo while also guaranteeing the safe return of the refugees from all communities. After five years without any major incidents, ethnic clashes occurred again in March 2004 after unfounded rumours about the drowning of three Albanian children provoked major riots across Kosovo, particularly in Caglavica and Mitrovica/Mitrovicë North, involving more than 50,000 Albanians.[36] The three days of rampage left 19 people dead, nearly 900 injured and over 4,000 people displaced while also damaging or destroying over 700 Serb, Ashkali and Roma homes, 30 Serbian churches and some public buildings.[37] The revolt only stopped after NATO transferred further 3,000 soldiers in the province and the Albanian leadership managed to calm things down. Nonetheless, the spontaneous and quick escalation of violence confirmed the fragility of the post-war situation:

> The violent explosion revealed Kosovo society to be deeply troubled, lacking institutions, leadership and the culture to absorb shocks and contain its violent, criminal minority. In its current state, this society will continue to push out minorities and ultimately consume its own wafer-thin layer of liberal intelligentsia.[38]

Therefore, the post-conflict domestic insecurity in Kosovo was marked by the perpetuation of ethnic division and the challenge to protect the Kosovo Serb community, now representing a decreasing minority in the province that was no longer under the authority of Belgrade. The situation of other minorities was also at risk, particularly Roma, Ashkali and Egyptian communities, who were trapped in the middle of the Serb-Albanian conflict. After 1999 they were generally perceived by the majority Albanians as having collaborated with Serbian and Yugoslav forces during the conflict and, thus, also became a target of discrimination and marginalization.[39] As a result, the hopes of the international community to reconstruct a multiethnic Kosovo still had many obstacles to surpass. Kosovo Serbs remained the largest minority group in the province and as the following empirical chapters will reveal, two key problems have been affecting the situation of the community since the end of the war: the mass flight of Serb population and the isolation of the remaining Serbs in mono-ethnic regional enclaves. It will be therefore very interesting to link this post-conflict environment with the de jure territorial enclavization of Kosovo after the 2008 declaration of independence.

Nevertheless, in addition to the multitude of domestic problems, the uncertainty of post-conflict Kosovo has also had an international side. The permanent statebuilding dilemma installed during the UNMIK period was embodied by the policy of *standards before status*: 'Although the resolution provides a clear mandate for the building of political institutions, it does not determine the scope of authority these institutions could eventually have. UNMIK was effectively tasked to engage in statebuilding without statehood.'[40] The problem of 'limited statehood' has been a key challenge for the international presence in Kosovo as it has created various problems at regional and international levels. Firstly, after 1999 Kosovo became a subject of international controversy in terms of the implications of the causes of the war, international law, NATO's involvement, relation with Serbia, ethnic tensions, regional context, issue of secessionism, and all these have been reflected by the ever contestation of Kosovo's status, territory, identity, legality and sovereignty. Given the context in which Kosovo has departed from the authority of Serbia, it has been put forward the argument that Kosovo has established 'the principle that states can lose their sovereignty over a portion of their territory if they so oppress the majority population there that they rise in revolt and successfully enlist international support for their rebellion'.[41] While this argument has been used by the Albanian Kosovars to reject any potential claim from Serbia to re-integrate Kosovo within its territory, it has also become a key test for Kosovo's independence and claim to build its legitimacy both domestically and internationally by securing the protection and integration of all its constituent peoples.

The multi-layered contestation of Kosovo has had both a domestic and an international character. The first period under the administration of UNMIK meant that standards in terms of governance and human rights had been set but with limited implementation in the absence of an agreement on the final status of the province. In other words, the limited statehood of Kosovo under UNMIK raised the questions of who would be the legal and legitimate guarantors and who would benefit of these standards and rights. In a similar fashion to the case of post-conflict statebuilding in Bosnia, implementation has been the main problem for a strategy that hurried to elaborate rules, laws, guiding principles, measures to be taken and so forth but with the challenges of legitimacy, capacity and means to implement it. The difficulty of transferring the authority to local actors is all the more highlighted by the fact that UNMIK's preliminary role was also to smooth the transition to local ownership but the prolonged external statebuilding gradually undermined the conditions for developing efficient and legitimate local ownership.

External actors face different challenges in building states after insurgent victory. Often the challenge is to provide security for the vanquished army and for the population associated with it. In Kosovo, for instance, NATO failed sufficiently to protect Serbs. Moreover, statebuilding here tends to focus on constraining or shaping the victorious groups occupying the state and on empowering the vanquished in both the design and the staffing of the post-war state.[42] Furthermore, the establishment of the Kosovo Transitional Council (KTC) with a purely consultative role was insufficient to prevent alternative sources of authority from taking over at the local level. The unrecognized 'Provisional Government of Kosova' that was led by KLA had the opportunity to appoint mayors and establish 'a parallel governmental structure reporting to its Minister of Local Government, not to UNMIK'.[43] The necessary democratic link between state and society and the creation of civil society were therefore instantly undermined by the external top-down control of the international administration, but at the same time a perennial state weakness was installed under the co-influence of illiberal non-state authority formations: 'What appears to have emerged is that the development of "civil society" has been monopolised by foreign internationals and exploited by local entrepreneurs.'[44]

The post-war context of Kosovo is therefore illustrative for the alternative characterization of the state failure model offered by the concept of 'hybrid political orders',[45] which captures the intersection of formal (modern state institutions) and informal (traditional, customary, social institutions) forces. This deviation from the standard state model of governance means that in order to make institutions work, informal networks and actors are utilized (indigenous societal relations and institutions). On the one hand, state institutions may become the target of power struggles between competing social groups and their leaders, who utilize them for their own benefit and disregard the wishes of the 'nation' or the 'citizenry'.[46] For this reason, 'the whole debate about neopatrimonialism, clientelistic networks and patronage, for example in postcolonial African states, revolves around this usurpation of imported formal governance structures by indigenous informal societal forces'.[47]

On the other hand, statebuilding impacts on non-state local orders too by re-forming customary systems of order when they are included in the central state institutions and processes. Non-state actors adopt then 'an indefinite position with regard to the state, appropriating state functions and "state talk", but at the same time pursuing their own agenda under the guise of the state authority and power. Taking state functions and state talk on board, however, also means changing one's original stance. Some governments also try to deliberately incorporate traditional authorities, in order to strengthen state capacities and legitimacy'.[48] This reaffirms the importance of conceptualizing the state as a process and a symbiosis of state structures (institutions, rules) and society. The idea of a hybrid political order highlights not only the impact of the various local contexts, but also that the state and society spheres do not exist in isolation from each other, 'but permeate each other and, consequently, give rise to a different and genuine political order'.[49]

The Ahtisaari Plan

> Kosovo shall be a multi-ethnic society, which shall govern itself democratically, and with full respect for the rule of law, through its legislative, executive, and judicial institutions. […]
>
> Kosovo shall guarantee the protection of the national or ethnic, cultural, linguistic and religious identity of all Communities and their members. Kosovo shall also establish the constitutional, legal and institutional mechanisms necessary for the promotion and protection of the rights of all members of Communities and for their representation and effective participation in political and decision-making processes […].[50]

In 2005 the talks on the status of Kosovo were relaunched and the UN Secretary General named Martti Ahtisaari was appointed as the UN Special Envoy at the Kosovo status process negotiations. The two parties involved in the Kosovo issue had completely different positions. While the Serbs were ready to offer Kosovo a large autonomy under the condition that it remained part of the Serbian territory, the Prishtinë/Priština officials considered that giving up the independent status was unacceptable. In February 2007 Martti Ahtisaari presented at the UN his plan for the status of Kosovo, which was designed to supersede UNSC Resolution 1244 (1999), establish Kosovo's internal settlement and minority-protection mechanisms, mandate a new international presence and allow for supervised independence. According to the Ahtisaari Plan, formally the Comprehensive Proposal for the Kosovo Status Settlement (CSP), the EU and the United States were going to be invested with the leading role in setting up Kosovo's future, which was supposed to become independent under the supervision of an International Civilian Representative with superior powers to the Kosovar government. For instance, the International Representative could have dismissed the members of government in case they did not respect the international accord. Furthermore, decentralization was at the core of the plan in the attempt to reduce the de facto influence of Serbia over the north of Kosovo.[51]

The plan was seeking for a compromise offering Kosovo Albanians the prospect of independence, Kosovo Serbs security, extensive rights and privileged relations with Serbia, and 'Serbia the chance to put the past behind it once and for all and realise its European future'.[52] However, even though this was considered to be an efficient way of governing multiethnicity in Kosovo, it was not what the Kosovo Albanian local leaders had envisaged:

> Decentralisation runs contrary to Kosovo Albanian ideas of achieving state 'functionality' through centralised administrative control. It is instead linked with contemporary European ideas of 'subsidiarity', devolving decision-making down to the lowest level authority, propelled by the idea that the closer governance is to the people it affects, the more likely it is to reflect their interests.[53]

After additional meetings with Belgrade and Prishtinë/Priština sides in Vienna, the UNOSEK status negotiations formally ended on 10 March. Ahtisaari declared that additional efforts would not bring them closer to a compromise and that 'a sustainable solution of Kosovo's status is urgently needed'.[54] During the discussions, Serbs and Kosovo Albanians kept their irreconcilable positions, Prishtinë/Priština asking for Kosovo to become an independent state, while Serbia and Kosovo Serbs wanted Belgrade to regain its sovereignty. Furthermore, prior to adopting the Ahtisaari Plan there was one more obstacle to surpass: the approval of a new UN Security Council Resolution and the unanimity of its five permanent members. The right to veto used by Russia on 26 March 2007 obstructed the plans of the United States and the EU as Moscow continued to oppose any potential threat to the territorial integrity of Serbia.

I have discussed earlier how the EU's involvement in Kosovo had from the start the goal of supporting local ownership not only as an implementation of the UNMIK interim administration's initial task to facilitate self-government but also as part of the strategy to assist Kosovo's regional and European integration. This strategy refers to the conditionality factor that has been motivating the Western Balkan countries to satisfy the EU's criteria for potential membership. The EU was therefore worried that after the failure to get the UN's authorization to put into operation the Ahtisaari Plan, there was a permanent risk that the indeterminate status and the unstable situation within Kosovo 'could again rekindle ethnic violence and destabilize the region'.[55]

In the second half of 2007 the trio of EU, United States and Russia attempted in a number of 'Troika'-led talks to determine Kosovo's future status as mediators between Serbia and Kosovo. The final troika report that was forwarded in December 2007 to Ban Ki-moon, the UN Secretary General, confirmed that even though they had not been able to reach an agreement, they were reaffirming Kosovo's degree of autonomy from Serbia. The report mentioned: 'There will be no return to the pre-1999 status ... Belgrade will not govern Kosovo .... Belgrade will not re-establish a physical presence in Kosovo [and] will not interfere in Pristina's relationship with international financial institutions ... Pristina will have full authority over its finances (taxation, public revenues, etc.).'[56] Kosovo's self-governing in the area of finance was also in accordance with EU's emphasis on the SAP. Therefore, despite the fact that it became clear that Russia would still veto against Kosovo's independence, the report also confirmed that the future of Kosovo was going to continue reducing Serbia's influence. A return to constitutional ties between Kosovo Albanians and Serbia was not an option given that Belgrade wanted to maintain Kosovo under its jurisdiction and it had not tried to integrate Kosovo Albanians or offer alternative autonomy arrangements. Instead, Serbia tried 'to establish the basis for an ethnic division of Kosovo and partition along the Ibar River, [...] Partition, however, would not only destroy the prospect of multi-ethnicity in Kosovo but also destabilise neighbouring states'.[57]

The independence of Kosovo: de facto vs. de jure

The Kosovo elections that took place in November 2007 and were won by the Democratic Party of Kosovo with over 34 per cent of the vote had a great significance as the elected Prime Minister, Hashim Thaçi, confirmed then that he would declare Kosovo as an independent state immediately after the 10th of December. Under the pressure of the international community and especially of the EU, the declaration of independence was postponed for 2008 in the waiting of the presidential elections in Serbia. As it happened, in February 2008 Serbia elected the pro-Western Boris Tadic as president and on 17 February 2008 the Assembly of Kosovo declared Kosovo an independent and sovereign state. Since then, Kosovo's unilateral declaration of independence has remained a matter of dispute at the international level and is still lacking the UN's recognition. To date, Kosovo has been recognized as an independent state by about half of the UN members, of which 23 are EU member states.[58] Therefore, the EU itself remains divided on the topic as Spain, Romania, Slovakia, Cyprus and Greece refuse to recognize Kosovo's independence.

The debate over the implications of Kosovo's unilateral declaration of independence is far too complex to be addressed in detail by this book. However, what must be underlined here is that just as important as the struggle for international recognition is the fact that Kosovo has also been trying to demonstrate *capacity* for self-governance before claiming independence. This refers directly to the opportunity for de facto local ownership in Kosovo in the absence of the official recognition of its statehood. This corresponds with the main argument of this chapter because it shows that statebuilding in Kosovo has been trying to become more functional by investing local actors with more authority. As Tansey has argued,

> Although it is not a sovereign state, and may not be recognised as one for some time (if at all), a process has been underway within the entity to establish the structures of a democratic political regime. Developments over recent years in Kosovo reveal significant moves in the creation of a political regime for democratic self-government, albeit in the context of significant levels of international creation of a political regime for democratic self-government.[59]

This suggests that the international debate over Kosovo's right to declare independence is not the only relevant aspect for evaluating the capacity of Kosovo to self-rule since state institutions are in place and have gradually become capable of governing outside the international authority of UNMIK. The Kosovo (under UNSCR 1244/99) 2008 Progress Report released by the European Commission outlined the situation in Kosovo since the proclamation of independence:

> Following the declaration, the security situation remained relatively calm, with the exception of two serious incidents in northern Kosovo. In February, two border posts in northern Kosovo were destroyed, and the storming of the court house in Mitrovica/Mitrovicë in March resulted in the death of an UNMIK policeman and several serious injuries. On 9 April, the assembly adopted the Constitution of the Republic of Kosovo, which entered into force on 15 June 2008. The Constitution is based on the CSP and envisages a significant role of the European Union in Kosovo. It also provides for the international civilian representative as ultimate supervisory authority as set out in the CSP.[60]

On the one hand, the post-declaration situation was generally stable and the fears over a possible exodus of the Serbs living in the north region of Kosovo were realized. This permitted the local authorities to adopt a Constitution and to continue reforms as regards political institutions, judiciary, police and public administration. On the other hand, the same EC report mentioned that Kosovo remained under international supervision as it had been established by the 2007 Comprehensive Status Proposal and also indicated the increasing responsibility of the EU during the transition from UNMIK. In relation to this, Tansey[61] analysed the relationship between democratization and statehood with reference to the political developments in Kosovo before the declaration of independence and identified three separate dimensions of statehood: recognition, capacity and cohesion. In the case of Kosovo, as a new political entity that emerged after the 1999 NATO intervention, all three dimensions have been either contested or limited by both endogenous and exogenous factors:

(a) Limited international recognition denying Kosovo's legal sovereignty
(b) The challenges of building a new state with new institutional, administrative, legislative and economic capacities
(c) The divided character of the new territorial entity with a multiethnic society living under the supervision of an international administration and a highly contested state authority.

This suggests not only that international recognition of statehood was not viewed as a prerequisite for democratization, but also that problems of state capacity or state cohesion present far more fundamental challenges to successful democratic regime change. The post-1999 Kosovo followed international standards of democratization and despite the external administration by UNMIK, local actors built and increased their authority progressively. Despite the lack of international recognition of statehood, domestic democratic structures have developed over time and have evolved into an unconventional hybrid political system, part domestic democratic regime, part international authority. Kosovo's recent political trajectory thus highlights the fact that processes of democratic transition are not unique to established states and can occur outside the state system.[62]

This overview of the post-conflict statebuilding in Kosovo highlights the dynamic character of the state under the impact of a multitude of external and internal processes. Nonetheless, Kosovo's international legitimacy has been contested from the moment it declared independence and it has continued to lack the support of the UN Security Council. In this regard, Kosovo's independence has paradoxically confirmed it as an 'unfinished state' given the layers of contestation, as outlined by Surroi:[63] territorial/regional (Serbia defending its territorial integrity in the post-Yugoslavian context), global (many of the UN member states have not recognized Kosovo as an independent state and hostility within the Security Council comes from both Russia and China) and the obstacles for Kosovo's perspective for European integration arising from the fact that five EU member states have refused to recognize its independence so far.

This latter obstacle has a major significance given the EU's leading role in Kosovo[64] as an agent of economic reform, as an institution-builder, as an actor in the domestic process of political reform and accommodation and as a provider of security. The EU presence in Kosovo has had three main components: first, the EU Special Representative in Kosovo (EUSR) has been the political factor supporting the local authorities to meet their obligations while promoting overall EU political coordination and who had a double-hatted role with extensive executive powers as the International Civilian Representative.

The second component has been the European Union Rule of Law Mission in Kosovo (EULEX) with an operational role to monitor, mentor and advise Kosovo's authorities on police, justice, correctional services and customs. The mission has aimed to develop and strengthen a Kosovo independent multiethnic rule of law system while prioritizing immediate problems regarding the protection of minority communities, corruption and the fight against organized crime.

The third entity has been a reform driving European Commission Liaison Office (ECLO) that helps Kosovo in its long-term reforms efforts and that has been deploying enlargement tools under the SAP in support of institution-building, economic development and meeting European standards (democratization, rule of law, legislation).

Therefore, while this book mainly looks at the limited domestic capacities of Kosovo's political and economic institutions, it also needs to be highlighted that Kosovo's future in terms of statebuilding progress and its path towards the EU indicates that 'for a variety of legal and political reasons, it seems highly likely that Kosovo will need to be fully and wholly sovereign, and its status uncontested, both within the EU and the wider international community'.[65] The mix of endogenous and exogenous factors considered here highlights not only that Kosovo is a post-conflict, post-communist political entity with contested statehood but that it also represents a unique example of statebuilding. Statebuilding in Kosovo has been combining efforts in support of international recognition, reconciliation, democratization and institutional capacity while highlighting the importance of developing sustainable local ownership and implementing a multiethnic model of governance capable of securing unity at the same time as enshrining far-reaching minority rights.

De jure integration and accommodation of minorities in Kosovo

We declare Kosovo to be a democratic, secular and multiethnic republic, guided by the principles of non-discrimination and equal protection under the law. We shall protect and promote the rights of all communities in Kosovo and create the conditions necessary for their effective participation in political and decision-making processes.[66]

After the declaration of independence on 17 February 2008, the Constitution was promulgated and defined the Republic of Kosovo an independent, sovereign, democratic, unique and indivisible state and as a 'multi-ethnic society consisting of Albanian and other Communities, governed democratically with full respect for the rule of law through its legislative, executive and judicial institutions'.[67] Given this book's aim to discuss the interplay between the de jure and de facto management of diversity in Kosovo, it is important to highlight from the start that declaring Kosovo a multiethnic society can be perceived as an overestimation of the ethnic diversity of its population. According to the 2011 Census,[68] Kosovo had approximately 1.7 million citizens, of which the Albanian majority represent approximately 93 per cent of the entire population while the rest 7 per cent consists of Serb, Bosniak, Turkish, Gorani, Montenegrin, Croat and Roma, Ashkali and Egyptian communities.[69]

In concrete terms, independent Kosovo was from the start a de jure multiethnic society with a de facto largely homogeneous population. At the same time, even if the emphasis of the Constitution is on establishing a multiethnic civic-based Kosovan identity, the formulation 'Albanian and other Communities' differentiates the majority community, the Albanians, from the rest of the communities, the minorities. As I will indicate later, a similar formulation that is used within several laws and other official documents singles out the Serb community from 'the other communities', therefore suggesting that the risk of installing a hierarchical order[70] of communities in Kosovo is of both de jure and de facto nature.

'Community' not 'minority'

The Law on Communities also provides a general definition of communities as

national, ethnic, cultural, linguistic or religious groups traditionally present in the Republic of Kosovo *that are not in the majority*. These groups are Serb,

Turkish, Bosnian, Roma, Ashkali, Egyptian, Gorani and other communities. Members of the community in the majority in the Republic of Kosovo as a whole who are not in the majority in a given municipality shall also be entitled to enjoy the rights listed in this law.[71]

This definition gives the notion of 'community' a clear meaning as the equivalent of 'minority' and, in consequence, differs from the text of the Constitution that includes the Albanians in the category by saying that communities are 'inhabitants belonging to the same national or ethnic, linguistic, or religious group traditionally present on the territory of the Republic of Kosovo'.[72] Moreover, by using this general understanding of 'communities', the Constitution further divides the notion into two categories: 'non-majority communities' and 'majority community' (Albanians), which are both also present in the constitutional text and in other laws and official documents of Kosovo. These inconsistencies of using the term 'community' instead of 'minority' and of also giving different definitions derive from the intention to avoid referring to any group as minorities.[73] This came as a consequence of Kosovo's unsettled status under Resolution 1244 and the symbolically important divisions of the past between 'constitutive and/or non-constitutive nations'.[74] Resolution 1244 preserves the sovereignty of the Federal Republic of Yugoslavia (FRY), suggesting that Kosovo Serbs identify themselves as the majority community in the general context of FRY. At the same time, Kosovo Albanians reject any legal connection with FRY and therefore define themselves as a majority within Kosovo.[75]

It is also important to say that, initially, both the Constitution and the Law on Communities mentioned only seven minorities in Kosovo (Serb, Turkish, Bosnian, Roma, Ashkali, Egyptian, Gorani) by omitting the Montenegrin and the Croat communities. As a result, until recently these two minorities were not protected by the Kosovo legislation in the post-independence period and, for instance, were not awarded guaranteed seats in the parliament and were not included as ethnic categories in the 2011 Census. After three years of lobbying and discussion on this issue,[76] Kosovo authorities agreed to include Montenegrin and Croat as minority communities and amended the Law on Communities on December 2011.[77] However, the two communities have remained unrepresented in the Assembly and the only visible inclusion after the amendment was on the list of representatives for the Consultative Council for Communities (CCC),[78] where Croats and Montenegrins shall each have 'two (2) representatives respectively, one (1) of each of whom may be a member of the Assembly of Kosovo'.[79]

Furthermore, using the notion of 'community' instead of 'minority' does not have any impact on the commitment to respect human rights and minority rights in accordance with international standards as guaranteed by Article 22 of the Constitution, which mentions the international agreements and instruments that are directly applicable in the territory of Kosovo and that in the case of conflict have priority over provisions of laws and other acts of public institutions.[80] Likewise, the constitutional chapter on 'Rights of Communities and Their Members', Article 58, specifies that Kosovo shall respect the standards set forth in the Council of Europe Framework Convention for the Protection of National Minorities and the European Charter for Regional or Minority Languages.[81] Therefore, by mentioning its commitment to international standards, the Constitution of Kosovo does have two direct references to the term 'minority': 'national minorities' and 'minority language'. Article 58 also describes the proactive responsibilities of the Kosovo state to help minority groups protect and promote their identities, to support reconciliation, to develop and enforce anti-discrimination measures, to promote socioeconomic, political and cultural equality, to preserve cultural and religious heritage of all communities and to ensure that all communities and their members exercise their constitutional rights. Moreover, 'the Republic of Kosovo shall refrain from policies or practices aimed at assimilation of persons belonging to Communities against their will, and shall protect these persons from any action aimed at such assimilation.'[82] Therefore, not only the Kosovo Constitution makes the state responsible and proactive in the promotion and protection of minorities, but it also specifies that policies or practices of assimilation are outlawed and against the multiethnic character of Kosovo.

Moreover, despite having been criticized by both supporters and opponents of Kosovo's independence, the provisions included in the CSP[83] document remain the cornerstone of the multiethnic democratic model of governance installed in Kosovo. Therefore, in addition to the constitutional framework, by signing several fundamental laws and especially the Law on the Protection and Promotion of the Rights of Communities and their Members, the Kosovo Government has constructed a solid system of rights that 'should meet Kosovo's international commitments and requirements for European integration, as long as they are effectively implemented'.[84] Kosovo has developed a complex system for minority rights protection that even though it was not envisaged by all its minority communities, it was necessary for dealing with the new position of Serbs in Kosovo.[85] After the war, not only did Serbs become isolated and had to live in small enclaves but their status also changed completely. Serbs needed to be provided with special rights because it was very difficult to become a minority after having been the majority and the community in charge of Yugoslavia and Serbia for such a long period of time.[86] From this point of view, Kosovo was defined as a multiethnic society so as to help with establishing power-sharing institutions and to give ethnic autonomy and representation as part of the international peacebuilding toolbox. Nevertheless, all these measures will have a great impact on the long term as they are also designed to help finalize the status of Kosovo.[87]

Constitutional and institutional provisions for minority rights protection

Kosovo has a solid legal basis for the protection of minorities and of cultural heritage. These guarantees are directly enshrined either in Kosovo's Constitution and regulated by the law on the protection and rights of minorities. As the Council of Europe Framework Convention for the Protection of National Minorities is directly applicable in Kosovo and takes precedence over Kosovo legislation, Kosovo has clear obligations to ensure that its own legislation, policies or practices meet the international requirements.[88]

The Constitution not only has a chapter on minority rights but also includes special guarantees for participation of non-majority communities in the decision-making process at all levels of governance. To start with, the power-sharing tools that have been included in Kosovo's Constitution can be identified as follows: grand coalition government (ministers from minority groups must be included in the executive; role of community consultative bodies), proportionality (composition of parliament and the judiciary, electoral system, local government and employment in public administration and state-owned companies), veto rights (right to veto on constitutional amendment procedures and on the adoption of vital laws and amendment procedures) and segmental autonomy (special cultural autonomy and protection for minorities as regards language, religion, education, media and symbols).The most visible political rights of representation are therefore the guaranteed seats in the Assembly and the less visible is their participation within other institutions (vice-president, deputy-mayor and deputy-chair or deputy-speaker in local assemblies). At the central level, Kosovo Serbs have held several important government offices, including a deputy prime minister, three ministerial and two deputy ministerial posts.[89] The Constitution follows the recommendations and responsibilities included in the Ahtisaari package, which emphasizes the rights and freedoms granted to minority communities living in Kosovo.[90] At the same time, Kosovo has not signed human rights treaties given its unsettled international status, but Article 22 in the Constitution obliges Kosovo to give priority over its laws to several of the main international agreements such as the Universal Declaration of Human Rights, the European Convention for the Protection of Human Rights and Fundamental Freedoms and the International Covenant on Civil and Political Rights as guarantee for election standards. Kosovo's constitutional commitment to these international agreements is even more important given that 82 per cent of Kosovo Serbs are dissatisfied with respect for human rights while they also mainly define democracy in terms of 'protection of human rights'.[91]

Furthermore, Article 58 of the Constitution affirms the responsibilities of the state in protecting and promoting the rights and interests of communities and mentions the areas in which Kosovo must have a proactive role towards minorities.[92] These responsibilities highlight the positive role that must be taken by state institutions and bodies not only to avoid discrimination but also to achieve equality among communities. Furthermore, Article 59 contains specific rights of communities and their members for maintaining and preserving their culture, receiving public education in one of the official languages or in their own language for preschool, primary and secondary education, using their language in public institutions where they represent a sufficient share of the population and having access to and special representation in public media.

In addition to the constitutional provisions, the Kosovo Government passed in 2008 the Law on the Protection and Promotion of the Rights of Communities and their Members in Kosovo, also known as the Law on Communities. Its purpose is to enable minorities to cultivate, preserve and develop their identity by taking affirmative measures to promote full and effective equality in all spheres of life.[93] The Law mainly repeats the protections laid out in the Constitution, making the state responsible to protect the identity, language, culture, religion, education, media access and health of all communities. The positive role of the state should especially be targeting areas of socioeconomic opportunities, education and political participation. Article 4 of the Law on Communities outlines the language rights for all communities in Kosovo that shall be respected and regulated in accordance to the provisions of the Law on the Use of Languages.[94] The Law on languages and Article 4 of the Law on Communities both confirm that Albanian and Serbian are the official languages in Kosovo and 'have equal status in its institutions'.[95] At the municipal level, other community languages (Turkish, Bosnian, Roma) are also languages in official use. Therefore, in addition to the rights of all communities to preserve, maintain and promote their linguistic identity and the local level language rights, Serbian can be equally used in all Kosovo institutions and all official records, documents and laws also have to be kept, issued and published in Serbian. The use of Serbian is guaranteed at all levels of government, from municipal to central level, public companies, schools and all other social environments.

The equal status between Albanian spoken by more than 90 per cent of the population and a minority language spoken by only about 3 per cent of the population[96] is another key privilege for Kosovo Serbs that is designed to help with their accommodation under the authority of Pristina. Regarding use of language in education, the law stipulates that 'all persons belonging to communities shall have the right to receive public education at all levels in one of the official languages of Kosovo of their choice ... [and] are entitled to pre-school, primary, secondary public education in their own language, even if it is not an official language'.[97] These provisions indicate that while non-Serb minorities should always also study one of the official languages, Kosovo Serbs have the right to undertake their studies exclusively in Serbian language. However, given the similarity between the Slavic languages of Kosovo, Bosniaks, Gorani, Montenegrins and Croats are also reported to pursue education solely in Serbian in Belgrade sponsored schools. Furthermore, the Law on Education in the Municipalities of the Republic of Kosovo grants municipalities the opportunity to develop education in Serbian.[98]

The law also requires the Ministry of Education in Kosovo to create an independent commission responsible for reviewing the educational material in Serbian, so as to ensure its conformity with the Kosovo legislation on education.[99] The commission is composed of three Serb representatives, one international member and three representatives selected by MEST.[100] Lastly, the Law on Education offers a special provision for the Serb municipality of Mitrovicë/Mitrovica North as it makes the University of Mitrovicë an autonomous public institution of higher education and gives the municipality the 'authority to exercise responsibility for this public Serbian language university'.[101] Funding for the university shall be ensured from the budget of Kosovo, but the law nonetheless mentions the possibility of support from the government of Serbia, which must be transparent and made public.[102]

Article 6 of the Law on Communities provides another guarantee for minorities regarding their right to information in their own languages and to establish their own electronic and printed media. As regards the Serb community, 'The Government of Kosovo shall be obliged to take all measures within its powers to secure an international frequency plan that will allow the Kosovo Serb Community access to a licensed Kosovo-wide independent Serbian-language television channel operating effectively and without discrimination in accordance with law'.[103] The establishment of a TV channel in Serbian is also guaranteed by the Law on Radio Television of Kosovo, which nonetheless ensures that 15 per cent of all programmes are broadcasted in the minority languages.[104] In terms of religious and cultural rights of minorities, it is noteworthy to mention that the Serbian Orthodox Church in Kosovo 'is afforded the protection and enjoyment of its rights, privileges and immunities according to the Law on the Establishment of Special Protective Zones'.[105]

The legal framework in Kosovo stipulates that non-majority communities should also be represented in the judiciary as the Constitution requires that at least 15 per cent of the judges of the Constitutional Court, Supreme Court and any other court established with appeal jurisdiction across Kosovo shall be from communities that are not in majority in Kosovo, out of which 8 per cent of positions should be allocated to Serbs.[106] District courts are required to reflect the ethnic composition of the municipalities constituting the district, thus allowing for a balanced representation even at the first instance level. Representation is also guaranteed in the prosecutorial system, Kosovo Judicial Council, Ombudsperson Institution and Central Election Commission. In jurisdictions where Serbs are the majority population, there is another extra privilege for their community as candidates for judicial positions within basic courts 'may only be recommended for appointment by the two members of the Council elected by Assembly deputies holding seats guaranteed or reserved for the Serb Community in the Republic of Kosovo acting jointly and unanimously'.[107]

Executive level institutions

As regards central level institutions, Kosovo has a Ministry for Communities and Return (MCT) founded in 2005 with the aim to protect the rights of minorities and returnees as defined in Articles 3 and 4 of the Constitution of Kosovo. Besides its task to create conditions for the return of members of all communities in Kosovo, the Ministry's mandate is also to promote inter-community dialogue, trust and reconciliation and to monitor and coordinate the activities of the government and other central and local institutions related to minority rights protection.¹⁰⁸ Another important body at the executive level is the Office on Good Governance, Human Rights, Equal Opportunities and Gender (OGG) that has been operational within the Office of the Prime Minister since 2002. This Office has operated in conformity with UNMIK Regulation No. 2001/19, and it has been mainly mandated with overseeing and advising ministries involved in matters of good governance, human rights, equal opportunity and gender, and with developing relevant policies and guidelines. It can also review legislation, policies, programmes and practices 'for compliance with applicable standards of human rights and good governance'.¹⁰⁹ Although the OGG is not a body explicitly dedicated to minority rights and interests, it is mandated to engage with all communities in relation to its commitment to protect human rights, encourage equal opportunities, address gender issues and sustain good governance.

Furthermore, since 2007, Kosovo has also established Human Rights Units (HRUs) in all ministries and municipalities of Kosovo.¹¹⁰ While closely cooperating and overseeing the implementation of the recommendations of the Ombudsperson Institution, these ministerial HRUs were created to monitor compliance with policies, legislation and activities with applicable human rights standards, which implicitly include minority rights. Each Kosovo municipality is also required by law to have a HRU mandated to monitor compliance of human rights at the municipal level: anti-discrimination, gender equality, children's rights, disabled persons, the rights of communities, use of languages and anti-human trafficking.¹¹¹

Legislative branch

Kosovo is a parliamentary democracy and according the Constitution, and repeated in the Law on General elections, its unicameral Assembly has 120 deputies. Representatives of minority communities have guaranteed a number of twenty seats. Ten of the guaranteed seats are for Kosovo Serbs and ten for the other communities.¹¹² Minority communities are also guaranteed one of five deputy presidents in the Assembly presidency. For the first two electoral mandates upon the adoption of the Constitution, minorities in Kosovo had an additional advantage of also participating in the distribution of the 100 seats outside the guaranteed ones.¹¹³ Moreover, the 5 per cent threshold necessary for regular political parties did not apply to minority parties, which helped the Independent Liberal Party (SLS) to become part of the governing coalition despite the fact that they received only 2.05 per cent of the votes in the elections.¹¹⁴ Therefore, because of the set-aside seat system for minority political parties, the 2010 general elections allowed Serb parties to win three additional regular seats, which meant that between 2010 and 2014 the Assembly had thirteen Serb deputies representing three parties, eight of which were from SLS.

Overall, the minority political parties had together 25 out of 120 seats in the parliament, representing 20 per cent of the total number of deputies and making them the second biggest parliamentary caucus. This opportunity for minority parties to have such strong decision-making power is even more noteworthy given that in 2010 they won the 25 seats with approximately only 55,000 votes altogether while, for example, the LDK Albanian party came second in the election by receiving around 170,000 votes and won 27 seats.¹¹⁵

The participation of minorities in decision-making was made even stronger by the consociational-like veto power offered for constitutional amendment procedures. In order to pass proposed laws affecting minorities' vital interests like language and education, concurrent majorities are necessary: not only a majority of the whole Assembly but also a majority of minority representatives. Repeal of any relevant laws must also have concurrent-majority consent. By having to be present and vote, minority representatives in the Assembly should be prevented from boycotting the adoption of legislation. Article 81, therefore, names the laws¹¹⁶ that in order to be adopted, amended or repealed require both the majority of the deputies present and voting and the majority of the deputies present and voting holding seats reserved or guaranteed for representatives of communities that are not in the majority. Furthermore, according to the Constitution, the amendment or adoption of laws must be validated by both a majority of the Assembly (two-thirds) and a majority of the parliamentary members representing minority communities present and voting (two-thirds). Therefore, the inclusion of two supermajorities in the Constitution made subsequent constitutional changes very difficult and unlikely. As Korenica and Doli explain this in their analysis of the rigidity of the Kosovo Constitution:

> It means that, a two-thirds majority at the level of ethnic minority MPs is not a monopoly of Serbian MPs alone, with Serbs being the largest ethnic minority in Kosovo. This, therefore, suggests that the two-thirds minority MPs' vote in Parliament is neither a prerogative of one ethnic community's MPs, say Serbian MPs, nor an easily reachable bar from the perspective of other ethnic communities' MPs.¹¹⁷

Consultative bodies for minorities

Another fundamental opportunity for the promotion and protection of minority rights in Kosovo has been the development of an institutional framework of minority consultative bodies composed of the Communities Consultative Council (CCC), the Committee on Rights and Interests of Communities (CRIC) and the Office for Community Affairs (OCA). The plan to establish these bodies was initiated by the international community with the purpose of 'ensuring that constitutional commitments on minority rights are effectively implemented through direct engagement with minority representatives in consultative, decision-making and coordination processes'.[118]

The CCC is based in the Office of the President of Kosovo and has a mandate defined by Article 60 in the Constitution and by the Kosovo Law for the protection and promotion of communities: to provide a mechanism for regular exchange between communities and state institutions, to afford the communities the opportunity to participate at an early stage on legislative or policy initiatives, to provide a forum for coordination and consultation among communities, to enable communities to participate in the needs assessments, design, monitoring and evaluation of programmes that are aimed at their members or are of special relevance to them, to make recommendations during the decision-making process concerning the apportionment of funds for projects aimed at communities, to raise awareness of community concerns within the Republic of Kosovo and to contribute to harmonious relations between all communities within the Republic of Kosovo.[119] The CCC was founded in 2005 as an informal body of minority representatives linked to the Kosovo Delegation to the status settlement process and since 2008, the CCC has been a constitutionally mandated institution that consists of civil society and political minority representatives as well as government officials.

Given the mixed composition of the Consultative Council and its strategic position within the cabinet of the president, minorities in Kosovo have been provided 'with a forum from which to monitor and influence the legislative process, and to advance their needs and interests within government programmes and policies'.[120] As defined by the law, the Serb community 'shall have five (5) representatives, up to two (2) of whom may be members of the Assembly of Kosovo',[121] while the other minorities have fourteen representatives altogether. Thus, the Consultative Council has been another body offering a privileged position for Serbs as the most important minority community in Kosovo. Nevertheless, the nomination and election of representatives within the

CCC have been difficult especially for Kosovo Serbs,[122] and this is reflected, for example, by the fact that on the list with civil society organizations accredited by the Council, there have been only two Serb organizations out of a total of thirty-six. In comparison there have been eight organizations from the Gorani community and nine from the Bosniak community.

A second minority body in Kosovo has been the Committee on the Rights and Interests of Communities (CRIC), which was created prior to the declaration of independence as one of the key committees in the Kosovo Assembly. The 2001 Constitutional Framework granted the body with co-decision powers and with the responsibility of reviewing laws and making recommendations on draft laws so as to protect the rights and interests of minorities in Kosovo.[123] Since 2008, CRIC has been reconfirmed by Article 78 in the Kosovo Constitution as a permanent committee in the Assembly with the purpose to be consulted about proposed laws that may affect the interests of minority communities and with the opportunity to propose laws to address the concerns of minorities or, in other words, 'to act as a legislative catalyst for minority rights in Kosovo'.[124] Regarding its structure, CRIC

> is composed of one third (1/3) of members who represent the group of deputies of the Assembly holding seats reserved or guaranteed for the Serbian Community, one third (1/3) of members who represent the group of deputies of the Assembly holding seats reserved or guaranteed for other communities that are not in the majority and one third (1/3) of members from the majority community represented in the Assembly.[125]

The OCA is another minority consultative body founded in 2008 under the authority of the Office of the Prime Minister.[126] OCA was established to advise the prime minister on all issues concerning all communities in Kosovo, including Albanians as a minority in some municipalities. The body aims to help the government in its efforts to implement the legal framework on the rights of communities and to ensure that governmental policies and measures meet the needs and interests of communities. Its mandate includes: advise the prime minister on communities related issues, coordinate governmental bodies, independent institutions and also donors and international organizations to ensure that communities' issues are being effectively addressed throughout Kosovo, monitor and evaluate the implementation of communities related laws and policy and address practical needs of communities by using available funds.[127] The first director of OCA was Srdjan Sentic, a Kosovo Serb former advisor for Minorities to the Special Representative of the Secretary General for

Kosovo[128] and his successor was another Serb representative, Srdjan Popovic, who was also a senior advisor of the prime minister on community issues. This is therefore another example of Kosovo Serbs holding key upper-level positions in institutions and bodies dealing with the protection and promotion of minority rights.

So far, I have outlined the legal extensive rights and opportunities that have formally established Serbs as the most important minority in Kosovo. Given the provisions offered by the Constitution and laws relevant for minorities, Serbs can be considered legally as the 'most positively discriminated community'[129] in terms of their political, language, cultural, religious rights. However, as the next chapter will illustrate, there are many challenges for further and permanent integration depending on the commitment, capacity and sustainability efforts provided by both the Serb community and Kosovan authorities.

3

The Integration, Accommodation and Protection of Kosovo Serbs

Can a post-communist, post-conflict, contested entity such as Kosovo, with little or no experience of parliamentary democracy or a market economy and, despite the best efforts of the international community, develop such a political system without reverting to ethnic exclusion, with all the inconsistencies, nuance and idiosyncrasies that have been long compensated for by the local processes of donor states?[1]

This chapter aims to explain how the adoption of the Constitution of Kosovo and the implementation of key legislation on minority rights protection have influenced the accommodation of the Serb minority in the post-independence context. The focus on promoting a multiethnic democratic model of governance with important consociational elements of power-sharing for Kosovo has pushed reforms to integrate minority communities. In the context of building a multiethnic Kosovo through legal, institutional and administrative reforms, a dilemma discussed here is regarding the balance between de jure measures for the integration of minorities with focus on Kosovo Serbs and the de facto implementation process targeting political, socioeconomic, legal and cultural rights of minorities.

As the largest minority community, and politically the most difficult ethnic group to integrate within the new state, it seems appropriate to begin an assessment of the development of minority rights protection in Kosovo from this empirical perspective. The overriding aim here is to explore the development of formal legal rights appertaining to minority protection and the actual implementation of such collective rights 'on the ground'. Recognizing the potential gulf between de jure and de facto minority protection and empowerment is at the core of this book. The task here is to consider such issues from the perspective of the Serbian communities across the territory. In the post-independence stage, the will and capacity to integrate minorities has become a condition for the development of domestic sovereignty in Kosovo. The analysis of the situation of the Serb community is discussed in relation to the institutional commitment, capacity and sustainability to implement the post-independence multiethnic model of governance. Furthermore, these elements can help explain better the different levels of effectiveness when implementing minority rights in Kosovo and the shared responsibility between state institutions and the Serb community for the success or failure of a comprehensive and sustainable integration. I have highlighted in the previous chapter that Kosovo Serbs have been the main target and the priority of designing the multiethnic framework under the guidance of the international community. I will now also discuss the interplay of progress and problems characterizing the Serb minority after independence and how this framework provides extensive political rights, social benefits, language and cultural rights. However, their implementation reveals the persistence of important shortcomings as regards the sustainable integration of Kosovo Serbs. After looking in detail at the political participation and representation of Kosovo Serbs, I also examine the socioeconomic challenges that influence the effectiveness of the measures adopted to integrate and accommodate the community.

Firstly, regarding the issue of commitment to foster the integration and implementation of minority rights, the level of understanding and the acceptance of the new context[2] by both the majority Albanians and the Serbs indicate that Kosovo's official pledge to multiethnicity has many limitations too. While the Kosovan authorities have been collaborating for the protection of minority rights as one of the key conditions for independence,[3] minority Serbs have been highly divided and even though they have shown some commitment to integrate, they are not willing to fully drop their non-constitutional ties with Serbia. Secondly, the institutional capacity to deal with the integration and accommodation of minorities plays a fundamental role in helping Serbs to assume their rights and integrate as equal political partners. However, this has not been fully developed and, as this chapter will show, Kosovo has a poor capacity to support its constitutional commitments to the management of diversity given its overall severe socioeconomic problems and its limited experience as a new state.

The domestic context of post-war Kosovo has been challenging not only for the Kosovo Albanians' aim to assume their new status and build a new state, but also for the Kosovo Serbs and the other smaller minorities affected by the conflict and by the secession from Serbia. In this divided and confusing environment, trying to construct and secure unity has been challenging. Nevertheless, Kosovo's path to independence and sustainable statebuilding has required stability and the construction of social cohesion. The point I am making here is that these domestic factors have made it very difficult for Kosovo to pursue the twofold task of integrating its citizens and promoting multiethnicity concomitantly. One of the conditions for Kosovo's partially recognized independence has been to show real and full commitment to respect and include Kosovo Serbs and the other minorities in the governance of the new state.[4] Furthermore, while achieving full international recognition (legal sovereignty) may remain the most difficult task for Kosovo, becoming capable of managing its minorities and, thus, protecting all its citizens equally regardless of their identity is a feature of functional post-ethnic conflict states (domestic sovereignty). The legitimacy of its independence and authority may depend more on a real and comprehensive inclusion of all communities.

Challenges and shortcomings of implementing minority rights

Kosovo Serb political parties after 2008: SLS and JLS

In the post-independence context, the Serb caucus in the Kosovo Assembly has been mainly divided between the pro-government Independent Liberal Party (Samostalna Liberalna Stranka, SLS) and opposition United Serb List (Jedinstvena srpska lista, JSL). None of the smaller Kosovo Serb parties managed to win more than 1,000 votes in the 2010 general elections.[5] SLS was initially the largest party representing the Kosovo Serb community within the political system of Kosovo. It was established in 2006 in Graçanicë/Gračanica during the Serb boycott of Kosovo institutions, and after several years since its foundation the party was still in the stage of growth and geographical expansion in all the regions of Kosovo. At that time, the international presence in Kosovo was seeking to support a new generation of Serb political elites and SLS focused on adapting to the new context and on what would be more beneficial for the Serb community rather than focusing on the political problems around Kosovo's unsettled status.[6] However, their attitude was perceived by Belgrade and its parallel institutions in Kosovo as an act of betrayal.[7] As a result, SLS had little support in the beginning and had to face opposition even from the Serb community in South Kosovo.

> We as a political party decided to participate in the Kosovo institutions because we believe that is the only way to protect the rights of the community. Otherwise, we would not have had any Serbs left in Kosovo after 2006. So, really

and honestly, we have been trying to keep Serbs here. There is no meaning of leading any kind of politics if there are no people here.[8]

As this statement indicates, one section of the Serb community in Kosovo has understood the fact that the post-conflict and post-independence context has inevitably changed their status and their position within Kosovo. Thus, SLS became the 'voice' of the Serbs who did not want to or simply could not depart and who realized that remaining in total opposition and silent within Kosovo politics would have been detrimental for themselves.[9] The SLS party has been involved in all areas with Serb population, apart from the northern region of Kosovo. Party representatives believe that they have shown it was the right decision to work with and for Kosovo institutions and that the positive steps to protect the rights of the Serb community and to improve the conditions of life have increased the confidence of the Serb electorate.[10] The growing support for SLS was evidenced by the number of votes received in 2010 (14,352) compared to 2007 when SLS participated in elections for the first time and managed to get only 855 votes.[11]

In the 2007 general elections SLS gained three Assembly seats with a limited number of votes and joined the government dominated by the Democratic Party of Kosovo (PDK) and the Democratic League of Kosovo (LDK). During that mandate, SLS ran two ministries, the Ministry for Communities and Returns and the Ministry for Social Welfare, and provided two deputy ministers. Even though SLS was benefiting from the support of PDK and of the international presences in Kosovo, the low number of votes won by SLS politicians in 2007 confirmed the difficulty to mobilize Serbs and gain their support for political integration within an independent Kosovo. The SLS candidates who were then allocated seats in the Kosovo Assembly were Bojan Stojanovic with 281 votes, Slobodan Petrovic with 248 votes and Kosara Nikolic with 172 votes.[12] Other important SLS politicians also had extremely low number of votes as it was the case of one future minister, Nenad Rasic, who in 2007 won only 163 votes.[13] Moreover, this problematic situation was accentuated by the contrasting high number of votes obtained by representatives of smaller minorities. For example, all Bosniak and Turk representatives elected in the 2007 Assembly had over 1,000 votes each and, thus, more than the votes won by all SLS candidates together.[14]

The breakthrough for SLS came in the 2009 municipal elections, when the Kosovo Serb (south of the Ibar) turnout 'was ten times higher than in the elections in November 2007',[15] with a number of over 10,000 Serbs casting their ballots in both rounds for the certified Kosovo Serb parties competing across Kosovo. Thereafter, the 2009 elections represented a great opportunity for SLS to strengthen its influence in the municipalities south of the Ibar after developing 'a powerful party structure and using their participation in the government of Kosovo'.[16] SLS mayors were elected in the newly formed Serb-majority municipalities of Gračanica/Graçanicë and Kllokot/Klokot, as well as in the existing municipality Štrpce/Shtërpcë. Another SLS mayor was elected in Parteš/Partesh, a Serb-majority municipality established in June 2010. This offered SLS the foundation from which to become the most successful Kosovo Serb party in the 2010 general elections.

Pragmatism and ethnic outbidding

After the encouraging results in the 2009 municipal elections, the SLS anticipated success in the forthcoming national elections was challenged by the emergence of a new Kosovo Serb party, the United Serb List (JSL). JSL was created with the support of Serbia as a coalition of prominent Serb politicians with links to parties in Belgrade and officials running the parallel institutions in Kosovo.[17] Among the JSL leaders have been Rada Trajkovic, the head of the Graçanicë/Gracanica medical centre, and Randjel Nojkic, who is the manager of the post office in Graçanicë/Gracanica. With this kind of assistance from Serbia and the support of Kosovo Serbs working for these institutions, JSL was expected to have an easy win.[18] Therefore, the 2010 campaign in Serb areas was dominated by the competition and mutual accusations between SLS and JSL. SLS focused on its achievements, including the infrastructure improvements it had made in Graçanicë/Gracanica and alleged that JSL leaders who are in charge of parallel institutions pressured employees to get their votes.[19] On the other hand, JSL campaigned against the SLS involvement in central and local institutions, its relationship with the PDK, the party of Prime Minister Thaçi, and 'alleged that it was buying votes and taking old people's ID card numbers'.[20] Nevertheless, the fact that JSL was participating in parliamentary elections for the first time did not help the party to win more than four seats in the Assembly (6,004 votes and 0.86 per cent electoral score), which 'lead many to question Belgrade's real influence over the Serbs south of the Ibar'.[21]

On the other hand, JLS tried to maximize their ethnic votes by choosing a more radical strategy in the competition with its main competitor, SLS. The clear refusal to consider cooperation with the main Albanian party in Kosovo, PDK, as well as the support for the parallel system in Serbian enclaves and the close links to Belgrade, put them in contrast with the more pragmatic strategy adopted by

SLS.[22] The two contrasting strategies of the main Serb parties in Kosovo indicate the application of the outbidding model of ethnic politics[23] according to which, in the case of intraethnic competition, parties prefer radical over moderate strategies so as to outdo each other in nationalist rhetoric and receive the support of the ethnic voters.[24] In these situations, each party seeks to prove that it is more nationalistic than the others by raising its electoral offer for its community. The radical position of JLS has thus created a risk of extremist politics among Kosovo Serb parties that could have destabilized the community and could have undermined 'ethnic conflict regulation within a democratic framework'.[25]

Moreover, as the outbidding thesis explains, extreme parties are expected to gain substantial votes from switches from previous supporters of more moderate parties, and this further explains the initial hopes for a JLS success in Kosovo. Nevertheless, the outbidding theory can also predict incorrectly in cases where the existence of power-sharing institutions and consociational arrangements may encourage ethnic parties to compete on more moderate platforms. Ethnic parties may gain support because they are seen as the strongest voice to represent their community because they reinforce 'the perception that they most effectively represent their group's ethnonational interests'.[26] Pragmatism and willingness to cooperate with the majority represented by Albanian parties have thus been transformed into an advantage for SLS.

> What is the point of being part of the Kosovo institutions and boycotting them? If you are part of the institutions you should try to get more support and make a change. You cannot help the community if you are boycotting the institutions.[27]

In this context, two elements influenced the performance of JLS in the elections. On the one hand, the support of Serbia and the popularity of the party leaders should have persuaded Kosovo Serbs to vote for JLS and maintain a more negative attitude towards Prishtinë/Priština. One of the party leaders and an important figure within the Serb community, Mrs. Trajkovic, highly criticized SLS' cooperation with PDK and declared she would not accept to be part of a government coalition led by Hashim Thaci.[28] On the other hand, the Kosovo context was not favourable for JSL because SLS had already developed as the representative political entity of the Serbs south of the Ibar. In the end, JSL won four seats in the Assembly and while this can be considered a success for 'a newcomer to the political scene',[29] it was also seen as an indicator of South Kosovo Serbs' decreasing loyalty to Belgrade and willingness to cooperate more with Prishtinë/Priština by supporting the pro-government approach of SLS. The fact that SLS entered the elections as part of the former governing coalition and as the winner of local elections in four Serb municipalities helped the party to get a 2.05 per cent score with around 14,000 votes in the elections (up from 0.15 per cent in 2007) and earn a total number of eight seats in the Assembly, two of which are seats through ballots and six are seats through quotas.[30] The 2010 results made SLS, together with the New Kosova Alliance (AKR), the fifth biggest party in the Assembly and the biggest minority party.

Furthermore, after the 2010 elections SLS had two ministers in the government, Nenad Rasic as a continuing minister of Labour and Social Welfare and Radojica Tomic as minister of Communities and Returns. This was again a great reward for SLS joining the governing coalition as holding such important positions exceeded constitutional rights. The Constitution says that the government shall have a minimum of two non-Albanian ministers (one Serb and one from another minority community) and four minority deputy ministers (two Serb and two from other non-majority communities). If there are more than twelve ministers, there shall be one additional minister and two additional deputy ministers from the non-majority communities.

Post-2013 politics: A new coalition and the growing influence of Serbia

A turning point for the political participation and representation of Serbs in Kosovo was the November 2013 local elections. These elections came five years after the declaration of independence and, for the first time, they covered the whole territory of Kosovo, including the four Serb-majority municipalities in the northern part of the country. Moreover, in the context of the agreement reached between Belgrade and Prishtinë/Priština in April 2013, Serbia supported and encouraged the participation of Serbs in these local elections with the general aim of securing control at the local level. Of the total 103 political entities[31] that participated in the elections, there were 27 representing the Serb community.[32]

A crucial change also came with the entrance in the elections of a new Serb political entity, the Civic Initiative 'Srpska' (GIS), created and financed by Belgrade and bringing together the Serb parties in Kosovo linked with the Serbian government.[33] The support of Belgrade for these elections proved to have a major impact on mobilizing the Serb minority in Kosovo as shown by the high turnout rates: over 50 per cent on average for the Serb municipalities with numbers as high as 64 per cent in Parteš/Partesh, clearly over the Kosovo average turnout of 46 per cent in the first round.[34] The results confirmed a strong dominance for the newcomer GIS Srpska as it won nine out of ten municipalities in mayoral elections and a total of 40 per cent of the seats held by Serb representatives in municipal assemblies throughout Kosovo.[35] Therefore, this victory marginalized SLS and the other Serb parties while also predicting that GIS Srpska would 'become the dominant political force of Kosovo Serbs in the 2014 national elections and most likely the third political force represented in Kosovo Assembly (through the guaranteed minority seats) and the next Serb party in the future government of Kosovo. This will make Serbia a de-facto governing partner of the next government of Kosovo'.[36]

Chapter 5 will analyse these results in more detail and will show why the 2013 and the subsequent 2017 elections confirmed a new political landscape for the Kosovo Serbs. The new dominant political representation for Kosovo Serbs has stimulated a more radical policy in its relationship with the Prishtinë/Priština authorities as suggested, for instance, by the declaration of the elected mayor of Mitrovica/Mitrovicë North, Krstimir Pantić: 'We have won nine municipalities where Serb citizens will never recognise the independence of Kosovo'.[37] However, the Serb community was still highly fragmented as indicated by the fact that only seven out of the twenty-seven political entities representing Kosovo Serbs managed to obtain more than 3 per cent of the votes, while fifteen others scored lower than 1 per cent overall.[38]

As regards the 2014 parliamentary elections, the impact of the 'normalization' of the relations between Kosovo and Serbia[39] was again visible in the participation of northern Serb municipalities and in the almost doubled number of recorded votes among Kosovo Serbs compared to the 2010 elections (from 24,138 to 46,663).[40] As anticipated, the Belgrade-backed G.I. Srpska coalition won the majority of votes from the Serbian community. As a result, they replaced the SLS' supremacy (eight out of fourteen Serb seats between 2010 and 2014) and gained nine of the ten guaranteed seats for Kosovo Serbs in the Assembly.[41] Moreover, among the list of the newly elected Srpska MPs were previous leading politicians of the SLS, including its founder and president, Slobodan Petrovic.[42] In 2017 Kosovo held snap elections, which although brought some major changes within the Albanian electorate had little impact on the political representation of Kosovo Serbs. The renamed Srpska List Party (The Serbian List – SL) came fourth with 44,578 votes or 6.12 per cent of the total number of votes and maintained the nine out of ten seats reserved for the Serb community.[43]

Furthermore, the recent elections in Kosovo have brought an increasingly volatile political climate with more competition between the Albanian parties and the rise in popularity of the Self-Determination Movement

(VV – Vetëvendosje).⁴⁴ The main Albanian party, PDK, was not capable to form again a government under its sole command and instead it has led a coalition of twelve parties (PAN) while also gaining the support of the AAK party and of the twenty minority MPs. The SL party has thus decided to join the most recent government under controversial and unforeseen circumstances that have cemented their role in Kosovo while having to support key Albanian stakeholders.⁴⁵ Altogether, the new political context of Kosovo has made the future role of the Serb political representatives more difficult to predict within the broader aims of accommodating, integrating and protecting minorities.

The effectiveness and legitimacy of Serb representation

By law, the extensive rights and powers that representatives of Kosovo Serbs and other minorities have been awarded give them the consociational option to block important government actions that may undermine their interests. In reality, the situation has been more modest as minority representatives have lacked the political will to put pressure on the central institutions because they depended on the support of the Albanian main parties, and they did not want to jeopardize their positions or create problems for the community they have represented.⁴⁶ Moreover, as regards the consociational character of the executive, despite minority representation at the highest level of governance, the system is weak. If ministers from minority communities are MPs, then they do not necessarily require majority support from minority MPs, meaning that 'the system is more concerned with minority representation than with minority consent'.⁴⁷ In order for minorities to represent a stronger and effective political force, there is need for more consensus among their representatives. This is difficult to achieve and maintain given that opportunism or self-interest can be exploited by the main parties to place different groups or politicians against each other. Although the public political debate is focused on policies and governmental strategies, voters of all communities in Kosovo believe that their political representatives are fighting to prolong their stay in power to maximize their own private gains at the expense of their constituencies.⁴⁸ This also applies to the public perception of the Serb politicians, as one Serb civil society representative observes:

> Serbian politicians are not real representatives of the Serbian community in Kosovo as they do not work for the interest of the people they represent but for their personal interest. Having to more or less limit your cooperation to representatives of your own community is inevitable in Kosovo.⁴⁹

For instance, the post-2010 government coalition depended on the votes of minority representatives who, despite constantly complaining about the position of their communities,[50] have not entirely used this political leverage to advance their influence and become more active in spite of having the institutional tools to protect their rights.[51] Instead, they continued to be fragmented and in competition with their political rivals. As regards the Kosovo Serb politicians, a 2012 Crisis Group Report concluded:

> Infighting, mutual accusations of corruption and cronyism and jockeying for better positions with Belgrade, Pristina and key embassies are the main features of Serb politics. The SLS and JSL accuse each other above all of corruption and not having Serb community best interests at heart. The JSL sees the SLS as sell-outs following Pristina's orders; the SLS sees JSL as politicians who have been in charge of Serbia-funded health care and other institutions for over a decade with only financial mismanagement as a visible result. Many in the Serb population are left disillusioned, while youth interested in social, economic and political development finds a home in the growing NGO sector.[52]

Another critical issue is the level of credibility of politicians, which nevertheless characterizes the entire political environment in Kosovo. The population has been reported to be more and more sceptical about politicians, viewing the disputes within and between parties as irrelevant, self-interested and far removed from their needs, while confidence in parties and political institutions has been plummeting. When Kosovars were polled in 2012 regarding their faith in political party leaders, results revealed that a majority of the population (33 per cent) did not trust any political leaders, up from 23 per cent in 2010.[53] An explanation for this situation was given by one of the key political figures in Kosovo at the time, the Serb minister Nenad Rasic:

> Democratisation and statebuilding take time. Firstly, education is necessary. Secondly, implementation depends on the attitude of both people and politicians (tolerance, patience). Politicians have a great responsibility and currently a key problem in Kosovo is that they lack consistency in their speeches, opinions or political views. As a result, Kosovo politics is not stable and does not have one direction when it comes to essential issues that should not even be disputed.[54]

Contestation from inside the Serb community has also affected the legitimacy of their representatives, who were advantaged by the existence of guaranteed seats despite the small numbers of votes that they won in elections. The reply to such accusations has normally been that they reflect resentment for not being in power or the lack of willingness and incapacity to understand the practical and inevitable need for collaborating with Kosovo authorities.[55] In the words of Suzana Andelkovic, advisor of the Minister of Communities and Return, 'there is a lack of capacity to use rights but also a need of better understanding of their rights'.[56] In the post-independence context of Kosovo, the fragile legitimacy of Serb representatives has been a key disadvantage for the wider aim of integrating the Serb community as a whole.

At the same time, the growing participation of Kosovo Serbs in local and national elections has been a positive development for building the legitimacy of both their political representatives and the institutions these work for. This positive trend nonetheless challenges the argument that the only obstacle to integration is the lack of will that characterizes the Serb community. As Briscoe and Price put it, 'There is no shortage of other institutions, provisions and procedures designed to safeguard and promote minority participation. The challenge is getting ethnic Serbs to use the mechanisms and participate in the political process.'[57] The idea of convincing Serbs to use political mechanisms is not only about how much willingness there is within the community but also about the capacity of Kosovo Serbs to actually take advantage of all their constitutional privileges that reach far beyond using elections to gain strong political representation. However, even in the case of total participation, the de facto integration and acceptance of the Serbs would continue to be a challenge, given the general non-recognizing position and perception of the community:

> No Kosovo Serb recognises the independence of Kosovo in reality and if they say the contrary it is only for personal interests and for creating a good image of themselves. Albanians affirm that if Serbs want to benefit of their rights then they must recognise the authority of Kosovo. Rights should not be the subject of one's political vision and they should not be violated in any way.[58]

Employment, education, cultural and religious rights as well as the decentralization of power for Serb-majority municipalities are the other key opportunities designed to help promoting and protecting Serb integration. Nevertheless, besides the integration progress that has been done in some of the Serb-majority municipalities, the participation of Serbs in public affairs outside these areas has been highly limited:

> Kosovo Serb community is neither represented in the legislative nor the executive branch of any of the municipalities in which they comprise a minority. The community relies mainly on minority community participation mechanisms, such as communities' committees, municipal community offices, deputy chairperson of the municipal assembly for communities, and deputy

mayor for communities where these have been established. This is partly due to neglect by Kosovo institutions, but also due to the ongoing lack of engagement of the community in local level elections.[59]

I have looked so far at the institutional set-up and some of the key policies on minority rights protection in Kosovo but also looked at some of the integration challenges deriving from within the Serbian community. Some of these are the lack of unity and cooperation, different views on how to help the community (participation or support the parallel system), lack of commitment from self-interested actors and representatives, contested support from Albanian parties and limited capacity to develop a self-sustainable strong position of the entire Serb community in Kosovo. Furthermore, the Serb community has been rather sceptical about their new status in post-conflict and post-independence Kosovo, and the idea of integration will be harder to penetrate beyond the elite level institutional forms of representation and participation. The next section will pay more attention to the capacity and sustainability challenges faced by the Serb community.

Kosovo Serbs: Between parallel institutions and integration

Before 1999, Kosovo Serbs made up around 10 per cent of the population.[60] They dominated urban centres and virtually monopolized employment in public institutions and state-owned industries. By 1999, the population had further declined relative to the Albanian population (down to an estimated 5 per cent to 8 per cent of the population). Following the flight of an estimated 200,000 Serbs and Roma after July 1999, 100,000 Serbs, including internally displaced persons (IDPs), were thought to remain in Kosovo.[61] A third of them were living in the predominantly Serbian municipalities of Zvečane/Zveqan, Leposavić/Leposaviq, Zubin Potok, Štrpce/Shtërpce and Mitrovica/Mitrovicë. These municipalities, with minority Albanian populations, are still helped by the Serbian government through parallel structures, which fund municipal and other services, including hospitals, schools and a parallel university in the divided town of Mitrovica/Mitrovicë North.[62]

> The role and influence of the Kosovo Serb community in the political and socio-economic landscape of Kosovo has changed significantly over the past 50 years. From playing a leading role during the early days of the Socialist Federal Republic of Yugoslavia, when Kosovo Serbs held key posts in the then, provincial administration, to the present day when the community's influence is primarily confined to the municipalities where the community is the numerical majority.[63]

Approximately 74,000 Serbs have been thought to live south of the Ibar,[64] in dispersed, generally small, rural settlements outside two bigger towns, Gračanica on the outskirts of Prishtinë/Priština and Štrpce/Shtërpcë on the border with Macedonia. The Office for Community Affairs (OCA) mentions that Kosovo Serbs make up about 6 per cent of the country's overall population, which corresponds to roughly 114,000 people.[65] However, if we consider the results of the 2011 Kosovo Census, the number of registered Serbs in Kosovo is 25,532,[66] data obtained without the northern municipalities of Zveçan/Zvečan, Leposaviq/Leposavić and Zubin Potok, where the Central Census Commission could not establish Municipal Commissions. The data from the census shows that the Serb community is significantly more represented compared to the other minority communities. It could also have important consequences in terms of quotas and proportionality of minorities given that official numbers now place the Serb community third after the Albanian majority and the Bosniak minority.[67] Nevertheless, after the 2008 declaration of independence the process of decentralization created new municipalities throughout Kosovo, raising the number of Serb-majority municipalities to nine. The new Serb-majority municipalities were Ranilug/Ranillug, Klokot/Kllokot and Novo Brdo/Novobërdë (enlarged) in the Gjilan/Gnjilane region, Gračanica/Graçanicë in the Prishtinë/Priština region and since June 2010 the new municipality of Parteš/Partesh was established in the Gjilan/Gnjilane region as well.[68]

After the war and in the new post-independence context, the position of Kosovo Serbs has remained dependent on Serbia. The installation of the parallel education, health, hospital and police systems in northern Kosovo close to the Serbian border and in enclaves where Serbs are a majority has been of great support for the Serb community.[69] However, this undermines the authority of Kosovo and as long as it cannot replace and competes with the parallel system, the integration of Serbs can remain unsustainable. Ongoing language barriers and separate Albanian and Serbian health and education systems are negative factors for integration, with the reality being that after the declaration of independence, many members of the Kosovo Serb community continue to live separately from the majority.[70] This is the dominant view among Kosovo Serbs as regards the tools for protecting and integrating them in the post-independence context and as one civil society representative observes:

> The provisions for minorities can also be seen from a different angle. After the war, Serbs have been actually become isolated in Kosovo and more or less forced to leave in small enclaves that are now being turned into municipalities.[71]

Moreover, post-2008 statistics indicated that while 58 per cent of Kosovo Albanians and 84 per cent of non-Serb minorities were satisfied with relations between different communities in Kosovo, 72 per cent of Kosovo Serbs were dissatisfied.[72] In the context of promoting minority rights that highlight cultural differences (language rights, religious rights), there is a need to balance them with integration so as to prevent people using them as an excuse to reduce social ties and segregate communities.[73]

> Reconciliation has not happened yet in Kosovo. We have a continuation of war by other means. As long as there is no reconciliation the situation cannot improve, despite the examples of Serbs who have integrated, who speak Albanian and who accept the new state. The problem is the position taken by the majority of Serbs and the impact of Serbia's determination to motivate them against integrating within Kosovo.[74]

The lack of contact between Serbs and Albanians also represents a problem for reconciliation and the improvement of interethnic relations. The UNDP Public Pulse Reports after 2008 showed that a big majority of all Kosovars were not having any constant contact with other ethnic groups.[75] For instance, in 2012, the proportion of those who did not have any contact with other ethnic groups for three months was the highest among Albanians (70 per cent), followed by Serbs (65 per cent as opposed to 46.5 per cent in polls from November 2011) and then other minority respondents (18 per cent).[76] Moreover, because this chapter highlights the role of pragmatic measures and socioeconomic incentives for integration, it is important to note that when those who had interethnic contacts were asked about the reasons for their contacts with other ethnic groups, the majority of 27 per cent stated that they met in the marketplace, followed by 25 per cent reporting to live in the same neighbourhood, while only 11 per cent had business relations with other ethnic groups.[77] Language barriers are, nonetheless, a key obstacle to sustainable reconciliation, and the legislation-implementation gap has been widely acknowledged by Serb officials:

> The legislation in Kosovo is very modern […] but the law has not been implemented and we face many shortcomings and deficiencies, lack of capacity and even when there is a will to put provision into practice, there is a shortage of staff.[78]

Serbia has continued to deny Kosovo's independence while supporting parallel institutions that undermine Pristina's ability to develop inclusive democratic institutions and convince Kosovo Serbs to fully accept its authority. Following the political developments of February 2008, many Kosovo Serbs withdrew from Kosovo's institutions and public sphere, reversing the trend of the previous nine years in which Kosovo Serbs had gradually started to participate in Kosovo's public life.[79] While in some regions the presence of parallel institutions has been mostly symbolic, in others, they have delivered the bulk of the local governance and services required by the Kosovo Serb community, including administration, education and health. However, the process of transferring competencies and the creation of new Kosovo municipalities with Serb majority reduced their influence.[80] In response, the Government of Serbia then began to streamline and restructure its institutions and service provision in Kosovo.[81]

> Kosovo Serbs access municipal services and public utilities through a combination of the Serbia-run and Kosovo institutions. The selection of a service provider is based on needs and pragmatism, particularly in relation to proximity, availability and cost.[82]

This indicates that, generally, Serbs have better opportunities to access Kosovo services especially in the new municipalities with a Serb-majority population. Unlike the Serbs in the north who live in a mono-ethnic environment, a growing number of Serbs in the south have been more willing to cooperate with Prishtinë/Priština; pending concrete and tangible measures of good will are offered by the Kosovo Government and the international community. The formula that some Serbs are in the process of adopting is to respect the laws of Kosovo without accepting its full independence[83] and to sustain decentralization as a vital process that will ensure their future in Kosovo. As many Serb political and civil society representatives in Kosovo highlight,[84] it is essential that Kosovo's leaders show openness and understanding to this political evolution.

However, an alternative local-level focused adaptation to life in the new context was confirmed by many Serb civil society representatives in Kosovo, including north of Ibar. In more precise terms, despite all the central level and external factors that have compromised interethnic cooperation, there have also been examples of grass-roots community-led social, economic and cultural projects. Such projects have tried to facilitate reconciliation by 'addressing real, concrete issues and community-focused, non-ethnic, non-political basic needs of what we call, local patriots'.[85]

Furthermore, despite the increasing turnout and the number of benefits gained by the Serb community within central institutions, the public perception of the political environment in Kosovo has not been positive. A 2011 post-election survey showed that Kosovo Serbs were more dissatisfied with the overall situation in Kosovo (80 per cent) than both Kosovo Albanians and non-Serb minorities

(61 per cent) and also that Kosovo Serbs identified general political problems as a main concern at triple the percentage of Albanians (39 per cent and 13 per cent, respectively).[86] Another contrast was revealed in relation to the assessment of democratization, as while the majority (57 per cent) of Kosovo Albanians and non-Serb minorities view Kosovo as a democracy, 90 per cent of Kosovo Serbs do not believe Kosovo is a democracy.[87] Such a drastic opinion of the most important minority community is significant in the context of Kosovo's focus on the multiethnic character of its democratic system of governance. It is nonetheless a worrying situation for the Serb politicians in Kosovo in their attempt to reach out to their community for electoral support and build up their legitimacy.

The government of Kosovo has been investing and offering support to the Serb minority in order to integrate them,[88] but at the same time it has also been challenged by Serbia's efforts to convince Kosovo Serbs to remain loyal and deny the authority of Prishtinë/Priština. As previously mentioned, the post-2013 emergence of a new main political force of Kosovo Serbs (SL) further complicates the de facto participation and integration of the minority. A key issue for the Kosovo Government has thus been the elimination of the parallel system that limits the integration of Serbs in the society, which is not easy to accomplish given that in practical terms the health centres and hospitals 'are larger and better equipped than their Kosovo rivals, and schools are almost entirely in the Serbian system'.[89] Access to health services, access to education and access to justice are fundamental rights that Kosovo needs to respect and provide for all its communities.

Since 2008, there have been about 40,000 people (mainly Serbs but also Roma, Goranis, etc.) in Kosovo receiving support from the Government of Serbia and around 21,000 individuals on payroll receiving at least minimal wages.[90] Nevertheless, Serbia has been pressured to cease its funding by both Kosovo authorities and the international community.[91] In this context, the alternative for Kosovo Serbs would be to find jobs in the Kosovo public or private sectors. In Kosovo there are three major possible areas of employment: public companies (PTK, the energy company, the airport), public institutions and private businesses. In this context, the private option is challenging given it is very difficult for Serbs to find an Albanian private employer as they do not have to meet quotas for employing minorities.[92] Consequently, there is much dissatisfaction among Kosovo Serbs about the lack of employment opportunities, and the gap between elite and community levels of integration is further highlighted by the fact that there has been little progress in this regard despite having Serbs holding key ministerial roles:

The minister of labour, who is an 'Albanian' Serb, has not been interested to change the legislation so as to help dealing with under-representation. He does not use his ethnicity for the benefit of its community, but Albanians are using his ethnicity for the national interest of Kosovo.[93]

As the next sections will illustrate, regarding the other employment options, the number of Serbs working for Kosovo public companies has been extremely low (approximately 0.74 per cent),[94] despite the constitutional guarantees for proportional representation for communities in public enterprises (Article 61). Moreover, in public institutions, the law on civil service provides that 10 per cent of communities should work in public institutions and be equally represented at all levels.[95] In practice, the number of Serbs working for public institutions is only about 5 per cent and besides some ministries that respect the quota, most of them have very small percentages of minority employees and some do not have any Serbian employees at all.

Socioeconomic challenges for the integration of Serbs

> Surrounded by Kosovo Government authority, the southern Serbs are constantly balancing their loyalties and adjusting their interests and emotions to reality. They depend on a mix of heavy Belgrade subsidies and small-scale agriculture, but relations with Pristina are improving. Serbs are taking Kosovo documents and registering with state authorities, paying electricity bills to the Kosovo Energy Company (KEK) and using Kosovo mobile phones after their power was cut and Serbian mobile service was forcibly dismantled. This pragmatic approach is based on need to remain safe and commitment to staying where they live. Confidence can grow gradually, but full integration in Kosovo society is harder to imagine.[96]

The passage above describes how the position of the Serbs in southern Kosovo in relation to accepting or not the steps towards integration has not been completely dependent on the unsettled status of Kosovo. On the one hand, the international presence in Kosovo has been a great factor through its constant financial and technical support directed especially towards the integration of the Serb community.[97] On the other hand, as this chapter explains, the situation of Kosovo Serbs south of the Ibar in the post-independence context has mainly been affected by practical issues and policies applied by both Kosovo and Serbia. The dependency of Kosovo Serbs on the support provided by Serbia could not have been instantly eradicated by the newly born state of Kosovo going through a multifaceted process of statebuilding, economic development and democratization. Kosovo

Serbs have also resisted employment in Kosovo institutions under the influence of the Serbian government's policy to boycott the authority of Prishtinë/Priština after the declaration of independence and the development of the Serbian parallel system. Therefore, this has been one of the main reasons for the high unemployment numbers within the Kosovo Serb community. However, the so far pragmatic measures and policies developed by Prishtinë/Priština, varying from constitutional and legal extensive minority rights to the inclusion of Serbs within public institutions and the implementation of decentralization, have determined some progress in regard with Kosovo Serbs' willingness to cooperate more with the authorities and participate within Kosovo's public life. Statistics showed that Kosovo Serbs expressed less confidence in Kosovo institutions than all other communities as only 28 per cent had confidence in the municipal assemblies, 24 per cent in the police, 23 per cent in the media, 8 per cent in political party leaders, 5 per cent in courts in Kosovo and, at the bottom of the list, only 4 per cent of Serbs have confidence in the Kosovo Assembly.[98]

The concern of Kosovo Serbs for their safety at the same time with their desire to stay where they live are fundamental issues that may require pragmatic policies and actions from the authorities so as to improve the communities' standards of life through socioeconomic development and cultural opportunities but also through equal representation and anti-discrimination measures.[99] While some key steps have been made in this direction, the main challenge for sustainable integration of Serbs may require not only enhancing the current strategy and support for high-level representation and participation but also extending the integration efforts at the community level even more. As Gjuljeta Mushkolaj, former judge at the Kosovo Constitutional Court, remarks, 'Kosovo leaders are not creative enough and do not discuss these possibilities.'[100] From this point of view, the will and capacity of the Kosovo state are key factors in progressing with the integration of the Serb minority. Therefore, Kosovo Serbs' decision to accept or not Kosovo's authority as their new state has much to do with pragmatism and the necessity to adjust to reality (rational choice). As the attitude of most Serbs living in south Kosovo shows, integration is not merely dependent on arguments about secession and losing Serbian citizenship.

Employment in the public sector

> Since the Public Sector in situation poverty is often the biggest employer, many groups will be vying for positions (jobs) not only in government but in the Public sector in general. […] Managing diversity in the Public Service is

critical in post conflict situations. If not well handled, it will disrupt any efforts in reconstructing capacities for Public service. Political leadership needs to take an integrative and strategic stand on this issue providing a political framework as well as a strategic objective of tapping and utilising the full potential and contribution of all segments of the population for development.[101]

As indicated by this extract from one of the UN reports on building capacities for public service in post-conflict countries,[102] in a divided post-war society such as Kosovo the number of minorities employed in the public sector can have great significance. To discuss this in relation to the consociational proportionality principle in public administration and the integration of Kosovo Serbs immediately after the declaration of independence, I will use the information provided by a policy study on community employment in Kosovo public institutions that was published in 2010 by the OCA within the Office of the Prime Minister.[103]

In this report, a number of measures have been recommended to increase employment of minorities throughout the public sector in Kosovo. Some of the main recommendations were related to (a) harmonization of recruitment procedures in publicly owned enterprises (POEs); (b) advertisement of positions through a newly established information sharing network between central and local levels; (c) development of guidelines and professional criteria for specific vacancy positions; and (d) application of quota system in which all communities would be represented equally in the Kosovo Civil Service and POEs. In practice, a more recent policy review of the Kosovo Government from 2012[104] indicated that the ethnic composition of Civil Service was as follows: out of a total of 20,531 civil servants, there were 18,480 Albanians, 997 Serbs and the rest belonging to other minorities. Kosovo Serbs therefore represented 4.9 per cent of the civil servants in Kosovo.

Moreover, according to the 2010 Policy Study the two representative institutions of Kosovo, the Assembly and the Office of the President, had together a total number of 182 civil servants, of which 160 were members of the majority community and 10 were Serbs. Percentages are as follows: 87.91 per cent are members of the majority community and 12.09 per cent belong to non-majority communities, respectively 5.49 per cent are Serbs. The Assembly of Kosovo had a total of 147 civil servants, out of which 128 were members of the majority community (87.07 per cent) and 10 belonged to the Serbs community (6.8 per cent).[105] As regards the Office of the President, all six political appointees were Albanian, while at the civil service level the Policy Study reported that there were no Serbs.[106] The Government of the Republic of Kosovo, without the

Office of the Prime Minister, employed a total of 5,489 civil servants, out of which 5,051 were members of the majority community and 438 belong to non-majority communities. There were 279 Serbs representing 5.08 per cent of the total employees and at managerial level there were 29 (3.2 per cent) Serbs out of 907 staff members in total. The Office of the Prime Minister confirmed it had only 2 Serbs from a total of 207 employees.

Another relevant example is that of the Ministry of Communities and Returns (MCR), where there were two Serbs (25 per cent) out of eight employees at the political level and twenty-eight Serbs (31.81 per cent) working as civil servants, making it the most positive example of Serb representation within ministries. Within other ministries, the numbers of Serb employees tended to be much lower,[107] while the independent institutions, executive agencies and regulators included in the 2010 study employed sixty-three Serbs (11.03 per cent of the total).[108] Altogether, the number of Serbs within central level institutions represented *5.08 per cent* of the total employees.

Regarding local level governance, combined, the municipalities included in the 2010 study employed a total of 9,197 civil servants, out of which there were only 280 employees belonging to the Serb minority.[109] In percentages, the Serb representation in municipality level was of *3.06 per cent*, out of which only seventeen were employed at the management level. In regard to POEs, the study showed that out of a total of 12,243 staff, there were only 91 Serbs (*0.75 per cent*) and 3 working at the management level.[110] Another positive example is however the composition of Kosovo Police (KP) as it reflected the ethnic diversity of the population of Kosovo. Out of the total 8346 KP officers and civil staff there were 758 Serbs representing 8.99 per cent.[111]

> While the quota system may have its flaws, without the quota system the numbers would be even lower. Today there is a growing realization that better representation across the board would contribute to political stabilization and the integration of minorities into all levels of Kosovo's public sector. The responsibility is manifold and lies primarily with the authorities to bring decision-making closer to the people. The Serb community has a major responsibility to be more assertive and engage in deliberation, not only in its most immediate interests but also on national priorities.[112]

Furthermore, the 2010 report indicates that the quota system should be based on UNMIK regulation 2001/19 which stipulates that 'the non-majority community representation in the composition of the Civil Service at all levels shall be closely proportionate to the representation of non-majority communities in the Assembly'.[113] Consequently, in order to respect the system of guaranteed seats in the Assembly, provided by Article 64(2) of the Constitution, communities should be represented as follows in the Civil Service and POEs: 83.33 per cent for members of the majority community and 16.67 per cent for members of non-majority communities, while the quota for members of the Serb community should be 8.33 per cent.[114] However, the Law on the Civil Service[115] mentions a 10 per cent quota that applies to all the non-majority communities as a single group. This made it possible for authorities to fulfil the quota by employing more of one minority at the expense of others. Serb representation is low and the Serb community is often represented in fewer numbers than the other communities. By comparing any of these two quota criteria with the actual level of representation, the Serb representation is clearly below what the legal documents say, with around 5 per cent at central level institutions, 0.75 per cent within public-owned companies and 3.06 per cent at municipal level.

Kosovo Serbs in the wider economic context

Although little can be done to improve the overall economic situation without political stability and substantial investment, there is sufficient room to activate the economic potential of the Serb community.[116] An economic activation of the community could bring great benefits like encouraging growth and utilizing the underused human resources.[117] Before the conflict, many Kosovo Serbs were working for both the public sector and socially owned enterprises, while in the present 'many remain unemployed or informally employed'.[118] Even though Serbs used to be the urban population most of them are now living in rural areas, relying heavily on agriculture and social and welfare assistance provided by Serbia for their survival.[119]

Moreover, their access to property and housing has been 'impaired by the illegal occupation of their homes, business and arable land',[120] a problem which still persists after all these years since the end of the conflict.

> Kosovo Serbs used to be the urban population, but most Serbs are now living in rural areas. This indicates capacity problems for the Serbian community: illiterate, un-educated population, lack of elites. How can then Serbs consume their rights and how can they be represented properly? They need to become aware of their position and understand their rights. There is sufficient legal basis for demanding respect of their rights. What is needed is for them to become educated in this direction and capable of consuming their rights.[121]

This situation indicates capacity problems for the Serb community in the new Kosovo context: poverty, illiterate and uneducated population and the lack of elites that prevent Serbs from assuming their rights and become properly represented.[122] Any community with such existential challenges cannot be defined as sustainable in the long run and while the state holds great responsibility in dealing with these community problems, Serbs also need to become aware of their position and understand how much legal basis there is for demanding respect of their rights.[123] However, self-sustainability of the Serb community in Kosovo should be considered within the wider economic context in Kosovo. Despite the economic growth in recent years (estimated to 3.8 per cent in 2012),[124] Kosovo's economy continues to be in a worrying situation especially with regard to poverty and unemployment. Kosovo remains the poorest country in Europe[125] with over 40 per cent of the population living in poverty with less than 1.42 euros per day and approximately 15 per cent in extreme poverty with less than 100 cents per day.[126]

According to the 2012 Analytical Report of the European Commission, the overall unemployment rate in Kosovo was the highest in Europe at about 43 per cent, and 80 per cent of all unemployed have been without a job for more than a year, more than 70 per cent of the youth (from 15 to 24 years) are without a job, most of the labour force is unskilled or semi-skilled and 'the lack of perspective for a job, especially among the young population, is putting strains on social cohesion and encourages emigration'.[127] Such statistics are very troublesome given that Kosovo has the youngest population in Europe, with 50 per cent under the age of 25, and 19.1 per cent considered youth (15–24).[128] The economic problems of Kosovo are also reflected by the public perception as unemployment has been constantly identified as the biggest problem facing Kosovo by all ethnic groups (92 per cent), while general economic problems and poverty are also among the top concerns of all communities in Kosovo.[129]

Key challenges[130] like inflation, underdeveloped private sector, reliance on the import of goods, low domestic growth and high trade deficit are correlated with Kosovo's problems highlighted in all of the European Commission's Progress Reports (2008–2012):[131] a large informal economic sector, widespread corruption, weak rule of law, organized crime and poor infrastructure.[132] In this economic context, not only minority communities but also the entire Kosovo society heavily relies on remittances from the diaspora[133] and foreign aid. The 2012 OSCE 'Community Rights Assessment Report'[134] highlights among the main obstacles for the integration of minorities in Kosovo are unemployment and absence of socioeconomic opportunities. The report also criticizes the government because its three-year strategy plan for economic development[135] published in 2011 does not mention 'individual communities within Kosovo, how their economic opportunities can be developed or how they can be utilised to improve the economic situation of Kosovo'.[136] This is a matter of serious concern because the labour market in Kosovo is also characterized by long-term unemployment of minorities (more than twelve months).[137] In 2011, out of the total 29,711 registered unemployed persons belonging to non-majority communities, 29,598 were long-term unemployed.

Official unemployment has also been high for Kosovo Serbs and many of them have been dependent on the social payments from the Serbian government.[138] According to a 2011 poll, 62 per cent of Kosovo Serbs thought unemployment was the biggest problem facing Kosovo and of most concern to them.[139] However, despite high unemployment, Kosovo Serbs have been relatively better off than other minorities, thanks to the subsidies granted by Belgrade, Kosovo institutions and international donors in the form of pensions, social welfare and donations. Moreover, the OCA stated that in municipalities where the Serb community represents over 40 per cent of the population, the rate of unemployment within the community has ranged from 40 per cent to 75 per cent. The reasons identified by the government for this situation have been lack of qualifications, language issues, an absence of investment in the development of small businesses and the agricultural sector, a lack of employment opportunities, as well as information on existing opportunities and a lack of public companies.[140]

As this chapter has illustrated, Serbs are represented at the visible political level within both central and local governance but underrepresented at the managerial and civil service level of public institutions and public companies. With the purpose of integrating its Serb minority in terms of employment in the public sector, post-2008 Kosovo adopted a strategy that began with Serb representation at the elite level (Assembly, government, consultative bodies, municipal governance), which is expected to become a positive example and stimulate integration at the wider level of the community:

> This is where political leadership is called up on to live by example in ensuring that there is no feeling of exclusion in employment in the Public service. [...] The way political leadership positions in all levels of government are filled will provide a hint to the public on the way diversity will be managed in the public sector. The political level therefore needs to set example of how diversity should be managed across the board in the Public Service.[141]

From this perspective, as the Kosovo Serb community grows more vocal about its rights through its representatives, there could also be an increase in the willingness at all levels of the community to work within the system. However, as the socioeconomic challenges for Serbs in Kosovo have shown, an adequate integration will require much more than access to upper-level positions. Even with more positive change in Kosovo Serbs' willingness to integrate, the vital challenge will remain to build sufficient capacity for both the community itself and the Kosovo state to secure a sustainable integration.

Conclusion

This chapter evaluated the progress of the integration of the Serb minority in post-independence Kosovo by looking at the development of the system of minority rights protection and at the challenges that have influenced its implementation so far. A first challenge derives from the Serb community's will and capacity to understand, accept and assume their rights. A second challenge for Kosovo Serbs is to find and secure the support of governmental institutions at both central and local levels of governance. Besides adopting the current constitutional framework, the Kosovo Government also needs to prove long-term commitment and build capacity to sustain its minorities.[142] A third challenge is the sustainability of the cooperation between Serbs and Albanians at both elite and community levels. The political cooperation built so far is contested not only by the Albanian opposition and the civil society but also by the Serb community itself.[143]

The first part of this chapter outlined the complex multiethnic institutional and constitutional framework of Kosovo, which was put in place after 2008 with the purpose of accommodating Serbs and other minorities under the authority of the new state. While this framework provides extensive minority rights at central and local levels of governance, political rights, social benefits, language and cultural rights, in practice there are still important shortcomings despite all the efforts that have been made so far. This was illustrated by the second part of this chapter, where I focused on political and socioeconomic challenges for the integration of the Serb minority in Kosovo. Overall, given the opportunities provided by the complex system of minority rights in post-independence Kosovo, there have been some positive results with the integration of Serbs living south of the Ibar. The main progress has however been made only at the upper level as shown by the political representation of Kosovo Serbs within the Assembly, the minority consultative bodies, the government and the municipal institutions. Even though signs of progress at the community level are indicated by the higher turnout in national and local elections, Kosovo Serbs continue to rely on the existence of the parallel system and have limited socioeconomic incentives to accept Pristina's authority. Pragmatic strategies and policies have been somewhat effective at the higher level of representation and participation of Kosovo Serbs. However, this has not been properly expanded at the community level in order to secure a sustainable integration and as the following chapters will also illustrate, the legislative framework and the formal provisions for protecting minority rights cannot fully compensate for practical needs.[144]

4

Non-dominant Minorities in Kosovo

A marginalized view on statebuilding

This chapter considers the situation of non-Serb minorities in Kosovo and the post-independence impact of adopting and implementing the legislation on minority rights protection. The aim here is to illustrate how promoting and protecting minority rights in Kosovo through legal and political provisions intersect with the complexity of needs and requirements coming from different minority groups. This may act in favour or not of minority groups depending on the particular characteristics and priorities, as well as the will and capacity of each of them. In order to illustrate this, the first part will complement the examination of the formal provisions for minorities started in the previous chapter and the second part will examine the different situations of the Bosniak, Turkish, Roma, Ashkali, Egyptian, Gorani, Montenegrin and Croat communities in Kosovo.

The legal and institutional framework in Kosovo vis-à-vis the integration of minorities requires two main areas of investigation. On the one hand, this chapter seeks to understand the incentives for providing far-reaching protection for even the smaller minorities in Kosovo as well as the immediate results and consequences of the relevant policies. It is vital to observe the immediate results and consequences of adopting post-conflict specific consociational measures that apply to all minorities, regardless of their implication in the conflict or their actual need of integration. On the other hand, what also cannot be neglected is that the primary purpose of developing a multiethnic institutional and legal framework has been to address the integration of Serbs. Kosovo has thus designed a multiethnic framework to mainly integrate its largest and most important minority while this inevitably also impacts on the other communities. Therefore, the individual data and results revealed here confirm the risks of creating a social and political hierarchy among minorities depending on the will and capacity to reach the smaller, less visible minorities as well.

Altogether, presenting the efforts made to integrate the non-Serb minorities will further emphasize the significance of the gap between formal and actual implementation of minority rights protection in Kosovo. While smaller minorities in Kosovo have equal legal collective rights with the Serb minority and could potentially benefit from this unanticipated status, on the ground their situation varies from case to case. Therefore, the main problem that this chapter investigates is the variation regarding minority rights protection towards the smaller communities in Kosovo as reflected by the possible discrepancy between excessive measures and facilities that could become counterproductive. Formal provisions and post-conflict specific measures like power-sharing consociational features cannot guarantee social cohesion and the legitimization of the state by all its constituent ethnic groups. This chapter argues that the inconsistency regarding minority rights protection towards the smaller communities in Kosovo indicates a potential discrepancy between impractical measures that could cause segregation and marginalization instead of integration.

Formal provisions for smaller communities in Kosovo

The previous chapter looked at some of the main components of the multiethnic constitutional and institutional framework adopted by Kosovo with the primary aim of integrating the Serb community under its authority as a new state in the post-independence context. This framework however needs to be further analysed by looking at the rest of provisions for minority rights protection incorporated in the Constitution and the Law on Communities as well as at the role of the Ministry for Communities and Return, the minority consultative bodies and the integration strategy through municipal decentralization. In terms of representation and participation of minorities as well as the protection of their identities, the legislation was developed for both the central and local levels of governance and deals with political rights (guaranteed seats in the parliament and municipal councils), proportional employment in public institutions and state-owned enterprises, socioeconomic benefits and education, language and cultural rights.

As regards the political participation of minorities at the national level, the most visible and important feature is the right to guaranteed seats in the Kosovo Assembly. As previously mentioned, out of the 120 seats in the Kosovo parliaments, 20 are guaranteed for the non-majority communities. Kosovo Serbs hold ten seats while the remaining ten guaranteed seats are divided among the other minorities included in the Constitution as follows:

The Roma community, one (1) seat; the Ashkali community, one (1) seat; the Egyptian community, one (1) seat; and one (1) additional seat will be awarded to either the Roma, the Ashkali or the Egyptian community with the highest overall votes; the Bosnian community, three (3) seats; the Turkish community, two (2) seats; and the Gorani community, one (1) seat if the number of seats won by each community is less than the number guaranteed.[1]

In addition, for the first two electoral mandates upon adoption of the Constitution, minorities were also allowed to participate in the distribution of the 100 seats outside the guaranteed ones.[2] This advantage, combined with the fact that the 5 per cent electoral threshold did not apply to minority parties, allowed minorities to win five extra seats in the general elections of 2010. While Serbs have been the most advantaged with three additional seats, Bosniaks and Turks also won one additional regular seat each. Despite a strong political lobby by minority representatives to extend this electoral privilege for the upcoming national elections,[3] the 2014 change to guaranteed seats only has limited the representation of minorities to twenty seats altogether.

Institutional representation

At ministerial level, the legislation says that at least one minister must be from the Serb community and another from a non-Albanian community, while at least two deputy ministers must be from the Serb community and another two from non-Albanian communities.[4] Moreover, if there are more than twelve ministers, 'the Government shall have a third Minister representing a Kosovo non-majority Community'[5] and two additional deputy ministers, one representing the Kosovo Serb community and one for another non-majority community. As regards specific bodies for communities, the primary mechanism of minority consultation for Kosovo is the previously mentioned Consultative Council for Communities (CCC), which functions under the authority of the president and should be composed of representatives of all minorities in Kosovo. Even though Montenegrins and Croats have been formally recognized since 2011 with the amendment of the Law on Communities, CCC is the only official body mentioning that the Montenegro and the Croat communities have one representative each, while the CCC list with accredited NGOs contains one Croat and four Montenegrins.[6]

The Kosovo Assembly should also play an important role in building more constructive majority-minority relationships. The Constitution established a Community Rights and Interests Committee (CRIC) of the Assembly with a mandate to examine and comment on all legislation affecting minority communities. Overall, it is a potentially effective check on the tendencies of the majority to advance legislation without thinking through the implications for Kosovo's minority communities. CRIC should be composed of two members from each community (MPs) and its recommendations to the Assembly are adopted by majority vote of its members. The composition of this committee can be given as another example of the inconsistency regarding the use of the term 'communities'. Given that it includes five members from Albanian parties, CRIC does not represent a minority body per se.[7]

The Kosovo Judicial Council is another fundamental institution that is tasked with ensuring not only that Kosovo courts are independent, professional and impartial but also that they fully reflect the multiethnic nature of Kosovo.[8] Moreover, the Judicial Council is also instructed by the Constitution to 'give preference in the appointment of judges to members of Communities that are underrepresented in the judiciary as provided by law'.[9] Therefore, these constitutional provisions represent another example of the emphasis on institutionalizing a multiethnic character of Kosovo. The composition of the Judicial Council is designed to combine the principles of professionalism and expertise with the issue of underrepresentation of minorities and the specific inclusion of Serb representatives in the appointment process. One essential aspect here is again the privileged position of Serbs in comparison with the other minorities in Kosovo given the distribution of power on the principle of splitting any number of seats for all minorities as follows: 50 per cent for Serbs and 50 per cent to be divided among the rest. The results of this may be not only the intended overrepresentation of Serbs through positive discrimination but also the unforeseen confusion and competition between the other minorities. The second challenge for implementing the constitutional rights given to minorities in the election of members for the Judicial Council is regarding the actual capacity of these communities to assume their right/responsibility. Firstly, the representatives of minorities in the Assembly should possess the necessary skills and experience to make valid and responsible nominations. And, secondly, finding and recommending qualified candidates for the positions will be an extremely difficult task given the scarcity of skilled labour force that characterizes some of the minorities in particular.[10]

Another example is the Kosovo Police, which needs to facilitate cooperation with municipal authorities and community leaders through the establishment of Local Councils as provided by law, and the ethnic composition of the police within a municipality shall reflect the ethnic composition of the population within the respective municipality to the highest extent possible.¹¹ The Ombudsperson office has one or more deputies, and their number, method of selection and mandate are determined by the Law on Ombudsperson, which also says that at least one Deputy Ombudsperson shall be a member of a community not in the majority in Kosovo.¹² The Central Election Commission is another key body, composed of eleven members. Six members are appointed by the six largest parliamentary groups represented in the Assembly, which are not entitled to guaranteed seats. If fewer groups are represented in the Assembly, the largest group or groups may appoint additional members. One member is appointed by the Assembly deputies holding seats reserved or guaranteed for the Kosovo Serb community, and three members are appointed by the Assembly deputies holding seats reserved or guaranteed for other communities that are not in majority in Kosovo.¹³

Community profiles of non-Serb minorities in Kosovo: The Bosniak community

Demographics

According to the results of the 2011 census,¹⁴ there were 27,533 (1.6 per cent) members of the Bosniak community living in Kosovo, which confirmed them as the second largest minority group after the Serb community. As indicated before, in the context where Serbs boycotted the census (exclusively in northern municipalities not included in the study and partially in the rest of Kosovo), the official data places Bosniaks above the number of Serbs (25,532).¹⁵ The exclusion of the mainly Serb-inhabited northern Kosovo meant that about half of the Serb population was not included at all in the final data, but it has also affected the census figures of Bosniaks and Roma minorities who live in that area.¹⁶ As a result, the census number for Bosniaks is around 18 per cent lower than previous OSCE estimates (33,524).¹⁷

Most Bosniaks in Kosovo live in the municipality of Prizren, south of Kosovo, where they constitute about 10.01 per cent of the local population (16,896 residents), mainly in the city of Prizren, in Zupa Podgor and also in the rural part of Prizren. It should be mentioned that the result of the census is with about 5,000 less people than previous estimates for Bosniaks in Prizren that provided figures of around 22,000.¹⁸ Other important locations are the municipality of Dragash/Dragaš, with 4,100 Bosniaks residing mainly in the Gora region, Pejë/Peć municipality with 3,786 Bosniaks and Istog/Istok with 1,142 members of this minority,[19] but also in three northern municipalities that were not fully included in the census: Mitrovicë, Leposavic and Mitrovicë North with representation between 2 per cent and 3 per cent of the local population as reported by the Office for Community Affairs (OCA).[20] In other municipalities, Bosniaks are in much smaller in number and make up between 0.02 per cent and 1 per cent of the municipal population: Deçan/Dečane – 0.57 per cent, Zvecan – 0.3 per cent, Prishtinë/Priština – 0.2 per cent, Ferizaj/Uroševac – 0.02 per cent, Fushë Kosovë/Kosovo Polje – 0.08 per cent, Gjakovë/Đakovica – 0.02 per cent.

Identity

Bosniaks are a Muslim Slav community that does not necessarily trace its origins to Bosnia and Herzegovina but with strong cultural and religious links to the country.[21] Consequently, Bosniaks can be divided in two groups. The first consists of those who migrated to Kosovo from Bosnia, Montenegro and, mostly, from the Sandzak region, especially after the end of Ottoman rule in the Balkans.[22] These are concentrated around the Peja, Istog/Istok and Mitrovice regions and, to a lesser extent, in Prishtinë/Priština. The second group includes those who have traditionally lived predominantly in the regions of Prizren, Dragash/Dragaš and Zupa.[23]

As speakers of a Slavic language, Bosniaks are believed to have converted to Islam during the Ottoman times and since then developed a sense of separate ethnic identity.[24] The group was first recognized as a distinct category in 1961 by a Yugoslav census that included them as 'Muslims in the ethnic sense'.[25] In the 1990s, during the Bosnian war, the term 'Bosniak' was adopted for this ethnic group of Slavic Muslims, and the Bosnian language promoted as different from Serbian and Croatian.[26] In this context, in the Prizren region, and especially in the municipality of Dragash/Dragaš, the divide between Kosovo Bosniak and Gorani (also Slavic Muslims) is porous, as both minorities share a number of key characteristics, with the main difference deriving from their political affiliations.[27] Generally, Kosovo Bosniaks have managed to live peacefully alongside both the majority of Albanians (religious ties) and Kosovo Serb community (linguistic ties). Therefore, the Bosniak community can be considered among the well-integrated minorities in Kosovo. In the words of a Bosniak representative:

> We are for integration but not for assimilation. But at the same time, this discussion is problematic because we are already integrated, we have been co-existed peacefully with the Albanians for a long time.[28]

The 'voice' of the Bosniak community is a good symbol for the marginalization of the non-dominant non-Serb minorities in Kosovo and of the problems resulting from the top-down artificial process of statebuilding:

> The main responsibility lies with each community as it mainly depends on them to foster inter-ethnic cooperation and diminish social division. The idea of integration itself is controversial given that we are already part of the Kosovo society. It is one thing to ask migrants for instance to integrate in a society that they emigrate to and another thing to ask communities that are already a substantial part of the society.[29]

This represents a powerful perspective on the meaning of integration and indicates a potential incompatibility between the rationale and political design of de jure measures for integration and de facto reality on the ground. The context of the war, the post-conflict developments and the more recent post-independence sociopolitical processes have all required the Bosniak community to reassess their position within the Kosovo society. Bosniaks have thus generally understood the need of institutional social integration as a problem and as a partial threat to their historical status within Kosovo.[30] Furthermore, the idea of a civic identity of Kosovars is hard to be accepted by Bosniaks and other minorities in the context where the majority population, Albanians, do not see themselves as Kosovo citizens before identifying with their ethno-national group.

Political representation and participation

The Kosovo Bosniak community is fairly well represented in public life compared to other non-Albanian communities. At the central level, the community has three guaranteed seats in the Assembly of Kosovo and four positions of deputy ministers within Kosovo Government. In addition to that, three seats are reserved for Kosovo Bosniaks in the CCC, the advisory body operating under the auspices of the Office of the President of Kosovo. The major two opposing Bosniak political entities have been VAKAT Coalition and the New Democratic Party (NDS). VAKAT Coalition is an alliance of three political parties which represent Bosniaks in Kosovo, formed in 2004 and covering all important regions with Bosniak population in Kosovo. After the national elections in 2010, VAKAT held two seats in the Kosovo Assembly and by winning 5,296 (0.76 per cent) votes it also managed to keep its electorate in comparison with the previous elections in 2007 and in 2004. It is important to say that one of its seats was won through ballot in addition to the one won through quotas, making VAKAT the second non-Serb party after the Turkish KDTP to win seats in parliament through threshold.[31]

VAKAT Coalition has been mainly challenged by NDS, whose leader Emilija Redžepi became an MP after winning the necessary votes for the third guaranteed seat for Bosniaks both in the 2010 and 2014 elections.[32] The fourth Bosniak seat in 2010 was won by Hamza Balje (816 votes) from the Bosniak Party of Democratic Action of Kosovo (BSDAK). At the same time, the Party of Democratic Action (SDA) was not allocated a seat in 2010, even though its main candidate, Numan Balic, won more votes (1,048) than the result of BSDAK's deputy in the parliament.[33] Nevertheless, the BSDAK MP lost his seat in 2014 after the new electoral system for minorities was introduced. Therefore, the results of these main Bosniak parties in the 2010 national elections indicated a total electoral score of 11,194 votes (1.6 per cent) for the community, a score higher than the 1.22 per cent result of the Turkish KDTP party, yet approximately half of the Serb minority parties' 3.05 per cent of the total vote.[34] In 2014 the Bosniak community slightly increased its total share of the votes and the snap elections of 2017 did not bring any major changes with two MPs for VAKAT and one for NDS. Overall, the Bosniak participation in public affairs would be even stronger if there was more unity among its political representatives, thus more on the model of the Turkish community that had only one main party representing the interests of its community prior to 2013.

As regards the local level, despite the constant lobbying by the community's leaders,[35] no Kosovo Bosniak majority municipalities have been established. The planned new municipalities would be formed in and around the villages of Recan (current Prizren municipality) and Vitomiricë (current Pejë/Peć municipality) and would give the minority a much-desired control over local affairs.[36] One particularly interesting observation here is that, in contrast with the Turks, Bosniaks lack the support of their kin-state, an opinion shared among some of the main Bosniak political representatives:

> Turkish have Turkey. We have Bosnia, but Bosnia is not interested in us Bosniaks in Kosovo [...] Turkey have economic influence in Kosovo. [...] Also, we actually have an important role at the local level and we have a big say on the political outcomes in places like Prizren, thus they don't allow us to get more power [...] Plus, unlike the Turks we are divided, and we are five political parties, which is why Albanians don't respect us.[37]

However, despite the absence of owning a municipality and continuous political division, the community's participation in public affairs in the municipalities where Bosniaks live has improved.[38] The community holds prominent positions in the legislative and executive branches and assembly seats in the more densely Kosovo Bosniak-inhabited municipalities of Prizren, Pejë/Peć and Dragash/Dragaš. In these municipalities where members of the Bosniak community constitute over 4 per cent of the local population there is additional Bosniak representation within the local institutions. For instance, in Prizren, three Bosniaks were elected to the Municipal Assembly in 2009 and VAKAT Coalition has been one of the four political entities that formed the municipal ruling coalition. However, the 2009 results in Prizren also confirmed NDS with the highest number of votes among Bosniak parties (2.36–4.27 per cent) in comparison with VAKAT's score of 1,826 votes (3.29 per cent).[39] The situation repeated in the November 2013 elections when NDS won again more votes than VAKAT and increased the number of Bosniak members of the local assembly to five. Bosniaks have therefore been well represented at local and central levels of governance. They are generally aware of the fact that although Kosovo Serbs have been the priority, the post-2008 framework has helped the other minorities too,[40] although legislation needs to be backed up by material provisions and benefits too.[41]

Language and education

Bosniaks speak a Slavic language, Bosnian, which represents a vital element for defining their position within the Kosovo society. While this characteristic is a reason of great cultural pride and distinguishes them from other minorities, it also has a negative impact on the community's integration, especially that 'the inability to speak Albanian among the majority of the Kosovo Bosniaks remains a determinant factor for the sense of insecurity and the level of freedom of movement exercised by the community'.[42] Moreover, Bosniaks have been reported as facing increasingly limited recognition of their language rights,[43] even though Bosnian is currently recognized as a language in official use in four municipalities, namely Pejë/Peć, Prizren, Istog/Istok and Dragash/Dragaš, which requires local authorities to provide interpretation, translation, municipal services and documents into Bosnian upon request.[44] There is also a shortage of textbooks in Bosnian for primary and secondary education, and some Bosniak children educated in Albanian have no option to learn in Bosnian or about Bosniak culture history and tradition, even in supplementary classes. These are important challenges for the community indicating unforeseen consequences of the legislation and focus on multiethnicity, as observed by Bosniak representatives themselves:

> Education is the main tool for preserving and promoting the identity of a community in the context where people have to live with both their ethnic/cultural heritage and their affiliation with the state through citizenship.[45]

Furthermore, the access to secondary mother-tongue education is further hampered by the lack of curricula translated into their own language and the low quality of textbook translations. Given that Prishtinë/Priština University mainly offers courses taught in Albanian and Bosniaks have also been excluded from attending higher education in Serbian in Mitrovice, Kosovo's only tertiary education options in Bosnian are a business school in Pêja and an education faculty in Prizren. In this context, Bosniaks feel that they need decentralization as much as the Serb community does, not only for their cultural survival but also for their sociocultural development.[46] The OCA indicates that in Prizren, for instance, public education is offered at preschool, primary and secondary levels in both Albanian and Bosnian,[47] but the lack of high-quality secondary education in Bosnian is considered a fundamental problem.

Overall, the possibility to study only in Bosniak and Serbian means that young Bosniaks have little incentive to learn the language of the majority population, Albanian:

> The students who attend universities abroad in Serbia or Bosnia to obtain valuable degrees and professional skills but upon their return to Kosovo they cannot employ these and cannot find work because they do not speak Albanian ... if we live in Kosovo we have to learn Albanian, it is normal.[48]

Thus, linguistic segregation is a real challenge for Bosniaks as shown not only by the difficulties experienced by young generations but also by the fact that Bosniak representatives and MPs themselves cannot speak Albanian.

Socioeconomic challenges

In the post-war and post-independence contexts, the socioeconomic situation of the Bosniak community in Kosovo has been difficult, with one of the key challenges being the access to employment, similar to all communities in Kosovo. The overall unemployment rate for Bosniaks in 2011 was reported at 37.68 per cent, which is a significant number, but, on the positive side, it indicates a better situation than all other communities, including the Albanian majority.[49] At the same time, the situation of Bosniaks varies depending on the region they live in. Bosniaks are employed mainly in the agricultural sector (Dragash/Dragaš), physical labour (Gjakovë/Đakovica), small businesses and also working in the public sector, though in small numbers as indicated by the data on employment of minorities in the civil sector.[50] In the Prizren area, where most Bosniaks reside, many challenges remain while many have their own commercial activities or engage in construction and seasonal work in Montenegro.[51] In Prizren, the 2010 Policy Report indicated that there were 26 Bosniaks working in the civil service, from a total of 298 employees and 54 belonging to all minority communities.[52] Moreover, the municipal court in Prizren reported one Bosniak judge as the only minority representative among the total ten judges while the district court had two Bosniak judges and the municipal prosecutor's office one Bosniak.[53] Bosniaks also have the highest number of minority police officers within the Prizren police station: 36 out of the total 210 officers.[54] As regards the security and freedom of movement for Bosniaks, the community has not had significant problems in the five regions of Kosovo besides a number of security incidents reported in the municipalities of North Mitrovicë and Pejë/Peć, where 'both men and women have been the targets of reported harassment and assaults'.[55] Furthermore, as OSCE reports, Bosniaks have enjoyed unhindered access to social services and social welfare and relatively good access to property and housing.[56]

> Bosniaks displaced during the war have not returned for reasons similar to those of many from other smaller minority communities: a combination of bad memories, mistrust of the ability and willingness of local authorities to protect them, and lack of economic prospects in Kosovo.[57]

Lastly, another fundamental issue for the Bosniak minority has thus been the situation of returns and reintegration, as a high number of Kosovo Bosniaks were forced to leave Kosovo during and after the conflict due to concerns for their own safety, lack of economic opportunities and the difficulty to find jobs.[58]

The Turkish community

Demography

The Turkish community represents the third largest minority in Kosovo with a population of 18,738 (1.1 per cent).[59] The results of the 2011 census are important especially because previous estimates had suggested that there were about 30,000 Turks living in Kosovo.[60] Kosovo Turks are mainly concentrated in the municipalities of Prizren (9,091 Turks), Mamuşa/Mamushë/Mamuša (5,128) that is also a Turkish municipality and Prishtinë/Priština with 2,156 Turks. There are also small Turkish communities in Mitrovicë/Mitovica North – 3 per cent, Gjilan/Gnjilane – 1.3 per cent (978 Turks), Vushtrri/Vučitrn – 0.45 per cent, Ferizaj/Uroševac – 0.02 per cent.

Identity

> Integration is a very, very wrong word. Nobody explains what it means to be integrated. I don't need to be integrated. I am here, I have always been here. To whom do I have to be integrated?[61]

As the above words of an important civil society representative of the Turkish community indicate, the grass-roots-level understanding of the idea of 'integration' represents a very powerful endogenous challenge to the top-down language and policies of integration. Moreover, this paradoxical feeling about the necessity of Kosovo-wide integration is shared by most communities and highlights once again the discrepancy between legislation and de facto situation in Kosovo. In other words, the rationale behind protection and promotion of minority rights in Kosovo does not necessarily take into consideration all cultural, social and regional particularities of each community apart. The Turkish community has had a significant presence and influence in Kosovo since the Ottoman conquest of Kosovo in the fourteenth century and it has been composed by both descendants of the Ottoman Empire and indigenous population that converted to the Muslim religion and adopted the Turkish language and culture.[62] Their privileged status during the Ottoman Empire, the fact that they share the Muslim faith and many cultural traits with Albanians and the notion of Turkish as an elite language among many people in Kosovo, have all helped Turks to become active and well integrated into Kosovo's society over time.[63]

It is worth mentioning that the 1974 Constitution of Yugoslavia, which granted Kosovo an autonomous status, also named Turkish as one of the official languages in the province,[64] thus equal status with Serbian and Albanian. However, the post-conflict UNMIK administration did not keep this official status, and after 2008, Turkish was only recognized as an official language at the local level.

Political representation and participation

The Turkish community in Kosovo has been almost exclusively represented by the Turkish Democratic Party of Kosovo (KDTP), which until 2010 was also the only party from the Turkish minority to participate in elections.⁶⁵ KDTP is a conservative party established in 1990 and registered in 1999 during the UNMIK administration. The party's head office is in Prizren and the other local branches are in Mamusë, Prishtinë/Priština, Gjilan/Gnjilane, Vushtrri/Vučitrn and Mitrovicë/Mitovica North.⁶⁶ The leader of the party is Mr Mahir Yahcilar, who was elected in 2000 and, during the UNMIK administration, was a member of the Interim Administrative Council, Minister of Health and also president of the Kosovo Assembly during the 2001–2004 legislative mandate.⁶⁷ KDTP's open statement to its supporters has been

> to preserve the identity of the Turkish community. In particular, this identity is reflected through preserving education, language and culture of the Turkish community in Kosovo. In addition, KDTP works for a tolerant life among all communities in Kosovo and is always willing to support this cause.⁶⁸

In the 2010 national elections, in addition to KDTP, the Kosovo Turkish Union (KTB) registered as the second Turkish party to take part and create internal political competition within the community. However, they did not manage to win any seats in the Kosovo Assembly as they gained 1,364 votes (0.2 per cent), while KDTP reconfirmed its dominance with a total score of 8,548 votes (1.22 per cent).⁶⁹ In the previous elections in 2007, KDTP had won 4,999 votes (0.9 per cent).⁷⁰ Therefore, the improvement in the 2010 elections made KDTP not only the second minority party in Kosovo after SLS but also the non-Serb minority party with the highest electoral score as it had over 3,000 more votes than the next non-Serb party, VAKAT from the Bosniak community.

The 2010 elections also secured for KDTP three seats in the parliament: two through quotas (guaranteed) and one through ballot (passed the minority threshold of 1 per cent). The Turkish deputies in the 2010 legislature were Enis Kervan, who won 2,303, Fikrim Damka with 2,187 votes and Müfera Şinik with 2,036 votes. These Turkish MPs held important positions, like the vice president of the assembly, head of the Committee for Health, Labour and Social Welfare and also four positions of vice presidents among other parliamentary committees. At the same time, the party's leader, Mahir Yahcilar, gained 3,570 votes but did not take his MP position as after 2008 he became the minister of environment and Spatial Planning (MESP). KDTP was part of the ruling coalition supporting the Hashim Thaçi government. After 2008, the deputy minister of communities and returns and the deputy minister of agriculture also came from the Turkish community. Overall, the political success of KDTP confirmed the benefits of the initial strategy of the Turkish community to avoid creating new political parties so as to ensure a greater representation in the Assembly of Kosovo:

For four mandates we entered as one party, and every time we improved our scores [...] we focused on unification and this has been very beneficial for the community.[71]

Moreover, three Turkish representatives were also selected to the Communities Consultative Council and a Kosovo Turk judge was member of the Constitutional Court. The 2014 national elections were marked by a small decrease in the total number of votes for Turkish representatives against the general trend across Kosovo. KDTP managed to win the elections among the Turkish community, although its votes dropped as a result of the challenge posed by the new Kosova Türk Adalet Partisi (KTAP, Kosovo Turkish Justice Party).[72] Same as the Bosniak community, Turkish representatives lost their extra seat in the Assembly after the introduction of the new guaranteed seats system.

At the local level, the most important gain for the Turkish community in the post-independence context has been the creation of the Turkish municipality of Mamuşa/Mamushë/Mamuša (Mamuşa in Turkish), located in the southeast region of Kosovo. As mentioned before, Turks are the only non-Serb minority in Kosovo to have been awarded a municipality where they are in majority. In the 2009 local elections, by winning 73 per cent of the votes, KDTP secured an overwhelming majority in the municipal assembly with eleven seats and Seylan Mazrek as its chairperson.[73] Moreover, the mayor of the municipality has been Arif Bütüç (KDTP) and the deputy mayor as well as all directors of different departments have been from KDTP. In 2013, however, the fracture within the political representation of Turks was confirmed by the new KTAP party's win in Mamuşa/Mamushë/Mamuša over KDTP (eight seats for KTAP and five for KDTP) and by the mayor's migration to the new party.[74]

The municipality of Prizren, where most Kosovo Turks reside, has also had a strong political representation for this minority. The municipal assembly has included three seats held by KDTP, which was also one of the four parties in the ruling coalition after the 2009 local elections.[75] These were important achievements for the Turkish representatives, especially that Prizren is the second largest municipality of Kosovo with 177,781 inhabitants, of which 145,718 are Albanians and 16,896 are Bosniaks. These facts will be further discussed in the next chapter, where I look at both Mamuşa/Mamushë/Mamuša and Prizren as case studies in relation to the impact of decentralization. In Prishtinë/Priština, the biggest municipality and the administrative, political, economic and cultural centre of Kosovo, the Turkish community has been the most numerical minority after 2008. After gaining 1.21 per cent in the 2009 elections,[76] Turks became the only minority represented in the local assembly of Prishtinë/Priština with one seat of the total fifty-one seats and with Engin Beyoglu (KDTP) in the position of assembly deputy chairperson for communities.[77] The same situation with Turks as the only minority holding a seat in local assemblies has been present in three other Kosovo municipalities: Mitrovicë/Mitovica North, Gjilan/Gnjilane and Vushtrri/Vučitrn.

> Our politicians are not thinking about Turkish people. They are working for their coalition and their positions in the Assembly. This is wrong. They were elected by us for our interests. We do not work for them, they work for us.[78]

As previously mentioned, the main force of the Turkish community has been its political unity[79] as reflected by the political gains at both central and local levels of governance in the 2009 and 2010 elections. Nevertheless, the subsequent fractions within the political leadership of the community and the creation of a new main party have destabilized the Turkish representation. The other challenge for the community is common to all non-Serb minorities in Kosovo and refers to the hierarchical division of the society and their marginalization by the relationship between Albanians and Serbs. Like during the late 1990s, the new situation in Kosovo has also placed 'the Turks and other minorities in the middle of the conflict between Serb and Albanian politics, which has nonetheless been in the detriment of our rights and has reduced the rights we had before the war'.[80]

Language and education

One of the fundamental aims of the Turkish community as a whole and of its political representatives has constantly been the protection and promotion of their language, given the pre-war constitutional status of Turkish as a state language next to Albanian and Serbian. Consequently, 'the Turkish minority now feels much more alienated because the 1974 Constitution of Kosovo had recognised them as equal with the now, positively discriminated, Serbs'.[81] Nevertheless, in accordance with the Law on the Use of Languages (Art 2.4), Turkish has gained the status of language in official use at the local level in four municipalities: Gjilan/Gnjilane, Mitrovicë/Mitovica North, Vushtrri and Prizren. Moreover, this law stipulates the linguistic rights of minorities and the specific obligations of the municipalities, such as providing interpretation and translation into Turkish upon request. According to OSCE, this task has remained largely unfulfilled.[82] As regards the access to education, like in the case of Bosniaks, a main concern is the shortage of textbooks in Turkish, which has a negative impact on 'the community's enjoyment of the right to education'.[83]

In more general terms, the main problems facing Turks in accessing education are a shortage of good school books, a lack of proper transport and poor educational infrastructure. Moreover, the increasing numbers of young Turks going abroad to study universities in Turkey may generate a new long-term problem.[84] While they obtain valuable degrees, upon their return to Kosovo their access to the job market is still limited because they do not speak fluent Albanian as a result of completing their full education cycle exclusively in their mother tongue.

Socioeconomic situation

In the context of the poor state of the economy as a whole, the socioeconomic situation and employment opportunities for the Kosovo Turk community are reported as relatively good.[85] Generally, the older generation's ability to speak Albanian and a high degree of integration have helped them to access the labour market and maintain the community's unemployment rate just above the one reported for Bosniaks but below the rest of the communities in Kosovo.[86] Moreover, the minority's high level of integration into the Kosovo society[87] is also demonstrated by the fact that Turks do not generally make use of the Serbian parallel institutions and services. Instead, Turks choose to use the services and facilities provided by Kosovo institutions and enjoy full access to social services and welfare throughout Kosovo.[88] Many Turks work in the private sectors and have managed to develop successful private enterprises, but there is also a significant presence of the community in the public sector.[89]

Furthermore, Turks have traditionally been residing in urban areas, which means that they generally do not participate in the economic opportunities available via agriculture. An important feature is that the Turkish community has been the minority with the most equitable representation in the public sector. While the overall representation of minorities cannot be considered reflecting the multiethnic character of Kosovo, the Turk community has been the only one with equitable representation within the representative institutions.[90] Moreover, unlike other minorities in Kosovo, the Turkish community has not been very concerned about the returns and reintegration of its displaced members, mainly because the 1999 conflict did not cause significant migration among Turks. The departures that have occurred after the war have been generally motivated by the poor economy.[91] Therefore, this represents another positive feature of the

Turkish minority as it absolves the community from dealing with this complex challenge that has such a big impact on most other Kosovo communities.

RAE communities: Roma, Ashkali and Egyptians

> Roma, Ashkali and Egyptians identify themselves as persons belonging to three distinct communities and are as such recognised by the Kosovo legislative framework, Kosovo institutions, and international organisations. The Organization for Security and Cooperation in Europe Mission in Kosovo (OSCE) fully recognises the existence of three distinct communities.[92]

As the OSCE statement suggests, after 1999 it has been very important to identify and treat these minorities as three different ethnic groups instead of including them all as one single group under the notion of 'RAE community'. While the grouping of these three communities together by both international and domestic actors has also had positive and practical motivations like creating a stronger social and political representation for them, 'the perceived attempt for the creation of a new identity has created serious identity and political troubles for these communities'.[93] Perhaps the most visible example of grouping them is the distribution of seats in the Kosovo Assembly, where besides one seat guaranteed for each of the three minorities, one additional seat is offered to either the Roma, the Ashkali or the Egyptian community with the highest overall votes. Another example is the Law on Communities, which in regards to the economic and social opportunities of minorities in Kosovo stipulates that 'special consideration shall be given to improving the situation of Roma, Ashkali and Egyptian communities'.[94] Furthermore, using the 'RAE' formula can be considered as against one of the basic constitutional rights of the Roma, Ashkali and Egyptian minorities to 'freely express, foster and develop their identity and community attributes'.[95] However, it should be observed that this constitutional right has a positive character, while before 2008, under the UNMIK Constitutional Framework there was a more firm and clear statement that 'no person shall be obliged to declare to which Community he belongs, or to declare himself a member of any Community. No disadvantage shall result from an individual's exercise of the right to declare or not declare himself a member of a Community'.[96]

These legal provisions have had a significant meaning in the context where, historically, the members of these minorities have either not been recognized belonging to three different groups, or they have not declared or expressed their identity clearly.[97] Moreover, while Kosovo Roma have traditionally lived in

Serb-populated areas and generally speak only Serbian in addition to the Romani language, another distinct feature of the Ashkali and Egyptian communities is that they generally speak native Albanian. Therefore, this linguistic characteristic has either facilitated the voluntary assimilation of Ashkali and Egyptians as Albanians or it has simply become the key element of differentiation from the Roma minority.[98] However, the common perception among Roma and the majority Albanians that Ashkali and Egyptians are 'Albanian-speaking Romas who do not want to acknowledge their origins and are looking for new identities'[99] complicates even more the identity problems of these communities.

> After the return of refugees in the summer of 1999, and still today, urban myth has it that 'the Roma were collaborators with the Serbs [against the Albanians].' Consequently, it has been important for many individuals to distance themselves from the undesired community for safety purposes.[100]

Until recently and especially prior to the 1999 conflict, only the Roma were largely recognized as one of the different ethnic groups living in Kosovo given that 'Ashkali and Egyptian communities were not yet widely referred to under their current names'.[101] During the former Yugoslavia and Serbia regimes their official marginalization was sustained through non-recognition, but at the same time, a major factor has also been the decision of a large number of members from all three communities to declare themselves as 'Albanians', making self-identification and social cohesion all the more difficult.[102] These issues, in addition to the massive migration of these minorities both before and after the 1999 conflict, are some of the key reason why population estimates for Roma, Ashkali and Egyptians have always been much higher than official statistics. In the late 1990s the best estimates indicated the total of these three communities to be between 100,000 and 150,000 Roma[103] (10 per cent of the population). However, the 1991 census reported that 45,745 (2.3 per cent) Roma lived in Kosovo,[104] and while it included the category of 'Egyptian' for the first time ever, the Ashkali community was not officially recognized before 1999. Furthermore, in the recent census organized in 2011, the aggregated figure for the three communities was of 35,784 individuals, which is around 20–30 per cent lower than that of previous estimates.[105]

> We are struggling with 99.9 per cent of Kosovo on this issue of not differentiating between the three communities. The government, the internationals, people are all treating us like one community, like a new one, R.A.E., which doesn't exist in any paper and this is a human right, to respect the identity of others.[106]

Therefore, the lack of social cohesion within the communities and their troublesome official recognition have contributed to the continued marginalization of Roma, Ashkali and Egyptian minorities in Kosovo and have affected their ability to 'participate in the civic and political life in Kosovo'.[107] Nonetheless, regardless of how these complex issues of ethnic identity and recognition have obstructed their integration, the fundamental concern is that all three remain the most vulnerable, disadvantaged and discriminated communities in Kosovo, with the worst education and the highest unemployment rates.[108] In this context, the constitutional provisions for the integration of minorities cannot be expected to have the same impact on these communities as in the examples of minorities that have a better socioeconomic or/and political situation like Serbs, Bosniaks and Turks.[109] I will now offer an overview of the particular situation of each of these communities.

The Roma community

Demography

The 2011 census indicated that there were 8,824 people in Kosovo belonging to the Roma minority. According to the same data, the municipality with most Roma is Prizren with 2,899 residents from this community representing approximately 4.2 per cent of the local population. Other municipalities with significant numbers of Roma are Pejë/Peć (993), Gračanica/Graçanicë (745), Gjakovë/Đakovica (738), Obiliq/Obilić (661) and Mitrovicë/Mitovica North (528). However, previous estimates declared around 21,300–27,000 Roma in Kosovo and, for example, at the municipal level the census indicated only 745 Roma inhabitants in Gračanica/Graçanicë as compared to 1,900–2,000 from previous estimates.[110]

These differences can be explained by several factors like the exclusion of northern Kosovo and the fact that a large number of Romas live in Serb-inhabited areas, such as Gračanica/Graçanicë, and have also partially boycotted the 2011 census.[111] Furthermore, it is often not easy to disaggregate the data on Roma, Ashkali and Egyptians, while migration trends can also be a factor: 'Around 10,000–12,000 Kosovo residents, including members from the Roma community, emigrate every year (overall, for each returnee, there are two residents emigrating abroad).'[112]

Identity, language and education

Roma people have lived in Kosovo since the thirteenth century and therefore represent one of the traditional communities in Kosovo. The Roma community traces its roots to India, from which they migrated between the eighth and tenth centuries.[113] Kosovo Roma are predominantly of the Muslim faith, but some identify themselves as Christian Orthodox. They speak mainly Romani as their mother tongue but most Roma are bilingual in Serbian, although, in some predominantly Albanian municipalities, they speak Albanian (Kaçanik/Kačanik, Malishevë/Mališevo).[114] Overall, there are little efforts made to protect and promote the cultural identity of Roma as, for instance, 'there are no designated protected sites of cultural or religious significance, nor plans to undertake the identification of such sites in the near future'.[115]

> I am the first and only Roma in Kosovo with a Masters degree. But I am not happy about this, I want all people to be educated. What is even worse is that I still cannot find work. This is a problem for all Kosovo.[116]

Roma children continue to encounter problems to access and complete their education as they face common factors like social exclusion, poverty, large number of cases of early dropouts from school and cultural tradition affecting many families, whereas Roma girls are particularly affected.[117] Improving education of the Roma community is therefore a critical issue, especially that reports found that the level of illiteracy among Roma is as high as 24.3 per cent.[118] Even though the Kosovan legislation guarantees members of minorities the right to receive public education in their own language and in 2011 the Ministry of Education adopted a new curriculum for Romani language classes,[119] there are no schools or classes in the Romani language in Kosovo. Moreover, despite provisions to review and draft textbooks and promote the values, heritage and identity of Roma, Ashkali and Egyptian communities,[120] between 2009 and 2011 the Kosovan educational system did not contain 'curricula and textbooks specific or adequately tailored to the culture and history of Roma, Ashkali and Egyptians'.[121]

Political representation

In Kosovo there was initially only one Roma party, the United Roma Party of Kosovo (PREBK), and the Roma minority has generally been underrepresented at both central and local levels of governance in Kosovo. The United Roma Party of Kosovo (PREBK) has been led by Haxhi Zylfi Merxha and was founded in 2000 with the main office in Prizren with the aim to promote the security, rights and employment of the Roma minority in Kosovo. At the central level the community has been represented by one deputy in the Kosovo Assembly holding the Roma guaranteed seat and by two members in the CCC. The Roma deputy for the 2010 legislature was Mr Allbert Kinolli, elected with 393 votes in the 2010 elections, while his party had a total of 690 votes (0.1 per cent).[122] The 2014 election results confirmed the ascendance of the newly created party New Kosovo Roma Party (KNRP), which secured the Roma seat in the Assembly by winning only three more votes than PRBEK.[123] At the municipal level across Kosovo, there has also only been one Roma representative, who was elected in 2009 in the Prizren municipal assembly by participating on the list of the Albanian majority party LDK.[124] At the same time, PREBK did not manage to win any seats in the 2009 elections despite its participation in four Kosovo municipalities. Moreover, the Roma minority does not have any representatives in the municipal executive branches.

> Our representatives are not efficient and do not know how to make use of their positions. They are not connected with the communities they represent. One key issue is that they do not collaborate with the civil society and they see us as being in opposition ... This means that important and potentially useful projects and recommendations from the civil society are completely disregarded ... The needs of the community are not respected.[125]

Therefore, the poor participation and representation of Romas in the public affairs of Kosovo represent for this minority both a cause and a consequence of marginalization. On the one hand, a critical factor influencing their participation has been 'the lack of professional and educational credentials that undermine the self-confidence of community representatives to actively engage in municipal politics'.[126] Generally, the Roma minority fails to organize efficiently and promote its political engagement and it rarely participates in public discussions organized across Kosovo at both central and local levels.[127] On the other hand, the low turnout among Romas in the elections has also deprived them of representation, even where they represent a significant part of the local population.[128] As the Prizren example of the only Roma deputy in local governance shows, when Romas do engage in politics, they tend to vote or participate for majority Albanian parties.[129] In the words of the Roma MP Albert Kinolli: 'It is very difficult to get the support of their community because the big Albanian parties convince Roma people to vote for them, most of the time with non-democratic means like buying votes.'[130] Moreover, local authorities 'have not proactively reached out to Roma to promote their participation in the electoral process and voter registration',[131] despite the fact that in 2009 the Kosovo Government adopted the Action Plan for the Implementation of the Strategy for Integration of Roma, Ashkali and Egyptian Communities.[132]

Socioeconomic situation

> While the legislation for minorities is excellent, the implementation is very poor because the Roma community lacks education, because we are discriminated and we have very little representation in both the private sector and the public sector … poor representation in public institutions and ministries.[133]

As mentioned before, the Roma community is one of the most vulnerable minorities in Kosovo with a large proportion of its population living in extreme poverty and with fundamental problems like discrimination, unemployment, lack of education and professional skills placing them in an even worse position than Ashkali and Egyptians. In this context, it is extremely difficult for Romas to obtain employment in either public institutions or private companies that are reluctant to hire them, which leaves 'many individuals and families to rely on social assistance and pensions paid either by Kosovo institutions, Serbian authorities or both'.[134] Roma thus access both Kosovo and Serbia-run institutions, depending on their place of residence and the availability of services, but the lack of civil registration documents prevents many of them from accessing social services. Similarly, the lack of correct documentation, destruction during the war of documents proving ownership, the recurrent malfunctioning of municipal cadastral offices and the misconception within the community about property rights are some of the issues preventing Roma to repossess their lost properties.[135] Moreover, the minority's access to municipal services remains a challenge across all regions in Kosovo and among the main concerns are 'the affordability of utilities and administrative fees, the lack of necessary personal documents, and limited awareness on relevant institutions and offices where Roma can address their concerns'.[136]

Some Roma engage in seasonal work in agriculture and construction, but the most common source of income is from informal labour like collecting scrap metal and low-paid cleaning activities.[137] Moreover, only a very low number of Roma work in the public sector in publicly owned enterprises or as civil servants in Kosovo or in Serbian parallel institutions. In 2011, the Roma community had an unemployment rate of 60.22 per cent[138] and it was among the least represented minorities in the public sector jobs. Moreover, local-level executive institutions employed across Kosovo a total of thirteen Roma (0.14 per cent) and only one of them holding a political position (municipality of Pejë/Peć). The municipality where most Roma live, Prizren, had five (1.68 per cent) Roma employed in the civil service.[139]

This low representation of Roma is even more problematic given that many of these municipalities 'have in some cases lowered the standards of the job requirements in order to give priority to applicants from a non-majority community'.[140] These socioeconomic problems characterizing the Roma community have been an even bigger burden in the context where about two-thirds of the estimated pre-war population of 150,000 Roma, Ashkali and Egyptian residents were displaced during and after the 1999 conflict.[141] Dealing with the return of such a large number of persons has created serious difficulties for Kosovo authorities given that 'returnees in Kosovo are adversely affected by inadequate housing, limited access to reconstruction assistance and uncertainty of tenure in informal settlements'.[142] In addition, the lack of security and difficulty of finding employment are also fundamental problems for returnees.

The Ashkali community

Demography

The 2011 census represented the first-ever inclusion of the Ashkali community in official statistics and the result confirmed the Ashkali community as the fourth largest minority in Kosovo with a population of 15,436. Unlike the situation for most of the other communities, this figure was higher than previous estimates suggesting that approximately 12,000 Ashkali are living in Kosovo.[143] The largest Ashkali communities are located in the municipalities of Ferizaj/Uroševac with 3,629 Ashkalis, and Fushë Kosovë/Kosovo Polje, where they represent almost 10 per cent of the municipal population (3,230).

Identity, language, education

The Ashkali is one of the recently recognized minorities in Kosovo and their name originates from the post-1999 conflict period since when it has been supported by UNHCR and the international community as a distinct minority community in Kosovo.[144] Ashkali are Albanian speakers, generally of Muslim faith, and identify their origins in Ancient Persia. The fact that the Ashkali community's mother tongue is Albanian facilitates their interaction with central- and local-level institutions and service providers and has a positive impact on their freedom of movement as well as on their access to information in electronic and media.[145] Nevertheless, 'continuing marginalisation suffered by the Ashkali community means that lack of engagement in institutional or grassroots dialogue processes and forums may have less to do with inter-community conflict and more to do with widespread prejudice and social exclusion'.[146]

Therefore, despite the closer connection with the Albanian majority community linguistically and religiously, in many areas of Kosovo Ashkali continue to live separately from mainstream Albanian communities. As regards their access to education, Ashkali children have been affected by non-enrolment and high dropout rates. The reasons for this situation derive both from the general limited capacity of Kosovo institutions to invest in education and also from the community's particular issues: 'Poverty, parental choices favouring boys, child labour, early marriage, and girls called to perform household work and care for younger brothers and sisters.'[147]

Socioeconomic situation

> What is the use of a nice constitution if implementation is not in place? If you do not have laws that cannot be implemented why is the constitution existing? ... One of the causes for poor implementation is the lack of budget. Another one is the lack of political will. Also, the lack of capacities among people and most important is the lack of coordination between different mechanisms at the local and central levels of governance.[148]

The socioeconomic situation of the Ashkali community remains precarious, with high levels of unemployment and social exclusion throughout Kosovo. The 2010 unemployment rate for the Ashkali minority was 60.46 per cent,[149] representing the second highest percentage after the Egyptian community in Kosovo. As regards the employment in the Kosovo public sector, the Ashkali minority is also characterized by a disproportionate and widespread underrepresentation. For instance, in 2010 there were no Ashkali working for the Kosovo Assembly, while the government of Kosovo reported seven Ashkali (0.14 per cent) civil servants: three Ashkali working for the Ministry of Justice, three for the Ministry of Labour and Social Welfare and one working for the Ministry of Communities and Returns. At the municipal level of public service, the institutions across Kosovo reported a total of thirty-one Ashkali (0.34 per cent).

High dropout rates from school lead to low literacy, and a widespread lack of educational or vocational qualifications among the community hampers the access to the labour market for member of the Ashkali community. However, a number of individuals are self-employed, while small numbers are employed in the civil service. Many Ashkali families rely on social assistance and pensions mainly from Kosovo, although some receive social assistance from Serbia or from both. Pensions and social assistance from Kosovo are not adequate to ensure dignified living conditions, especially for those living with extended families. In addition, the law sets strict criteria for inclusion in the social assistance scheme and many Ashkali, although socially vulnerable, are excluded from it often due to a lack of civil registration documents. Ashkali women continue to be among the most disadvantaged groups in society.[150] The majority of the Ashkali population continues to rely extensively on the social welfare assistance. In some cases, the Kosovo department of social welfare delayed the provision of monthly social assistance, but no discriminatory actions have been noted. However, the effect that social assistance has on reducing poverty among Ashkali is very limited. Many complain that the scheme is not comprehensive enough to reach out to the very poor, leaving most without support owing to the narrow criteria for eligibility.[151]

Regarding the return and reintegration problem, a large number of Ashkali remain displaced both internally and throughout the region and in Western European countries.[152] The Ashkali residing outside of Kosovo continue to be mainly forcibly repatriated as the voluntary returns process has been slow under the impact of the lack of opportunities for employment and the poor economic integration of returnees.[153] Between 2000 and 2012, UNHCR reported only an aggregated figure of 6,537 Ashkali and Egyptians who returned voluntarily, representing 27.21 per cent of the total number from all Kosovo communities,[154] but nevertheless a small figure given the 150,000 estimated population of Roma, Ashkali and Egyptian residing in Kosovo before the war. Other factors affecting the return and reintegration of Ashkali include 'difficulties in repossessing property due to their widespread lack of registered property titles and personal documents; security concerns; insufficient donor support; and insufficient representation in returns elated bodies at the local and central level.'[155]

Political representation and participation

> Minorities are not respected equally. Putting Serbs first and the others after that is not fair. This is a major obstacle in the attempt to implement the constitution ... The representation of Ashkalis in public institutions is a disaster and does not

respect the constitutional provisions. For instance, in Fushe Kosovo Ashkalis represent 10 per cent of the local population with only 2 employees in the municipality, while Serbs are 1 per cent of the population but have 13 people working for the municipality. Is that fair?[156]

The Ashkali community is generally underrepresented politically, although the situation has been slightly better at the local level as a result of the 2009 municipal elections. There have been two Ashkali deputies in the Kosovo Assembly and two Ashkali holding guaranteed seats in the CCC. The Ashkali community has been represented by two political parties: the Democratic Ashkali Party of Kosovo (PDAK) and Ashkali Party for Integration (PAI). PDAK was founded in 1999, after the end of the conflict in Kosovo to represent and protect the interests of the Ashkali minority. The first leader of PDAK was Sabit Rrahmani, who was also one of the three Ashkali deputies during the first two legislatures of the Kosovo Assembly (2004–2007 and 2007–2010). In the 2007 national elections in Kosovo, PDAK got three seats in the Kosovo Assembly with 3,433 votes. The party experienced some difficulties between 2007 and 2008 when Mr Rrahmani, the party leader, was arrested and then sentenced for six months of imprisonment of unpaid debts and fraud charges.[157] Moreover, he resigned from his party and in December 2008, the Assembly also decided to end his mandate as representative of the Ashkali community, as he had reached the limit of six months of abstention from Assembly proceedings.[158] This was the first time that the Assembly of Kosovo decided to end the mandate of one of its members. Danush Ademi was PDAK's president and led the party in the 2010 national election to win 1,411 votes out of the party's total of 2,871 votes and secure one seat in the Assembly.[159]

The Ashkali Party for Integration (PAI) was founded in 2010 and took part in the elections, thus challenging the supremacy of PDAK within the Ashkali community. PAI obtained a good score in 2010 of 1,386 votes (0.2 per cent) and entered the assembly with one seat as well held by Etem Arifi who had an individual number of votes of 1,003.[160] The results of the 2014 elections did not change anything as the number of votes for Ashkali parties was again higher than that for the Roma or Egyptian minorities, which secured an additional guaranteed seat in the Assembly like in the previous elections.[161] In the 2009 elections, the community won a total of three municipal assembly seats across Kosovo in the municipalities of Ferizaj/Uroševac and Fushë Kosovë/Kosovo Polje, where the community has a significant presence. In Ferizaj/Uroševac there have been two Ashkali from PDAK, and the municipal assembly deputy chairperson for communities has also been Ashkali.¹⁶² In Fushë Kosovë/Kosovo Polje, the municipal assembly has included one Ashkali from PDAK.¹⁶³ Given the significant number of registered Ashkali voters in Lipjan/Lipljan, a higher turnout would have enabled the community to gain an assembly seat in this municipal as well. Furthermore, the community is not generally represented in the executive branches of the municipalities, but they are represented in the municipal offices/committees for communities.

Overall, the factors influencing the community's low participation in public affairs include the lack of professional and educational credentials that undermine the reputation of Ashkali representatives and their motivation to actively engage in local politics and the lack of initiatives by municipalities to support and promote their participation.¹⁶⁴

The Egyptian community

Demography

The 2011 census reported that the Egyptian minority in Kosovo had a population of 11,524 members, almost half of which live in the municipality of Gjakovë/ Đakovica (5,117 Egyptians), where they also represent the largest minority group. The municipality of Pejë/Peć is second with a number of 2,700 Egyptians, followed by Istog/Istok (1,544) and Klinë/Klina (934). Nevertheless, it should be mentioned that for the Egyptian minority there have been discrepancies in the data provided by different sources (Kosovo census, ECMI and OSCE data), mainly 'also due to the fact that data on the Roma, Ashkali and Egyptian communities often cannot be easily disaggregated'.¹⁶⁵ Nonetheless, unlike the Ashkali community, the Egyptians were previously included as one of the ethnic categories in the Yugoslav census of 1991 when 3,307 people (0.2 per cent) declared themselves as Egyptians.¹⁶⁶

Identity, language, education

The Egyptians represent one of the communities considered to have lived traditionally in Kosovo despite having started to declare their identity only in the early 1970s, claiming ancestry in ancient Egypt.¹⁶⁷ Kosovo Egyptians speak Albanian as their mother tongue and are predominantly of Muslim faith.

Moreover, the fact that Egyptians speak Albanian facilitates their access to services and information and to electronic and print media and contributes to their freedom of movement.[168] This also means that pupils from the Egyptian community can make use of the official public education system with no language barriers. However, similar to the Ashkali and Roma minorities, the Egyptian community is affected by social exclusion and poverty that hamper the school attendance and performance of children in Kosovo, while girls also remain the most affected: 'Many Egyptian families can rarely afford basic school textbooks and supplies, contributing to high numbers of dropouts and the frequent choice to keep only boys in school.'[169] Most Egyptian pupils do not continue their studies after the compulsory-level education and only a few enrol in university, even though there are quotas of guaranteed seats for Egyptian students in Kosovo.

Socioeconomic situation

The Egyptian minority has a similar situation to that of Roma and Ashkali communities in Kosovo as it is also facing fundamental problems like poverty, unemployment, social exclusion, discrimination, lack of education and professional skills.[170] Furthermore, the lack of information regarding job opportunities, the lack of investment in the development of small businesses and the agricultural sector, the lack of qualifications as well as the poor state of the economy as a whole are key reasons why the Egyptian minority was reported with the highest rate of unemployment in Kosovo (69.14 per cent).[171] The community has been relying on social assistance, on contributions from relatives residing abroad and donations from aid agencies, while 'seasonal agricultural works and self-employment activities are still the dominant types of employment for this community'.[172] As regards the Egyptians employed in the Kosovo public sector, the community is clearly underrepresented at both central and local level of governance. In 2010, there were no Egyptians employed within the central representative institutions while the central executive institutions confirmed only two Egyptians (0.03 per cent), representing the lowest representation from all minorities in Kosovo.[173] At the local level, all Kosovo municipalities combined employed only seven Egyptians (0.08 per cent), one more than the Gorani minority. The situation is even more worrying given that the municipality of Gjakovë/Đakovica did not report one single Egyptian within its members of staff despite having a population of over 5,000 members of this minority.

In this context, the previously mentioned problem of returnees also affects the improvement of the situation of the Egyptian community. The process has been slow for this minority even though a number of initiatives dedicated specifically to the return and reintegration of Egyptians have been undertaken in the Pejë/Peć region, where most Egyptians reside. It also appears that the 'representation and participation of Egyptians in relevant returns-related mechanisms is hampered by the fact that many municipalities failed to establish them or to convey regular meetings'.[174] Another crucial problem for the community is the fact that many Egyptians do not have birth or civil registration certificates that generally prevents them from enjoying full access to social services like employment assistance, healthcare and social welfare.[175]

Political representation and participation

The Egyptian minority in Kosovo has been mainly represented politically by one party, the New Democratic Initiative for Kosovo (IRDK). IRDK was established in 2001 under the leadership of Bislim Hoti and it has been aiming to protect the identity, traditions, culture of Egyptian.[176] The IRDK is a western Kosovo regionally based party and has been in close relations with the Alliance for the Future of Kosovo (AAK), one of the main Albanian parties in Kosovo. IRDK represents an interesting case among minority parties in Kosovo given it has been in coalition with a majority party (AAK) having formed a parliamentary group together in all three legislatures so far. In the first two legislatures of the Assembly, IRDK had two deputies each time, while after the last elections in 2010, there was one deputy (guaranteed seat) representing the Egyptian minority in the parliament.[177] At the central level, Egyptians also have had two representatives in the CCC. The 2014 elections confirmed the position of the newly founded Liberal Egyptian Party (PLE) as the largest party representing the Egyptian minority by taking over the one guaranteed seat from IRDK.[178]

The participation of the Egyptian minority in public affairs is better at the local level as the 2009 municipal elections were deemed a success for the community.[179] Egyptians gained a municipal assembly seat in each of the municipalities of Fushë Kosovë/Kosovo Polje, Gjakovë/Đakovica, Istog/Istok and Pejë/Peć. In Gjakovë/Đakovica and Istog/Istok the municipal assembly deputy chairpersons for communities have been Egyptians.[180] Nevertheless, the Egyptian minority has been unrepresented in the executive branches of the municipalities where they reside.[181]

The Gorani community

Demography

The Gorani minority has 10,265 residents in Kosovo and is mainly concentrated in the municipality of Dragash/Dragaš where there are 8,957 Goranis.[182] This means that together with the Bosniak community, they make up almost 50 per cent of the population of the Dragash/Dragaš municipality. In other municipalities, the Gorani community accounts for less than 3 per cent of the local population: Prizren, Mitrovicë/Mitovica North, Prishtinë/Priština and Pejë/Peć. In the past it was difficult to estimate the numbers of Gorani accurately because they have traditionally been migrant workers and also because in the pre-1999 censuses, Gorani (together with Bosniaks and Torbesh) had been generally categorized as 'Muslim Slavs'.[183] As a result, the 2011 census figure is higher than that of previous estimates and 'the changes in figures for Bosniaks and Gorani may potentially be linked: despite being separate ethnic groups, each of them with a separate cultural identity and speaking different Slavic dialects, figures concerning Bosniaks and Gorani are often merged or confused'.[184]

Identity, language and education

The Gorani are closely related to Bosniaks but constitute a separate Slavic Muslim community that originates from, and resides primarily in, Kosovo's mountainous and most southern municipality of Dragash/Dragaš (Prizren region). Moreover, the name 'Gorani' derives from the Gora area, which is also a Slavic word meaning mountain.[185] Gorani speak a Slavic language referred to as Našuski (roughly meaning 'ours'), which is similar to the language spoken in the western part of Macedonia and different from other Slav dialects spoken in Kosovo.[186] The language has not been standardized and no descriptive scholarly work on the Gorani dialect is available. This, together with continuous fights between two political factions, one supporting the usage of Serbian and the other the usage of Bosnian, prevents the Gorani community from advancing a coherent demand for language rights.[187] As a result, the language is not recognized as a language in official use in any of the municipalities of Kosovo. Furthermore, the 2011 census questionnaire did not include Gorani as one of the surveyed 'mother tongues'. Therefore, in the municipality of Dragash/Dragaš, where the largest Gorani community resides, 6,978 individuals indicated 'other' as their mother tongue.[188]

People have been declaring themselves as either Gorani or Bosniaks depending on their interests: political or for employment. They say they are Gorani at the local level and then declare themselves as Bosniaks at the central level.[189]

Therefore, within the community there are those who identify themselves as Gorani and a smaller number who identify themselves as Bosniaks.[190] This split is also caused by the political division between the two groups as the main distinguishing feature between them continues to be that of political affiliation.[191] Nevertheless, the Gorani identity has also been claimed by Macedonia and Bulgaria by providing passports.[192] Moreover, in post-conflict Kosovo the Gorani minority educated in Serbian was caught in the middle of the political stand-off between Kosovo Serbs and Albanians that included the creation of two education systems in Kosovo. Education in Serbian is available in regions where Serbs, Gorani and Roma reside and it is currently managed and funded by the Serbian Ministry of Education and follows a Serbian curriculum that differs from that in other Kosovo schools. Most Gorani in the Dragash/Dragaš municipality 'prefer to enrol their children in Serbia-run schools where instruction is in the Serbian language, which in turn affords greater opportunities for enrolment in Serbian Universities'.[193]

Socioeconomic situation

The 2010 OSCE report on minorities in Kosovo evaluated the socioeconomic situation of Gorani in Kosovo as 'relatively good'.[194] Given that half of the Gorani people are unemployed[195] and the number of Gorani working in the public sector is very small, the main source of income within the community is from private family-run businesses. Moreover, Dragash/Dragaš municipality, where most Gorani live, is one of the most underdeveloped municipalities in Kosovo.[196] In this context, marginalization is a challenge for Gorani people as well, especially that a part of the community complains 'to face discrimination when seeking employment in Kosovo institutions or the private sector due to their ethnicity. Thus, they often declare themselves as Kosovo Albanians and take advantage of their frequent proficiency in the Albanian language'.[197] Other sources of income for this minority group are pensions and social welfare from both the Kosovo and Serbian systems, as well as remittances from the diaspora.

The Gorani have also been underrepresented in the civil service. The central representative institutions do not have any Gorani employees, while the central executive institutions reported in the 2010 Policy Study have only four Gorani (0.07 per cent) in total.[198] At the local level across Kosovo there were indicated only six Gorani (0.06 per cent) employees, the lowest representation of all minorities in municipal institutions. Moreover, the poor access to employment and livelihoods and the challenges in relation to the choice of an educational system represent the main obstacles for the sustainable return and reintegration of Gorani displaced persons.[199] Overall, the main problems facing Gorani in the municipalities where they reside have been a lack of qualifications, a lack of information regarding job opportunities, language issues, an absence of development in industry, as well as the poor state of the economy as a whole.[200]

Political participation and representation

The Gorani community has been mainly represented by the Gora Citizen's Initiative (GIG) created as a citizens' association that took part initially in the 2000 municipal elections.[201] In 2002, under the leadership of Rustem Ibiši, GIG became a political party based in the municipality of Dragash/Dragaš with the main purpose of advancing the rights and interests of the Gorani minority in Kosovo. GIG held the Gorani guaranteed seat in the Kosovo Assembly after Mr Murselj Haljilji won 427 votes in the 2010 elections.[202] He subsequently joined the Serb parliamentary group of SLS in the Assembly, which indicated the party's and the community's close links with the Serbs.

> The political representation of the Goranis is fragile as a lot of issues that happen at the top level of governance influence the smaller communities significantly. Moreover, division within the community itself, political division and the fact that many voters have been co-opted by other parties like the Serb JLS, are all factors weakening our representation in Kosovo.[203]

GIG has been one of the minority parties in Kosovo that has gradually lost ground as its support fell from 1,789 votes in the 2000 local elections and 1,358 votes in the 2004 parliamentary elections to 454 votes in the 2009 locals and 787 votes in the national elections of 2010.[204] In this context, their votes went 'to the better organised and funded Bosniak parties',[205] while no new Gorani party was created. However, in the 2014 elections, the newly established Koalicijaza Gora (KG) won the majority of the increased number of votes for Gorani representatives and secured the one seat of the community in the Assembly.[206] At the local level, the Gorani community only plays a relatively active role in the public life of Dragash/Dragaš municipality, where two Gorani have been elected to the twenty-seven-seat municipal assembly, and three participate in the nine-member committee for communities.[207] Although all minorities are represented by the municipal committees and offices, in no municipality does a member of the Gorani community chair these institutions.

The Montenegrin community

> We are part of the Kosovo society as we have always been here. But we do not feel as part of the society.[208]

Kosovo Montenegrins and Croats were not included in the 2008 Constitution of Kosovo or the initial Law on Communities and both minorities were officially recognized only in December 2011.[209] As a result, they have been generally excluded from most legal provisions regarding the promotion and protection of minority rights in Kosovo and therefore they are not represented politically and have not been yet granted the right to guaranteed seats in the Assembly. The situation of these two very small communities is illustrative for some of the key problems with the legislation on minority rights in Kosovo. On the one hand, the focus on developing a framework for the main minority, the Serbs, combined with the inconsistency of the understanding and application of the notion of 'community', has undermined the equal inclusion of all minorities and, in the cases of Montenegrins and Croats, their exclusion through non-recognition.[210] On the other hand, the development of a far-reaching system of minority rights protection has stimulated the very small communities to ask for recognition and inclusion in the political life of Kosovo in accordance to the constitutional provisions for minorities. This could become, at least formally, a clear example of overrepresentation and excessive rights leading to segregation rather than integration of minorities.

Demography

Given the circumstances described above, Montenegrins and Croats were not included as ethnic categories in the 2011 census and as a result there is still no accurate data on the population of these two minorities. They had the possibility of declaring themselves as 'other' in the question on ethnic/cultural background, a category which resulted with a figure of 2,352 persons, but without representing a valid basis for comparison and analysis.[211] Kosovo Montenegrins are known to have mainly lived in the Kosovo regions of Pejë/

Peć and Prishtinë/Priština, in the municipalities of Deçan/Dečane, Istog/Istok, Lipjan/Lipljan, Obiliq/Obilić, Klinë/Klina, Fushë Kosovë/Kosovo Polje, Gračanica/Graçanicë and Prishtinë/Priština. However, because they have lived alongside Serbs 'no specific settlements/neighbourhoods have been identified due to difficulties in distinguishing the two communities'.[212] OSCE has estimated a population of about 5,000 Montenegrins in Kosovo, with most of them living in the Prishtinë/Priština region.[213] The Montenegrin population was included in the past in censuses completed by former Yugoslavia and over time the figures varied between 20,000 and 30,000 persons, but since the last official estimate (1991: 1 per cent of the population), there has been a dramatic fall in the numbers of Montenegrins living in Kosovo in the context of war and massive migration in the region due to security and to socioeconomic concerns.

Identity, language, education

Montenegrins are a South Slavic community that originates from Montenegro, they are predominantly of Christian Orthodox faith, and they speak Montenegrin or Serbian as their mother tongue. Montenegrins were recognized as one of the constituent nations of the Socialist Federal Republic of Yugoslavia and they share with Serbs a similar history as well as 'many cultural, linguistic, religious, and traditional traits'.[214] The development of a different Montenegrin identity has been mainly inspired by historical reasons (some parts of Montenegro were not under the rule of the Ottoman Empire), geographical reasons (its remoteness) and then their recognition as separate ethnic group and the proclamation of its territory as one of the constituent republics of Yugoslavia.[215] The most important and recent development was the independence of Montenegro from Serbia as a new state in 2006.

> We are an old and traditional community in Kosovo. But after the war, it was a big mistake to be associated with the Serb community. This was not true. We are our own community, this is our country too, and we are diaspora of Montenegro. We have tried to integrate for the last ten years by participating and getting involved in the public sphere in Kosovo.[216]

Even though the Kosovo Montenegrin political leaders strongly advocate for disassociation from the Serbs, 'many are still reluctant to publicly self-identify as Kosovo Montenegrins, particularly in areas where they are integrated into the Kosovo Serb community, and benefit from institutions financed by the Republic of Serbia'.[217] As a result the situation of Montenegrins is similar to that of Kosovo Serbs, and given the linguistic resemblance with Serbian, children from this community in the Pejë/Peć and Prishtinë/Priština regions follow the Serbian curriculum system and attend classes in the Serbian language.

Socioeconomic situation

As indicated above, Montenegrins face similar problems to those of the Kosovo Serb minority and a poor socioeconomic situation given the limited employment opportunities, the limited freedom of movement and the poor knowledge of the language spoken by the majority community in Kosovo, Albanian. Nevertheless, there is no specific data on the dominant types of employment or level of unemployment for the Montenegrin minority, although the community 'receives social welfare assistance from Serbia and minimum salaries derived from pre-1999 employment by state-owned enterprises'.[218] Therefore, the existence of the Serbian parallel institutions in Kosovo has had an essential role for the Montenegrins living in Kosovo as well.

Participation and representation

Despite the deferred recognition, the Montenegrin minority in Kosovo has developed a political presence from which to promote and protect the community's interests. Initially, they created in 2008 an Association of Kosovo Montenegrins, which helped them to participate in public affairs and gain a seat within the Communities Consultative Council, held by Snežana Karadžić. The main political problem for the Montenegrin community remains the fact that they still do not have a guaranteed seat in the Assembly despite the recognition of their status as non-majority communities.

> We are feeling very unhappy as we still do not have a seat in the parliament. We were promised a seat, but this has not been respected. How can we prepare our political campaign in this context? ... In any case, in order to gain our seat in the Assembly we need to cooperate with all communities in Kosovo.[219]

However, in 2009 and 2010 there were established three Montenegrin political parties: the Montenegrin Democratic Party (CDS), the Montenegrin People's Party (CNS) and the Montenegrin Liberal Party (CLS).[220] CDS has been the most important Montenegrin party under the leadership of Predrag Despotović and took part in the 2009 local elections and the 2010 national elections. CDS ran in five municipalities and managed to win 470 votes[221] and secure one seat in the municipal assembly of Fushë Kosovë/Kosovo Polje, where its candidate, Radoman Doderović, gained 377 votes (4.63 per cent).[222] In the 2010 elections, CDS won 771 votes (0.11 per cent) in total and 513 votes for its main candidate Predrag Despotović,[223] which gave CDS no chance for a seat in the Assembly given the Montenegrins were not then allocated a minority guaranteed seat. The result was nevertheless significant as it represented the same percentage as the one obtained by the Gorani party GIG and even better than the number of votes won by the Roma party PREBK (0.1 per cent), both of which have had a minority seat assigned in the Kosovo Assembly since 2010.[224]

The Croat community

Demography

The Croat minority was not included either as a separate ethnic group in the 2011 census but represents by far the smallest community in Kosovo with an estimated population of only 259 residents.[225] The few Kosovo Croats live in small villages located in two different regions: the Gjilan/Gnjilane region, municipality of Viti/Vitina (villages of Letnicë, Shashar, Vërnavokollë and Vërnez), where they constitute approximately 0.05 per cent of the population and in the Prishtinë/Priština region, Lipjan/Lipljan municipality (Janjevë village), where they represent approximately 0.29 per cent of the local population.[226] In the past, several thousand Croats used to live in these two regions as the 1991 census reported 4,331 Croats in Viti/Vitina and 2,914 Croats in Lipjan/Lipljan.[227] However, most Kosovo Croats left Kosovo in the 1990s and especially during the 1999 conflict because of the lack of security and economic opportunities in combination with the support for relocation offered by Croatia.[228]

Identity, language, education

Kosovo Croats are Catholic Slavs thought to originate from fourteenth-century traders who came to Kosovo from Dubrovnik and who speak Croatian as their mother tongue. Therefore, their religious background and the local Roman Catholic Church represent the key elements for preserving the distinct Kosovo Croat identity. In general, Kosovo Croats make free use of their mother tongue in most public spaces, but the community does not feel completely at ease to do so in all public spaces and use Serbian to interact with public authorities, 'thus at times experiences difficulties in relation to the lack of adequate translation and interpretation in the two municipalities where the community resides'.[229] Moreover, the very few Croat children who are still in Kosovo attend the Serbian-supported educational system.

Socioeconomic situation

The employment and socioeconomic situation of the Croat minority are extremely worrying, especially that the majority of the population are elderly.[230] As OSCE reported, the Croat community is a 'vulnerable and isolated community [that] lives in extreme poverty and inadequate housing conditions'.[231] In the Gjilan/Gnjilane region, most Croats are pensioners receiving assistance from Croatian, Kosovo and Serbian pension funds and social welfare. Moreover, there are no Croats employed in the Serbian parallel institutions in the Viti/Vitina municipality, while the Kosovo Croats in the Prishtinë/Priština region have almost no employment opportunities. A few people have found work in the Janjevë primary school, including seven school teachers and, generally, 'other sources of income for the community include trading in items, crafts, farming and agricultural activities'.[232] In this context, other problems like the lack of public transportation and access to healthcare, lack of access to telecommunication services and lack of property titles are all contributing 'to a marked sense of isolation amongst the community'.[233]

Representation and participation

There is no participation of Croats in public affairs mainly because of the small size of their community, the late official recognition of their status as one of the Kosovan minorities and the absence of a guaranteed seat in the Assembly. Moreover, the community has no representation in the municipal executive and legislative bodies or civil service in the Gjilan/Gnjilane region, while in Viti, the contracts of the only two Kosovo Croat civil servants employed in the municipal administration were terminated in 2009.[234] In addition, 'neither municipality has been involved in any outreach activities to the community to promote their participation in public affairs and break the isolation of this small, vulnerable and aging community'.[235]

Conclusion

As this chapter has illustrated, the process of integrating non-majority communities in Kosovo has been accelerated in the post-independence period by the promulgation and adoption of a strong legislation vis-à-vis the protection and promotion of minority rights. However, the implementation of the multiethnic legal and institutional framework at both central and local levels of governance has had an asymmetrical impact on the different minorities in Kosovo. The first factor has been the overall priority to integrate the Serb minority, which I discussed more largely in the previous chapter. The second element has been the will and institutional capacity of the state not only to target the integration of all minorities but also to implement the constitutional provisions as equitably as possible. This was exemplified by the second part of this chapter that analysed the proportional employment of minorities in the public sector. The third and core element of this chapter has been the particular will and capacity of each minority community to accept, assume and take advantage of the far-reaching set of minority rights.

The in-depth investigation of each of the non-Serb minority in Kosovo therefore helped to better reflect on the various interpretation and application of minority rights. This has been dependent not only on the support of the Kosovo authorities but also on the individual socioeconomic and political situation of each community apart, as well as their different needs and demands. While it is important to underline the benefits and positive impact of the promotion of diversity and the protection of all minorities in Kosovo, this chapter has indicated why instead of integrating communities, the institutional focus on multiethnicity may also foster new divisions by promoting an ethnopolitical identity. There is evidence presented here of competition not only between the Albanian majority, the Serbs and other minorities, but also among the non-Serbian minorities themselves. Promoting multiethnicity with an actual main purpose to integrate only one dominant minority has brought the risk of a worsening trend as regards the situation of other smaller communities. In other words, to promote ethnic diversity by emphasizing each group's own identity, disregarding its appropriateness and assuming the uniform need of integration, may actually nurture division. The issue of what kind of 'identity' is promoted (cultural or political) explains how multiethnicity permits actors to reinterpret or exploit the concept when it reaches areas beyond its real scope.

5

Managing Diversity through Decentralization

Minority rights at the local level of governance in Kosovo

Within the myriad of post-conflict statebuilding mechanisms and strategies, decentralization has become particularly popular for dealing with the management of diversity at the local level of governance.[1] This novel intersection of concerns for good governance with those aiming to foster minority protection and accommodation has also been visible within the statebuilding missions emerging after the 1990s ethnic conflicts in the Balkans. Broadly speaking, local governance was always going to be a highly delicate issue for the post-conflict social, political, institutional, economic, demographic and territorial changes brought by the breakup of Yugoslavia. The challenges for local governance have been somehow similar to other post-conflict policies and tools in the sense that statebuilding from scratch often faces the dilemma of harmonizing state capacity with democratization, which may also include the diffusion of power through decentralization.[2]

Ten years after its unilateral declaration of independence and almost twenty years since the 1999 war, Kosovo is still facing significant challenges in developing self-rule and sustainable capacity at both central and local levels of governance. This chapter reflects on the task to merge decentralization as a purely administrative tool (building devolved, accountable, legitimate, efficient local governance) and decentralization as a tool for post-(ethnic)conflict reconciliation and power-sharing governance. I will thus discuss the measures taken to integrate, accommodate and protect minorities at the local level in Kosovo while mainly addressing the situation of the Serb community as the key target of the process of decentralization. The first part of the chapter takes into consideration general arguments that show both positive and negative aspects of using decentralization as a tool for managing diversity. This may involve, for instance, the creation of decentralized governance on ethnic lines by empowering minorities that are in majority in a certain area. One positive outcome can be determining minority communities to accept and legitimize the authority of state institutions in exchange of a high degree of local autonomy. However, a key risk of this strategy is to cause territorial and institutional isolation of minority municipalities[3] on the long term. Furthermore, the practical and non-ethnic benefits of decentralization (good governance, local democracy, etc.) may not be compatible with the ethnic criteria of establishing or empowering minority municipalities because the new administrative units may lack the necessary capacities for sustainable local self-governance.

This chapter then looks at the legislation starting with the comprehensive proposal for the Kosovo Status Settlement (CSP), which represents the foundation of the decentralization strategy in Kosovo. This document had as priority addressing the needs of Kosovo Serbs by empowering them at the local level so as to gradually diminish the influence of parallel structures sponsored by Serbia and encourage them to accept the authority of Kosovo. The evident influence of the Ahtisaari Plan on drawing the post-independence legislation is analysed in the section on the post-2008 legal framework that has been regulating local government and decentralization in Kosovo. This will confirm the de jure high degree of transfer of powers from central government to municipal level in terms of political, administrative and fiscal responsibilities and competencies. Nonetheless, the particular provisions for Serb-majority municipalities further demonstrate that the Serb community has been the main target of decentralized governance.

Overall, the creation of new municipalities in post-independence Kosovo is the most important case study that this chapter employs to illustrate the empowerment of Serbs at the local level. This has consisted of a territorial and administrative reorganization of Kosovo so as to increase the number of Serb-majority municipalities to ten. In comparison, Kosovo Turks are the only other minority community with their own municipality, while only two other Albanian majority municipalities were newly established as a result of decentralization.

The last section of this chapter will examine not only the Serb-majority municipalities located south of the Ibar River, but also the Turkish municipality of Mamuşa/Mamushë/Mamuša and then the most ethnically diverse municipality in Kosovo, Prizren. This will consist of looking at the demographics, economic, administrative and political situations of each municipality so as to explain both the benefits and the challenges faced after decentralization, as well as to evaluate its impact on the levels of integration and accommodation of minorities at the local level. It will be essential to examine how the situation varies from one municipality to the other depending on the capacity of local actors, the support of Kosovo central institutions, the local economic opportunities, the willingness of the local population to integrate and the particular role of the Serbian parallel structures.

Why decentralization?

Local self-government is based upon the principles of good governance, transparency, efficiency and effectiveness in providing public services having due regard for the specific needs and interests of the Communities not in the majority and their members.[4]

Decentralization has thus been the primary element in regards to the management of minorities at the local level of governance in Kosovo. This has had the aim of transferring powers from central to municipal level and of redefining territorial boundaries for municipalities in Kosovo in the advantage of all minority communities.[5] This section will combine Kosovo-specific examples and measures with theoretical arguments so as to explain how decentralization can be used as a key instrument for conflict management and integration of minorities in divided societies.

As in the case of the power-sharing arrangements at the central level, the strategy for developing an enhanced and sustainable system of local-self-governance has mainly targeted the Serb minority. Consequently, there are currently ten municipalities in Kosovo that have a Serb majority but given the lack of implementation and the de facto administration by Serbian institutions of the four Serb municipalities in North Kosovo, this chapter will only examine the six Serb municipalities south of the Ibar River. As regards the other minorities, only the Turkish community has also benefited directly from decentralization through the establishment of the municipality of Mamuşa/Mamushë/Mamuša in 2008. The Bosniak community has also been lobbying for the creation of two municipalities where they would be in majority, one in Vitomiricë and one in Recane, but they have not been approved.[6] Furthermore, the last case study of this chapter will be the Albanian-majority municipality of Prizren, which has the most ethnically diverse population in Kosovo.

In the context of statebuilding, decentralization in Kosovo has become a key part of the administrative, political, economic and territorial reforms that have two main objectives: (1) the pure organizational purpose of developing the most efficient and accountable model of government and institution-building and (2) to act as a post-conflict solution to the problems caused by a centralized system and build a legitimate and effective government, which in the case of Kosovo mainly needs to address the integration of the Serb minority. On the one hand, the overall strategy to transfer power at the local level by strengthening the status and capacity of municipalities aims, therefore, to secure an increased space for decision-making by local authorities and also a better provision of public services for citizens of these localities.[7] In other words, this concerns the non-ethnic generic needs of all citizens that can be better managed through more control at the local level of governance and by bringing decision-making closer to the people. The transfer of authority away from the central level is thus planned to assure a better efficiency and accountability of local governments, limit the size of the public sector, reduce corruption, respond better to citizen preferences, enhance democracy and protection of rights and stimulate local development as well as intergovernmental competition.[8] Furthermore, this transfer of powers to lower governmental tiers is part of the 'global trend towards devolution [that] is based on subnational legitimacy and implies greater transfers of authority and resources from the centre to the states or regions. In most cases, and as in previous waves of decentralisation, regional legitimacy has historic, linguistic, religious, and/or cultural roots'.[9]

On the other hand, the particular purpose of decentralization in Kosovo has been to address the situation of minorities and the protection and promotion of their rights at the local level (ethnic reasoning). Thus, the strategy has incorporated the idea that a decentralized government has a better potential to protect minority communities and, thus, offer equal participation for all minorities in the socioeconomic and political life of Kosovo.

> If minorities inhabit an area with a certain degree of self-government, decentralization essentially grants them the right to be free as a collective. Thus, decentralization offers the possibility of combining democratic ideals with guarantees for minorities and can provide a means of accommodating problems arising from ethnic diversity. By guaranteeing local autonomy, especially to questions considered important to ethnic identity, the potential for conflict within the national political arena is reduced.[10]

Much of the literature that discusses the role of decentralization in post-conflict contexts[11] does not include significant research on the specific impact of decentralization on the integration and accommodation of ethnic minorities. However, as also discussed in the first chapter, the post-conflict studies of power-sharing have generally been in favour of either group-building (consociational) or integrative approaches and have revealed the difference between more traditional top-down methods that target the central-level (quotas, electoral reform, veto power) and local-level mechanisms (decentralization) that 'can contribute to the bottom-up transformation of conflicts'.[12] By employing substantial primary data obtained through fieldwork, this chapter offers a bottom-up portrayal of local governance in Kosovo and its relevance for the broader argument that there is a varying gap between de jure and de facto conditions for the accommodation, integration or protection of minorities.

Ethnic vs. territorial models of decentralization

Given that the ethnic problems that motivated decentralization in Kosovo are the focus of this chapter, it is useful to mention a distinction made by Loew[13] between the *ethnic* and *territorial* models of implementing decentralization based on the way the borders of local administrative units (municipalities) are drawn. Ethnic decentralization creates ethnically homogeneous entities by using the distribution of ethnic groups as criteria of territorial demarcation. By contrast, territorial decentralization builds ethnically heterogeneous units (municipalities) by drawing 'borders based on traditionally and socioeconomically defined territories [...] in which ethnic minorities constitute an important percentage of the overall population of the municipality'.[14] The territorial decentralization model can be described as an integrative tool for constructing power-sharing that aims to 'de-ethnicize' politics and secure the transformation of conflict. Rather than focusing on mechanisms that give autonomy and empower ethnic minorities as unitary groups at the local level, territorial decentralization has the purpose of creating heterogeneous administrative-territorial units that work in favour of interaction, cooperation and trust-building between individuals belonging to different ethnic minorities.

Nevertheless, a fundamental challenge for this model is not addressing the issues of self-determination and of finding quick solutions for the mediation/integration of conflicting groups in the immediate context of post-conflict societies. This is affected by the lack of security for minorities as regards their participation in the decision-making, the peril of assimilation and of falling under the control of the majority population and not prioritizing the specific minority issues at the local level. In cases of post-conflict statebuilding like

Kosovo the focus is on reconciliation and on creating the necessary conditions for sustainable peace. Nonetheless, as this book has been showing too, all ethnic minorities in such plural societies are affected by the process regardless of their level of implication in the conflict. Therefore, in relation to the use of decentralization as a tool of conflict management/transformation, the *ethnic* model of decentralization has generally been chosen as a potential solution for post-conflict societies.[15]

The main advantage of ethnic decentralization is that it creates the conditions for a high degree of autonomy and ethnic self-determination. On the downside, ethnic decentralization creates homogeneous territories that can trigger segregation rather than integration of different ethnic minorities. Local ethnic elites can set up their own power bases[16] allowing them to secure their legitimacy based on ethnicity and perpetuate ethnic politics in the detriment of democratization.[17] Furthermore, the benefits of ethnic decentralization are unlikely to be uniformly distributed among all minority groups or even among all members of the same ethnic group. The smaller ethnic communities might not be in the capacity to constitute a majority at the local level which would thus exclude them 'from this instrument of conflict resolution and will in consequence also lack an important instrument for the representation of their interests at the central level'.[18]

In other words, not only ethnic decentralization does not benefit the integration of smaller ethnic groups, but it can obscure the overall protection and promotion of their rights. The empowerment of a certain group at the local level can also create new minorities and thus complicate the interethnic relationships. Benefits of ethnic decentralization are thus conditional on factors like geographical spread of the population and the model proves desirable for groups spatially concentrated or that have a local majority, while for other it may have no effect or be harmful.[19] Ethnic decentralization may target the immediate empowerment of ethnic minorities at the local level and thus create strong conditions for the protection of their rights and stimulate integration in the post-conflict environment (temporary conflict management). However, this may not be the best solution for the long-term aim of conflict transformation. Therefore, while territorial decentralization may be less effective on the short term and is not directly targeting the integration of minority groups, it cannot be evaluated as a post-conflict tool per se. On the other hand, the ethnic model of decentralization is particularly designed to target the situation of minorities at the local level and for this reason it requires more consideration. As the analysis of Kosovo illustrates, the fact that ethnic decentralization may negatively affect the transformation of conflict through territorial polarization represents a matter of great concern.

The legal framework on decentralization and minority rights at the local level

Decentralization in Kosovo has consisted of policies mixing both ethnic and territorial models for the demarcation of local units of governance and has thus established both ethnic heterogeneous and ethnic homogeneous municipalities. As the arguments discussed in the previous section suggest, decentralization can have a positive effect in post-conflict environments mainly by guaranteeing local autonomy and for this reason it 'had been long discussed as a potential mechanism for resolving some of Kosovo's ethnic differences'[20] and it became a central point on the international agenda during the interim period under UNMIK. Before the war and the breakup of Yugoslavia, decentralization in Kosovo had a different role. During the communist period, decentralization had the same ideological purpose as in other communist regimes to strengthen the effectiveness of political control exerted by the party over local affairs.[21] The two basic constitutive elements of Yugoslav federalism were *communism* and *nation* reflecting an interdependent relationship that while it supported the regimes' principles, structure and functioning it also caused its eventual disintegration.[22] At the same time, decentralization in Kosovo was also used in the past by the Belgrade government 'as a means to influence the ethnic power balance in the region in favor of the Serbian community'.[23]

After the 1999 conflict the Serb community in Kosovo became gradually isolated from the Albanian majority and the provisional administration and institutions in Kosovo and settled in geographical, sociopolitical and economic enclaves with the fundamental support of the parallel system sponsored by Serbia. Moreover, before the 2008 declaration of independence, the integration of Kosovo Serbs clearly became a matter of great concern as indicated by the declining participation of Serbs in southern Kosovo and the successful boycott of the 2007 local and general elections.[24] UNMIK created municipalities to coordinate humanitarian aid and the development of local administrative units, and afterwards, decentralization became a key point of discussion during the negotiation process over the future status of Kosovo between the international community, Serbia and Kosovo representatives that started in 2006.[25] The failure of these negotiations led to the proposal for the status settlement (the

Ahtisaari Plan) that set up 'a far reaching decentralisation policy designed to achieve acceptance of the Kosovar authorities and the population of all ethnic communities, to reduce the struggle for dominance and legitimacy over the territory and to enable peaceful coexistence of all ethnic communities on its territory'.[26] Therefore, this was perceived as an additional efficient way of governing multiethnicity in Kosovo, but it was not what the Kosovo local leaders had envisaged:

> Decentralisation runs contrary to Kosovo Albanian ideas of achieving state 'functionality' through centralised administrative control. It is instead linked with contemporary European ideas of 'subsidiarity', devolving decision-making down to the lowest level authority, propelled by the idea that the closer governance is to the people it affects, the more likely it is to reflect their interests.[27]

Decentralization was thus considered as a key tool for post-conflict reconciliation and an opportunity to convince the Serb minority to accept Kosovo institutions in exchange of a high degree of local autonomy. But while decentralization has been utilized to primarily deal with the integration of Kosovo Serbs, the situation of the other minorities in Kosovo has nevertheless been affected. In addition to the general legal and institutional tools developed to address the protection of minority rights at the local level (participation and representation in political structures, decision-making powers, consultative bodies), of particular significance is the ethnic-based creation and empowerment of (minority) municipalities. All these factors indicate a major challenge for Kosovo's use of decentralization as a key tool for integration of minorities at the local level. Success in the long term might depend on whether the implementation process is capable of linking together the minority rights protection strategy with the general aim of dealing with crucial non-ethnic issues like poverty, unemployment, underdevelopment, unemployment and quality of public services. Decentralization in Kosovo may serve as a positive element for effective post-conflict and post-independence statebuilding in Kosovo but at the same time there is a risk of entrenching ethnic divisions through geographical, social, political and economic segregation. Once again, differentiating between immediate and long-term results is essential for understanding the efficiency and sustainability of decentralization.

The Ahtisaari Plan and decentralization

The process of decentralization has been mainly initiated and designed on the same lines with some of the key provisions from the 2007 Ahtisaari Plan or the

Comprehensive proposal for the Kosovo Status Settlement (CSP). Annex III of the proposal was entitled 'Decentralisation' and its purpose is clearly outlined in the first paragraph:

> To address the legitimate concerns of the Kosovo Serb and other Communities that are not in the majority in Kosovo and their members, encourage and ensure their active participation in public life, and strengthen good governance and the effectiveness and efficiency of public services throughout Kosovo, an enhanced and sustainable system of local self-government in Kosovo shall be established

Therefore, the text promotes the principle of local self-government as a solution for the particular needs of minority communities in Kosovo and correlates the participation and protection of minority rights with conditions for good governance, as well as with effective and efficient public services, 'based upon the principles of the European Charter of Local Self-Government and, in particular, the principle of subsidiarity'.[28] The priority of this document was certainly to address the needs of the Kosovo Serbs by empowering them at the local level and creating the necessary conditions for them to be in charge and manage issues that are of particular interest for the Serb community. This had the aim to limit the influence of the Albanian majority while at the same time it offered the possibility for Serb self-rule at the local level in exchange of recognition of the authority of the Kosovo Government.[29] Therefore, integration was supposed to be facilitated by developing a system of local self-government that would also incorporate the ethnic (minority) criteria. As the implementation of the decentralization plan shows, the ethnic criterion was applied as much as possible to secure self-rule for Kosovo Serbs. Moreover, in addition to the general lists of competencies, certain municipalities were going to have enhanced competencies, such as three particular cases of Serb-majority municipalities of Mitrovicë/Mitrovica North, Gracanicë/Gracanica and Shtërpce/Štrpce, with extensive control over education and healthcare. However, the enhanced competencies were solely meant to address concerns of the Serb community given that all municipalities where Serbs constitute the majority were going to have:

a. Authority to exercise responsibility for cultural affairs, including protection and promotion of Serbian and other religious and cultural heritage within the municipal territory, as well as support for local religious communities ...
b. Enhanced participatory rights in the appointment of Police Station Commanders, as set forth in Article 2.6 of Annex VIII of this Settlement.[30]

Furthermore, the Article on Education of the Decentralisation Annex in CSP solely addresses issues regarding education in the Serbian language in schools and the University of Mitrovicë/Mitrovica as an autonomous institution.[31] Another key proposal of the CSP chapter on Decentralization focuses on the cooperation of municipalities with institutions of the Republic of Serbia, which 'may take the form of the provision by Serbian institutions of financial and technical assistance, including expert personnel and equipment, in the implementation of municipal competencies',[32] thus also entitling municipalities to receive financial assistance from Serbia.[33]

Lastly, the decentralization provisions offered by the Ahtisaari Plan also address the establishment of new municipalities: Gračanica/Graçanicë, Novo Brdo/Novobërdë, Ranilug/Ranillug, Parteš/Partesh, Kllokot/Klokot and Mitrovicë/Mitrovica North. Among the steps indicated in this article, it is worth mentioning that 'Kosovo shall engage in consultations with a non-majority Community where that Community makes up at least 75 per cent of the population of a concentrated settlement with a minimum total population of 5,000 inhabitants, with a view to establishing other new municipalities'.[34] This specific criteria for the establishment of new municipalities could be of great help not only to compare CSP with the present legislation but also to analyse the practicality and results of the actual implementation of decentralization in Kosovo. Altogether, the provisions of the Ahtisaari package were set to use decentralization as an instrument of gradually limiting the presence of Serbian parallel structures in Kosovo or at least changing the way they function by consolidating the authority of the Prishtinë/Priština government while also providing autonomy, rights and particular linkages with Serbian institutions for Kosovo municipalities with a Serb majority.

The post-independence legislation

> Local self-government is based upon the principles of good governance, transparency, efficiency and effectiveness in providing public services having due regard for the specific needs and interests of the Communities not in the majority and their members.[35]

The legal framework regulating local government and the process of decentralization in Kosovo consists therefore mainly of three laws: the Law on Local Self-government, the Law on Administrative Municipal Borders and the Law on Local Government Finances. Therefore, the post-independence context of statebuilding has also comprised of a complex process of political, administrative and fiscal decentralization. Furthermore, in the Action Plan on the Implementation of Decentralisation, the Kosovo Government presented its strategy to create a sustainable system and effective local government meant to ensure good living conditions for all citizens while paying particular attention to special needs and concerns of the minority communities in Kosovo.

Both the Constitution and the Law on Local Self-government confirm that the municipality represents the basic unit of local self-government in Kosovo 'made up of community of citizens of a specific territory defined by law and shall exercise all powers which are not explicitly reserved for the central institutions'.[36] This law immediately indicates that municipalities should have policies and practices designed to promote coexistence and peace between citizens while creating the necessary conditions to enable 'all communities to express, preserve, and develop their national, ethnic, cultural, religious, and linguistic identities'.[37] Therefore, the proactive character of the constitutional provision for minorities is also clearly reflected by the legislation concerning the process of decentralization. As previously mentioned, subsidiarity is the principle in accordance to which all the competencies of municipalities shall be exercised. The significant number of competencies transferred to the local level suggests that 'the Republic of Kosovo can be regarded as highly decentralised'.[38] Furthermore, the competencies of municipalities fall into three categories: own, delegated and enhanced.

The *own competencies*[39] at the local level of administration cover all key areas, starting with economic development and continuing with education, healthcare, culture, environment and, of course, human rights issues. All these confirm the challenging and wide-ranging responsibility of municipalities to build up and promote good governance, economic development and efficient delivery of public services. The second category is that of *delegated competencies* that are passed on by central authorities in Kosovo to municipalities, which mainly have to deal with cadastral records, civil registries, voter registration, business registration and licensing, distribution of social assistance payments (excluding pensions) and forestry protection on the municipal territory within the authority delegated by the central authority.[40] These competencies require specific capacities adding on more challenges especially in the case of new municipalities, and, as a result, the law also mentions that delegated competencies must be accompanied by necessary funding 'in compliance with objectives, standards and requests determined by the Government of Kosova'.[41]

The support of central institutions is thus vital for the development and sustainability of municipalities in Kosovo.

The third category of *enhanced competencies* applies to certain municipalities in the areas of health, education and cultural affairs, while also offering participatory rights in selecting local station police commanders.[42] Given that the capacity of municipalities has been a key test for the sustainability and practicality of decentralization, it is worth mentioning that the law specifies how central authorities are meant to monitor the exercise of enhanced competencies in accordance with 'minimum quality and quantity standards in the provision of public services [and] minimum qualifications of personnel and training facilities'.[43] The article on enhanced competencies nevertheless reproduces the suggestions of the Ahtisaari Plan and names the municipalities of Mitrovicë/Mitrovica North, Graçanicë/Gracanica and Shtërpcë/Štrpce in charge of the provision of secondary healthcare, while Mitrovicë/Mitrovica North is also given the competence for the provision of higher education.[44] Nonetheless, all Serb municipalities in Kosovo with a Serb majority have the right to select the local police commander and 'shall have authority to exercise responsibility for cultural affairs, including, protection and promotion of Serbian and other religious and cultural heritage within the municipal territory as well as support for local religious communities in accordance with the applicable law'.[45]

Moreover, the cross-border cooperation of municipalities permitting the direct support of Serbian institutions is also derived from the Ahtisaari Plan.[46] As a result, the purpose of CSP to accommodate the Serbs in Kosovo by providing rights and competencies at the local level that solely target the Serb community was adopted by the Kosovo legislation. The promulgation of these special provisions for Serb-majority municipalities is very important in the context of the continuing presence of Serbian parallel institutions. As a result, the legislation clearly empowered Kosovo Serbs to be in charge of their own affairs at the local level, but while this should be in exchange of full recognition of the authority of Prishtinë/Priština, the dependency on parallel institutions will require great efforts to be gradually diminished and eventually replaced.[47] Kosovo institutions need to be capable of substituting the role of the Serbian parallel system in order to accomplish a proper implementation of the legislation. In this context, the capacity problem could be just as impactful as the willingness of Kosovo Serbs to accept the authority of Prishtinë/Priština.

In this multilayered process of decentralizing powers, the Law on Local Government Finances focuses on the principles of financial autonomy and mentions that municipalities in Kosovo are entitled 'to adequate financial resources of their own that they may dispose of freely in the discharge of their municipal competencies in accordance with the applicable laws of Kosovo'.[48] As a result, the law allows municipalities to raise their own revenue through local taxes, services and donations, while it also takes into consideration the special conditions that may be necessary for the municipalities with enhanced competencies.[49] These specifications can only highlight again the importance of enhanced competencies that mainly target municipalities with a Serb majority and thus the needs and interests of Kosovo Serbs. It is also worth mentioning that the law includes financial assistance from the Republic of Serbia on the list of financial resources for Kosovo municipalities.[50] Another significant information that was included in the law on finances at the local level is regarding the data used for the allocation of the General Grant for each municipality. The General Grant is meant to assure a reasonable degree of stability in municipal income, an appropriate measure of equalization between municipalities, while considering the particular ability of the inhabitants of each municipality to access public services and provide an adequate allocation of resources for the non-majority communities in the respective municipalities.

According to the national and municipal legal framework, the following municipal institutions/posts are envisaged for minority communities at the level of municipal executive and assembly: deputy mayor for communities, deputy chairperson of the municipal assembly for communities[51] and the assembly committee on communities that has the status of permanent committee. The introduction of the deputy chairperson of the municipal assembly for communities aims to promote inter-community dialogue and serve as formal focal point for addressing concerns and interests of minorities in meetings of the assembly.[52] On the other hand, the deputy mayor has a rather vague role to 'assist the Mayor and provide him/her advice and guidance to the Mayor on issues related to the non-majority communities'.[53] Moreover, the communities committee was created to include at least one representative for any community living in the municipality and has the responsibility to review compliance of the municipal authorities with the legislation and to oversee the municipal policies and activities concerned with the rights and interests of the communities.[54] In 2009, a year after the declaration of independence, it was reported that the total number of representatives for each minority in communities committees across the twenty-six municipalities of Kosovo was as follows: Bosniaks (twelve members), Turks (eight members), Roma (seventeen members), Ashkali (twelve members), Egyptians (ten members), Gorani (three members), Croats (two members) and no representatives for the Montenegrin community.[55] Such statistics indicate that although in heterogeneous municipalities minority representatives cooperate more in the local administrations and assemblies, in homogeneous municipalities the small minority communities are often not represented at all in these institutions.[56] Although the committees for communities should act as permanent platforms for interethnic contact, they 'do not provide regular contact and are often exclusively attended by representatives of non-majority communities, being perceived as an institution only representing the interests of these communities'.[57] This can marginalize the minorities and prevent them from developing common interests and objectives.

As regards the Law on the Use of Languages, Article 2(3) defines the official language in the municipality as the language of a community which is not official (not Albanian or Serbian), when this community constitutes at least 5 per cent of the population of the municipality. In addition, when a community within a municipality represents above 3 per cent of its population, and its language is not an official language, based on Article 2(4), this language has the status of the language in official use in the municipality. The same Article gives the same status, of the language in official use in the municipality, to languages of the communities that have been traditionally spoken in a municipality. As a result, Turkish, Bosnian and Roma languages have the status of the official languages at the municipal level or will be in official use at all levels as provided by law.

The Law on Administrative Municipal Borders was adopted in February 2008 and its opening statement explains again the aim of bringing decision-making closer to citizens while the focus is clearly on the 'special needs and concerns of the non-majority communities in Republic of Kosova'.[58] It then motivates the adoption of the law:

> A democratic society is sustainable and functional when all the communities are integrated in the existing system and take part in the democratic and political life of the country, [...] For the purpose of integrating the non-majority communities, especially the Serb community, establishing of a functional state throughout the whole territory and creating a sustainable system of the self-government, to improve the efficiency of public services.

This statement resumes the rationale behind the process of decentralization in trying to develop a multiethnic democratic model of governance through administrative reforms and measures meant to facilitate self-government for minorities, while especially targeting the areas populated by Kosovo Serbs. The establishment of new municipalities, delineating the territory and boundaries of each municipality, has thus been included in this law. The law included the following changes to the previous territorial: an extension for the municipality of Novo Brdo/Novobërdë with residency in Bostan/Bostane and the division of the municipality of Mitrovicë/Mitrovica in two new municipalities, Mitrovicë/Mitrovica North and Mitrovicë/Mitrovica South and the establishment of seven other completely new municipalities. Altogether, changes were confirmed for a total of nine municipalities:

- Municipality of Novo Brdo/Novobërdë with residency in Bostan/Bostane
- Municipality of Mitrovicë/Mitrovica North with the residency in Mitrovica
- Municipality of Mitrovicë/Mitrovica South with the residency in Mitrovica
- Municipality of Junik with the residency in Junik
- Municipality of Hani i Elezit with the residency in Hani i Elezit
- Municipality of Mamuşa/Mamushë/Mamuša with the residency in Mamuşa/Mamushë/Mamuša
- Municipality of Gračanica/Graçanicë with the residency in Gračanica/Graçanicë
- Municipality of Ranilug/Ranillug with the residency in Ranilug/Ranillug
- Municipality of Parteš/Partesh with the residency in Parteš/Partesh
- Municipality of Klocot/Kllokot with the residency in Klokot/Kllokot.

As a result, the law confirmed six new municipalities with a Serb majority in addition to the already existing four Serb-majority municipalities (three North of Ibar: Zubin Potok, Zveçan/Zvečan and Leposaviq/Leposavić, one South of Ibar: Shtërpce/Štrpce). Therefore, ten of the current total thirty-eight municipalities in Kosovo have a Serb-majority population. Among the new municipalities there also is Mamuşa/Mamushë/Mamuša, making Kosovo Turks the only non-Serb minority with a municipality where they are in majority. In addition, two new Albanian-majority municipalities were established by the law: Junik and Hani I Elezit. Another key legal provision[59] is in regards to the possibility of establishing new municipalities in the future for minority communities. This addresses explicitly the 'Consultation with Non-Majority Communities' on the issue and adds two more precise elements for future projects of establishing new municipalities with minority communities in majority at the local level: firstly, the minimum percentage of the minority

Table 2 Municipalities with minority communities in majority (excluding North of Kosovo)

Municipality	Population		Ethnic majority
	Census	previous estimates	
Gračanica/Graçanicë	10,675	18,392	Serb
Shtërpcë/Štrpce	6,942	14,500	Serb
Novo Brdo/Novobërdë	6,729	9,670	Serb
Ranilug/Ranillug	3,866	5,150	Serb
Parteš/Partesh	1,787	N/A	Serb
Kllokot/Klokot	2,556	5,145	Serb
Mamuşa/Mamushë/Mamuša	5,507	6,007	Turkish

population (75 per cent) and, secondly, the minimum size of the total population being 5,000 citizens. Overall, the ethnic composition of population at the local level in Kosovo indicates a predominance of ethnic homogeneous municipalities (ten with Serb majority, one with Turkish majority, fifteen with Albanian majority) over the approximately twelve municipalities that can be regarded as heterogeneous.[60]

As Table 2 indicates, the outcome of the decentralization design reveals different standards for Serbs and for other minorities. As regards the Serb community, the legislation has key elements of ethnic decentralization that may separate the different ethnic groups and secure self-determination through far-reaching competencies at the municipal level.[61] Nevertheless, an important number of Serbs still live in Albanian-majority municipalities. In the case of other minority groups, the legislation follows the model of territorial decentralization as 'a significant number of individuals belonging to non-majority groups live in heterogeneous municipalities in which they enjoy a special representation in the municipal assembly and the administration who is supposed to represent their interests at the local level.'[62]

Lastly, the ethnic criteria of decentralization in Kosovo and the subsequent delineation of the municipal territories can be analysed as a legal and administrative precedent to the controversial 2018 talks about 'borders correction' between Serbia and Kosovo.[63] From the perspective of the arguments put forward in this book, this would also fall under the broad category of unintended consequences of the statebuilding process in Kosovo and the top-down adoption of the multiethnic framework for governance.

Particular challenges for the creation of new municipalities

The design of the decentralization process reflects its origin as a solution for the international conflict on the status of Kosovo. It is obvious that the aim of decentralization has been to establish municipalities with Serb majorities. To achieve this aim, municipal borders have been altered cutting across socioeconomically linked areas [...] and very small municipalities have been established which, in the long run, are hard to sustain given the high costs of municipal structures and services.[64]

The implementation of decentralization in Serb-majority municipalities has been troubled by several issues. Firstly, the continuing presence and influence of the Serbian parallel institutions has been successfully substituting Kosovo's delivery of services in the key areas of health, education and justice. Changing this situation will depend not only on Belgrade's willingness to continue supporting Kosovo Serbs in the same manner, but also on the capacity of Kosovo institutions to offer Serbs the same quality of public services. Secondly, the passing of competencies from central to local level has faced problems like inadequate funding, lack of qualified staff, limited cooperation between different levels of government, abuse of political positions, lack of proximity to citizens, strong control of municipalities by central government as well as limited efforts and support by the Kosovo Government to increase the local administrative capacity to manage public affairs.[65]

Furthermore, the creation of new municipalities made the local government system more fragmented and the Serb-dominated municipalities are among the smallest in Kosovo. Other vital capacity challenges that municipalities in Kosovo must face are lack of necessary infrastructure, the weak economy and a high unemployment rate, a context that is even more problematic given that the newly established municipalities lack a long-term strategy and action plan to develop capacity or natural resources so as to increase economic development and create new employment opportunities for their citizens.[66] Furthermore, while some residents of Serb-dominated areas have complained because after the demarcation of municipal borders they remained in Albanian-majority municipalities, others have opposed losing access to the social services offered in their Albanian neighbourhood.[67]

The lack of long-term strategies to stimulate economic development is a clear indicator of how implementation has been so far focusing more on setting up the institutional framework that formally empowers Serbs and other minorities at the local level while disregarding the practicality and efficiency of decentralization, especially on the long term. The new and small municipalities in Kosovo have been so far mainly co-financed by international and governmental donors with large investments in infrastructure and capacity-building.[68] Therefore, given the temporary nature of external funding, the limited budget of Kosovo, the dependency on the mother municipalities and the potential cut of funding of the Serbian parallel structures, these new municipalities will be facing great challenges of becoming self-sustainable. The integration of the Serb community and other minorities would be highly affected by a possible decline of local services and economic backwardness.[69]

> The full and effective implementation of competences by municipalities is running into difficulties. In the first place, municipalities have limited capacities to embrace and carry out all the responsibilities assigned by the law. In the second place, there has been a lack of sufficient resources and support by the central government, including line ministries. As a result, responsive and effective service delivery at the local level has been heavily challenged.[70]

Moreover, in addition to the specific capacity challenges at the local level, there is also the element of central-level institutions accepting the transfer of competencies as the government and some of the political elites continue to exert control over local municipalities.[71] Other matters of concern are the top-down structure of some political parties, the delayed transfer of financial competencies as well as the general transfer of competencies from the mother municipalities to the newly established ones.[72] Therefore, 'despite the relatively broad competencies set by the law, the scope of real local autonomy is limited. The actual municipal powers are constrained by the central control over municipal decisions and by the methods of fiscal planning and allocation of public funds'.[73] The official empowerment of minorities at the local level risks to be limited to a formal institutional arrangement that may be detrimental as regards the socioeconomic situation of these communities, which, in consequence, can also harm the integration process.[74] These problems derive from the top-down character of a decentralization process that transfers competencies to municipalities that lack the capacity and the mechanisms 'to carry out these new responsibilities efficiently and democratically'.[75]

Municipal profiles

With the exception of Mitrovica/Mitrovicë North, all planned new municipalities in Kosovo were established and became operational quite quickly after the declaration of independence. As a result, the November 2009 municipal elections included three new Serb-majority municipalities, Graçanicë/Gracanica, Ranilug/Ranillug and Kllokot, while separate elections for Parteš/Partesh were delayed until June 2010 in order for all necessary conditions to be ready. The November 2013 local elections in Kosovo included all new municipalities and, for the first time, the Serb municipalities located north of the Ibar River.

New Serb-majority municipalities

Municipality of Gračanica/Graçanicë

The municipality of Gračanica/Graçanicë is located in the central part of Kosovo and consists of sixteen cadastral areas with seventeen villages or settlements and a total of 131 km^2, bordering the municipalities of Prishtinë/Priština, Lipjan/Lipljan and Fushë Kosovë/Kosovo Polje.[76] The municipality represents the largest Serb-majority municipality in south of Ibar Kosovo, with an official population of 10,675 residents as confirmed by the 2011 census, while the ethnic composition in Graçanicë/Gracanica according to the census is as follows:

1. Kosovo Serbs: 7,209
2. Kosovo Albanians: 2,474
3. Kosovo Roma: 745
4. Kosovo Ashkali: 104
5. Kosovo Gorani: 22
6. Kosovo Turkish: 15
7. Kosovo Bosnian: 15
8. Kosovo Egyptian: 3
9. Other: 45
10. Not specified: 43[77]

However, due to the partial boycott of the census, the real numbers are considered to be much higher and 'according to the special advisor to the mayor and the Municipal Development Plan the total Kosovo Serb population in the municipality is estimated at 21,534'.[78] Previous estimates also indicated that out of the total inhabitants of Graçanicë/Gracanica, Serbs constituted 85.7 per cent, Albanians 3.7 per cent and other communities 10.6 per cent.[79] Graçanicë/Gracanica was the first municipality created from the process of decentralization and several reports[80] have indicated to be one of the municipalities that have made significant progress since its establishment, 'ranging from technical reforms, capacity-building, of human resources and capital investments, all of which are closely related to the transfer of power'.[81] This period of transition has mainly been consisting of a complex transfer of powers from the so-called 'mother municipalities', in this case those of Prishtinë/Priština, Fushe Kosove and Lipljan. More precisely, this has included a transfer of documents regarding archives, cadastral areas, property taxes, spatial and urban planning, the use of property and the civil register. However, the more challenging task has definitely been to build the necessary capacity of municipal officials to take over the responsibilities and duties of new municipalities.

In regards to the provision of public services, the municipality of Graçanicë/Gracanica created seven executive directorates of administration, finance, urban planning and cadastre, health, public services, culture, youth and sports and inspectorate.[82] The MLGA 2012 report on decentralization mentions that Graçanicë/Gracanica administration consisted of sixty civil servants who worked in the municipality, 'whereas the overall number of the employed staff in the municipal administration which is paid from the budget of the Republic of Kosovo is 441'.[83] However, these numbers are low and indicate the lack of capacities to make the municipality fully functional given the increasing number of competencies and responsibilities.[84] The budget of the municipality of Graçanicë/Gracanica increased annually from €2,719,850 in 2010, €4,538,780 in 2011 and €4,978,470 in 2012, showing not only a transition from a budget fully supported by government grants, but also that 'Graçanicë/Gracanica had budget rise from year to year and that is revenue collection capacities rose, too'.[85] Graçanicë/Gracanica has thus been considered the biggest and the most successful municipality established by the decentralization process as it has become capable of generating own-source revenues, initiating and implementing more local projects, and 'in which local businesses – especially the construction sector – have shown interest in expanding their local investments'.[86] In addition, the economy is based on agriculture and small-trade businesses with about 500 registered private businesses in the municipality.[87]

Nevertheless, an important aspect discussed by the previously mentioned HLC (2011) report is that public investments in the Albanian villages of Graçanicë/Gracanica are scarce, as the example of Kishnicë/Kišnica, where 'not much has been invested, even in road infra-structure and sewage, despite the fact that such investments have been made in other localities with a majority of Serbian residents'.[88] Therefore, if villages with Serb majority have better living conditions and more investments than Albanian ones because of the different ethnic composition, decentralization could produce discrimination and segregation between communities at the local level depending on who controls the municipality.

OSCE[89] also reported that the health and education systems in Graçanicë/Gracanica continued to be mainly provided by Serbia-run institutions, thus still outside the control of Kosovo local or central institutions. The municipality has not been participating in the management of secondary healthcare and this 'is partly due to lack of attempts by the central government and partly due to challenges that the situation on the ground presents'.[90] Given that the influence of parallel structures in the healthcare sector has been stronger here in comparison with other Serb-majority municipalities, the medical staff have refused to cooperate with the officials and have not recognized the authority of Gračanica/Graçanicë municipality.[91] Despite all efforts of the Ministry of Health to establish talks and start cooperating with them, the situation has been hard to improve. In addition, having the head of the parallel primary healthcare institution as an MP in the Kosovo Assembly should have helped with integration.[92] However, Rada Trajkovic's and her party's complicated strategy to be part of the Kosovo parliament while also boycotting and rejecting the legitimacy of Kosovo as an independent state has also been reflected in the concrete functioning of the parallel healthcare system. The municipality has nonetheless been run by representatives of the SLS party who have agreed to cooperate with the authority of Kosovo. Therefore, the political division within the Serb community between SLS and JSL, between cooperation and boycott of Kosovo institutions, has been found at the local level as well.

At the same time, education has mainly been provided by schools following the Serbian curriculum not approved by Kosovo, and the three pre-primary schools, eight primary schools and eight secondary schools in Graçanicë/Gracanica have all been operated by employees and teachers paid by the Serbian government.[93] The lack of finance and the refusal of Serb employees to cooperate with the legitimate local authorities make it very difficult for Kosovo institutions to take concrete steps in improving the situation. The example of the Albanian village of Kishnicë/Kišnica is relevant again as it represents an exception through its Prishtinë/Priština municipality-run small health centre and primary school, thus under the authority of Kosovo. Moreover, the elementary school in Kishnicë/Kišnica has been operating under bad conditions and the HLC 2011 report emphasized that the municipality of Graçanicë/Gracanica did not invest in schools located in Albanian-majority villages:

Even though unification of schools remains a political issue, this step could create the necessary platform for needed dialogue. In other words, the schools under the influence of the parallel structures could see possible benefits from Kosovo institutions.[94]

Therefore, the lack of willingness from the Serb community and the lack of capacity characterizing Kosovo institutions seem to represent the key obstacles in trying to reduce and replace the role of Serbian parallel institutions at the local level of governance.[95]

Political representation

The municipality of Graçanicë/Gracanica held its first elections during the November 2009 local elections that took place in Kosovo. The total number of voters registered then was 16,317 and the voter turnout was 23 per cent (3,532 people).[96] The elections were won by SLS (33 per cent of votes) and its candidate Bojan Stojanović became the mayor of Graçanicë/Gracanica, while also securing twelve seats in the municipal assembly. As regards the ethnic composition of the municipal assembly after these elections, eighteen were Serbs and only one member was Albanian. Furthermore, despite the fact that the Law on Local Self-government requires a municipality with more than 10 per cent of residents belonging to communities not in majority in that municipality is required to appoint a deputy municipal assembly chairperson for communities, the Graçanicë/Gracanica municipal assembly did not appoint a deputy chairperson for communities and did not establish a permanent human rights unit.[97]

The November 2013 local elections had a major significance for the Serb minority in particular given the official involvement of Belgrade that encouraged Kosovo Serbs to vote, triggering political mobilization and a clearly higher turnout among the community. In Grancanica, the turnouts for the two rounds of elections were 54.6 per cent and 49.37 per cent.[98] The results meant Graçanicë/Gracanica had a newly elected mayor, Branimir Stojanović, from the new party G.I. Srpska, who secured his win over the ex-SLS mayor with 58.48 per cent of the votes.[99] However, G.I. Srpska was forced to make coalition with another Serb party given it was one seat short of the absolute majority in the municipal assembly. It must be highlighted here that SLS lost nine seats in comparison to the previous mandate when it held an absolute majority in addition to the mayoral post. The latest elections of 2017 reconfirmed the dominance of the new wave of Kosovo Serb representatives, now as part of the Serbian List (SL) party, which secured the post of mayor (Srdjan Popovic) and twelve seats of the municipal assembly.[100] These developments confirmed not only a significant increase in turnout of Kosovo Serbs but also an important political shift away from the dominance of SLS, the Serb party that had been active in Kosovo politics prior to Prishtinë/Priština and Belgrade trying to reach an agreement. The external support coming from Serbia for the 2013 and 2017 local elections in Kosovo therefore has a visible impact in Graçanicë/Gracanica, one of the key municipalities populated by the Serb community.

Municipality of Ranilug/Ranillug

The municipality of Ranilug/Ranillug is situated in eastern Kosovo in the Gjilan/Gnjilan region and covers an area of 77.62 km^2, including the town of Ranilug/Ranillug and twelve villages.[101] As a new municipality, Ranilug/Ranillug was created out of 15 per cent of the territory of the municipality of Kamenicë/Kamenica[102] and it also borders the municipalities of Novo Brdo/Novobërdë and Gjilan/Gnjilan. Ranilug/Ranillug was officially established on January 2010 when the municipal assembly was first held after the 2009 elections. The population of Ranilug/Ranillug was 3,866 according to the 2011 census; however, the estimates suggested higher numbers and the municipal information office approximated a total of 5,800 inhabitants.[103] This is one of the smallest municipalities in Kosovo but the most remarkable demographic aspect here is that the Ranilug/Ranillug is almost completely populated by Kosovo Serbs, making it one of the most ethnically homogeneous municipalities with only 1–2 per cent residents belonging to non-Serb communities:

1. Kosovo Serbs: 3,692 (the number of Serbs is higher in reality: about 5,718)[104]
2. Kosovo Albanians: 164
3. Kosovo Bosniaks: 1
4. Other: 3
5. Not specified: 6

Nonetheless, the municipality of Ranilug/Ranillug has also been presented as a positive story of decentralization.[105] A reason for this has been the smoother transfer of competencies from its mother municipality, Kamenicë/Kamenica, in contrast to the situation in Graçanicë/Gracanica and Kllokot/Klokot. At the same time, the new municipality started to see relatively quickly the benefits of decentralization and the investments that can come with it.[106] Ranilug/

Ranillug has thus been used to 'illustrate that Kosovo municipal institutions can generate acceptance and support when they are able to provide efficient social services and are actively shaping municipal policies'.[107] However, as in the case of other municipalities in Kosovo, Ranilug/Ranillug has been facing a shortage of professional staff that makes it very difficult to handle the responsibilities of a new municipal administration and local governance.[108] The budget of the municipality of Ranilug/Ranillug has increased annually, similar to the case of Graçanicë/Gracanica – from €693,634 in 2010 (all governments grant) to €997,071 in 2011 (only €40,000 were own revenues) and €1,090,365 in 2012 (€59,000 own revenues).[109] This indicated a yearly budget rise but not accompanied by a reduction of the dependency on government grants. This represents a long-term challenge for all new municipalities in Kosovo given that the support of governmental funds and international donors should be gradually replaced by local self-sustainable resources.[110]

On the negative side, the 2011 HLC report on decentralization underlined that there was significant control and influence over the municipality by central institutions, preventing 'the proper functioning of the new municipality to create greater opportunities for new working places and local implementation plans'.[111] Moreover, the municipality had a high unemployment rate, the economy was mainly based on dairy production and small-trade businesses,[112] while the main investments in Ranilug/Ranillug have been used for infrastructure, such as roads, sewage and water supply.

As regards the health and education systems, the role of the Serbian parallel structures has been evident as its employees have been paid by Belgrade and have refused cooperation with local authorities legitimized by the 2009 municipal elections. But despite the reluctance to cooperate all health workers, for example, have received double salaries from parallel structures and from the Kosovo Ministry of Health. The removal of parallel structures has been one of the priorities for the municipality of Ranilug/Ranillug, next to reducing youth unemployment, development of agriculture as the main potential resource for economic development, attracting new investments from abroad and development of economy and more support for the NGO sector.[113]

Political representation

One of the key challenges for the ethnically homogeneous and newly established municipality of Ranilug/Ranillug has been to improve its legitimacy undermined the very low level of public support.[114] Thus, the rejection by the local Serb community and the presence of parallel structures manifested both before and after the 2009 elections, given that 'the elected officials were faced with distrust and even threats from their community'.[115] Prior to decentralization, there were also elections in 2007 but the locals had no interest to participate.[116] At the local elections held on 15 November 2009, out of the total number of 4,822 registered voters, the turnout was very low (OSCE[117] reports 17.92 per cent (895 voters)). The elections were won by Citizens Initiative for Ranilug/ Ranillug Municipality (GIZOR) with 78.70 per cent of votes that secured eleven out of the total fifteen seats in the municipal assembly, while four seats were won by the Serbian Party of Kosovo and Metohija (SKMS).[118] It should be remarked that Ranilug/Ranillug is one of the Serb municipalities that did not have SLS in power in the post-independence context. Another interesting fact about the local representatives is that although Ranilug/Ranillug has less than 10 per cent residents from communities not in majority at the local level, in 2010 the municipal assembly appointed a Kosovo Albanian as the municipal deputy mayor for communities.[119]

Despite the very low participation in the 2009 local elections, a positive sign was the much higher turnout in the 2010 parliamentary elections when the percentage of voters increased to 34.12 per cent.[120] This indicated that the local population started to develop trust in the Kosovo institutions even though '34 per cent for a small municipality such as Ranilug/Ranillug is still a low turn-out, underscoring the importance of good services and improvements of economic life in the municipality as determinants for increasing the legitimacy of the municipality'.[121] Furthermore, the 2013 elections indicated an approximately tripled turnout percentage in Ranilug/Ranillug compared to 2009: 57.66 per cent for the second round.[122] This illustrated once again the crucial impact of the changing attitude of Belgrade to encourage Kosovo Serbs to take part in the elections organized by Prishtinë/Priština. As regards the results, Gradimir Mikić was re-elected with 52.34 per cent of the votes,[123] but now as a representative of G.I. Srpska. The party also won six of the total fifteen seats in the municipal assembly, which, however, did not guarantee the mayor the support of a majority in divided assembly that included SLS representatives.[124] The situation became less complicated after the 2017 elections, given the overwhelming success of the SL party in securing twelve seats and almost 80 per cent of the vote.[125] In the context where SLS has now been reduced to only one seat in the municipal assembly, Ranilug/Ranillug symbolizes another important win for the Kosovo Serb political grouping backed by the ruling SNS party in Serbia.

Municipality of Kllokot/Klokot

The municipality of Klokot/Kllokot is located in southeastern Kosovo and consists of four cadastral areas that include the town of Kllokot/Klokot and three villages, covering a total area of approximately 24 km².[126] Moreover, Kllokot/Klokot is an enclave inside the territory of Viti/Vitina municipality, to which it belonged before the decentralization process (mother municipality). The 2011 Kosovo Population and Housing Census indicated that Kllokot/Klokot had a total population of 2,556 inhabitants, which is however approximately half of the actual number, estimated at about 5,145 residents.[127] Kllokot/Klokot has a Serb-majority population but due to their partial boycott of the 2011 census the results do not offer a reliable ethnic composition:

1. Kosovo Albanians: 1,362
2. Kosovo Serbs: 1,177
3. Kosovo Roma: 9
4. Kosovo Turks: 1
5. Others: 6
6. Not specified: 1.[128]

Kllokot/Klokot has proved to be one of the most, if not the most, challenging decentralization process in Kosovo[129] not only because of the resistance of the local Serb community but also because of the opposition of the Albanian population to the establishment of the new municipality on the territory of Viti/Vitina, 'because of the strong influence of the Self-Determination Movement'.[130] As a result, the municipality of Kllokot/Klokot experienced some initial difficulties in cooperating and communicating for the transfer of competencies from its mother municipality and 'experts registered intimidations, extortions and few cases of violent acts'.[131] Meanwhile, the situation improved after the two municipalities signed a Memorandum of Understanding and Viti/Vitina municipality started to help with the exercise of the new competencies of Kllokot/Klokot and transfer of powers ranging from civil registry and cadastral documents to spatial planning, transfer of archive and property taxes. The shortage of professional staff has nonetheless been a key challenge for making the municipality fully functional.[132] The inaugural session of the municipality was held on 8 January 2010, when the mayor and the members of the municipal assembly were sworn in.

The role of Serbian institutions has been significant, particularly in the health and education sectors, but 'the success of decentralisation and decrease in the impact of parallel structures are best observed in the municipality of Kllokot/Klokot.[133] The primary healthcare system includes a municipal health centre in Kllokot/Klokot town and one health house in Vrbovac village. Most significantly, all communities have access to healthcare facilities.[134] Kllokot/Klokot has four elementary schools, three being taught in Serbian following the Serbian curriculum and one following the Kosovo curriculum as a mixed Serbian-Albanian school.[135] Problems have remained in the education sector as some teachers have refused to cooperate with local authorities because of political reasons despite the fact that they have received double salaries:

> The feeling of belonging to the Serbian State is evident in this municipality, along with lack of trust in Kosovo Institutions. Citizens integrated into the Kosovo system are considered traitors by the Serbian community.[136]

The economy of the municipality of Kllokot/Klokot is mainly based on natural resources (mineral water), tourism (spas), agriculture and small-trade businesses,[137] but the high unemployment rate has been the biggest problem for the local population. The budget of Kllokot/Klokot for 2010 was €719,601, all government grants; for 2011 it was €855,745, of which only €8,390 as own revenues and for 2012 the budget was €929,097 with €43,300 as own revenues.[138] Similar to the other new municipalities, Kllokot/Klokot has had thus a yearly budget rise accompanied by a rise of its collection capacities too. Furthermore, the municipality has received multiple funds not only from the Kosovo Government but also from different international donors like USAID, LOGOS, UNCHR or the EU,[139] making Kllokot/Klokot in 2010 one of the municipalities with the biggest funds reaching around €3 million in total.[140] These funds have started several projects in the municipality in numerous sectors and the municipal assembly approved on April 2011 a Strategy for Sustainable Development and Integration 2011–2014 in the fields of economy, education, employment, health and social welfare. This has made Kllokot/Klokot 'the first municipality to have such a long-term strategy'.[141]

Political representation

In the 2009 elections, Kllokot/Klokot had a total number of 2,706 registered voters and the turnout was 25.2 per cent.[142] There were two parties competing in the elections (SLS and LDK), and as a result of winning 68.2 per cent of the votes, SLS was given ten of the fifteen seats in the municipal assembly.[143] In the mayoral contest there was only one candidate, Saša Mirković (SLS), elected with

510 votes.[144] Given the ethnic composition of the municipality, with Albanians in minority at the local level, the municipal assembly deputy chairperson for communities in Kllokot/Klokot has been an Albanian, Nasip Sinani, from LDK.[145] The 2013 local elections in Kllokot/Klokot marked a substantial increase in the turnout numbers during the two rounds of voting with 61.2 per cent in the first round, respectively 56.12 per cent in the second round.[146] The political contest here resulted this time in a more complex situation for several reasons. On the one hand, the G.I. Srpska candidate was elected as mayor (54.80 per cent of the votes) in the detriment of the ex-mayor Saša Mirković (SLS), who came second.[147] On the other hand, SLS managed to win most seats in the municipal assembly (5), thus one more than G.I. Srpska, while the other six seats were distributed among other five different political parties. Potentially, SLS could have built a majority coalition with Albanian parties and 'make the daily administration of the municipality relatively challenging'.[148] Despite the positive turnout in the latest elections, more competition at the local level between Serb politicians could actually increase the role of Albanian representatives even in Serb-majority municipalities. Nonetheless, the 2017 elections in Kllokot/Klokot also confirmed the growing dominance of the Serbian List (SL), which not only won six seats in the assembly but subsequently benefited from a 'collective transfer' of the representatives of the Civic Initiative (CI) to SL.[149]

Municipality of Parteš/Partesh

The municipality of Parteš/Partesh has been the last municipality with a Serb-majority population to be established as a result of decentralization. Parteš/Partesh is located in the eastern part of Kosovo, covering an area of approximately 18.3 km² with three small cadastral zones: Parteš/Partesh town and two villages.[150] According to the 2011 census, the total population of Parteš/Partesh was 1,787, but the real number is much higher given that the approximate figures mention a total of 5,300 people living in the municipality.[151] Moreover, the census indicated only two non-Serb people living in Parteš/Partesh, making it the most homogeneous non-Albanian municipality with almost all of its inhabitants belonging to the Serb community. Parteš/Partesh was thus established later than the other new municipalities, on 19 August 2010, when the first municipal assembly constitutive session was held.[152] The delay was caused by the incapacity to organize local elections in 2009 because of the very strong opposition from the local Serb population.[153] The elections were eventually held on 20 June 2010, which then permitted starting the implementation of the decentralization process in Parteš/Partesh, which previously belonged to the municipality of Gjilan/Gnjilane. Meanwhile, the mother municipality of Gjilan/Gnjilane has successfully transferred powers over property, competencies and other assets to the new administration.

The economy of the municipality of Parteš/Partesh is mainly based on agriculture (dairy production) and small-trade businesses, but same as in the rest of Kosovo, the high unemployment rate of approximately 60 per cent of population[154] is the main problem along with the worrying emigration rate indicating that about 50 per cent of the young people and 70 per cent of the overall population have moved abroad.[155] The presence of parallel structures is less visible in Parteš/Partesh within its healthcare facilities (one municipal family health centre and three health houses) and schools (two primary schools and five secondary schools), but teachers and support staff are nonetheless also paid by the Serbian Ministry of Education.[156] The 2010 budget of Parteš/Partesh municipality was €410,652, all of which were government grants; for 2011 it was €905,424, with all being government grants as well and in 2012 the budget was €922,459 out of which only €35,000 are own revenues.[157] This means that the budget of Parteš/Partesh has been rising but remains even more than in the case of other new municipalities, very much dependent on investment and funding provided by the central government.[158]

Political representation

Despite the initial problems with decentralization in Parteš/Partesh and the delay of its inauguration, the 2010 local elections had an impressive turnout of approximately 56 per cent of the 3,426 registered voters.[159] Therefore, this represented a great achievement for the establishment of Parteš/Partesh as a new Serb municipality of Kosovo, especially in the context of previous resistance by locals and the examples of much lower turnout rates in other new municipalities. The results confirmed the Citizens Initiative Zavičaj (GIZ) as the party with most votes (40 per cent), giving them six seats of the total of fifteen municipal assembly seats.[160] The rest of the seats were distributed as follows: three for JSL, three for the People's initiative (NI), two for the Citizens Initiative Together for Survival (GIZO) and one for the Serbian Social Democratic Party (SSDS).[161] Thus, in addition to the very positive turnout, local elections in Parteš/Partesh were also distinctive because of the higher number of political parties that took part.

The 2013 local elections in Parteš/Partesh were marked by the only major incident that actually took place in southern Kosovo, as on the evening after the count, the ballot boxes were set to fire and a TV crew was attacked.[162] These events meant that a revote was necessary in the polling stations involved. The rerun was successful and, overall, Parteš/Partesh had the highest turnout of all municipalities in the first round (63.8 per cent) and 64.07 per cent in the second.[163] The results here also changed the mayor as Nenad Cvetković, now representing SLS, lost to the representative of G.I. Srpska, Dragan Nikolić (52.16 per cent of the votes).[164] However, like in Kllokot/Klokot, SLS secured most seats in the local assembly of Parteš/Partesh (six seats), thus three more than G.I. Srpska.[165] The difference is that the assembly was composed exclusively of Serb representatives from SLS, G.I. Srpska and other four parties.[166] Nevertheless, it has been challenging for the new mayor to secure a majority given the fragmented composition of the assembly. In the context of SLS not taking part in the 2017 municipal elections, the Serbian List managed to win nine seats in the assembly, while the remaining six seats were secured by the GI – Civic Initiative People's Party.[167] Like in 2013, the 2017 elections in Parteš/Partesh were controversial and 'problematic because of the involvement of political subjects in the process'.[168] This resulted in a repeat of the mayoral vote that reconfirmed the initial win of the SL representative and the failure of one of the only challengers for the political supremacy of the SL within the Serb community in Kosovo.

Other Serb-majority municipalities

Municipality of Novo Brdo/Novobërdë (extended municipality)

Located in central Kosovo, the municipality of Novo Brdo/Novobërdë is not a new municipality but its territory was enlarged in 2009 to cover Serb settlements in neighbouring municipalities: nine cadastral zones of Gjilan/Gnjilaneë municipality with 90 per cent Serb population and five cadastral zones of the municipality of Kamenicë/Kamenica.[169] Therefore, after an expansion of its old territory by 120 per cent, at present the municipality of Novo Brdo/Novobërdë covers an area of approximately 204 km² that includes Novo Brdo/Novobërdë town and thirty-one villages,[170] which also makes it the largest Serb-majority municipality in terms of territory. As regards the population, the 2011 census indicated a total of 6,729 inhabitants in the municipality, but the municipal office for communities and returns offered more accurate numbers: total population of 9,670 and the following ethnic composition:

1. Kosovo Serbs: 5,802 residing in town and 24 villages
2. Kosovo Albanians: 3,771, residing the town and 14 villages
3. Kosovo Roma: 97, mainly residing in the village of Bostan/Bostane.[171]

Given that the municipality was extended, the decentralization process was different from the cases of new municipalities and did not require, for instance, a transfer of competencies from mother municipalities or the full development of a new administration. However, the executive branch of the enlarged municipality was constituted in January 2010 and it then consolidated ten directorates while also making 'significant progress compared to other municipalities, in service areas such as social welfare, road construction, sewage system construction, youth, culture and sport activities, as well as in citizen participation in all these activity areas'.[172] Despite all this, the economic situation of Novo Brdo/Novobërdë has not been very good with a particularly high unemployment rate. Moreover, after failed attempts to improve conditions for business development, investments have been limited by the poor infrastructure and unfavourable geographical position of the municipality.[173] The economy remains based on agriculture, rural tourism and small-trade businesses,[174] and the healthcare and education systems have been in need of much support for both developing the infrastructure and raising the necessary funds to assure salaries for its employees, while many doctors, teachers and other medical staff have been receiving second salaries from Serbia.[175]

Political representation

The situation at the political level in the municipality of Novo Brdo/Novobërdë has been unique mainly because despite the large majority of the population being Kosovo Serbs, the city has had an Albanian mayor and Albanian parties have dominated the local assembly. After 1999, Novo Brdo/Novobërdë was one of the first municipalities in which Serbs and Albanians began to cooperate within local institutions and Serbs even securing a majority in the municipal assembly after the 2003 elections.[176] However, under the strong pressure of Belgrade local Serbs started boycotting elections and in the 2009 municipal elections the results gave Albanian parties a clear majority in the assembly: LDK (34 per cent of votes and five seats), PDK (13 per cent and two seats) and AKR (13 per cent and two seats).[177] Altogether, ten members of the Novo Brdo/Novobërdë municipal assembly were Albanians and only five were Serbs. Nonetheless, the Albanian mayor of Novo Brdo/Novobërdë, Bajrush Imeri (LDK), was generally perceived positively by many members of the Serb community who even voted for him in the elections given his commitment to help all citizens of Novo Brdo/Novobërdë regardless of their ethnicity[178] and his efforts to include as many Serbs as possible in the local governance.[179] The post-2008 situation in Novo Brdo/Novobërdë was therefore unique to Kosovo as it did not follow the same trend of ethnic politics and Serb-domination of political representation in places where they constitute the majority population.

However, the different context of the 2013 local elections in Kosovo had a significant impact on the political situation in Novo Brdo/Novobërdë too. Like in the other Serb municipalities, the turnout was high (58.3 per cent in the first round and 56.94 per cent in the second round)[180] and while LDK won again most seats in the assembly (four seats), the increased Serb participation brought a clear majority for the Serb representatives and the election of a new mayor from G.I. Srpska, Svetislav Ivanović (57.05 per cent of the votes)[181] – an important change given that the previous mayor was Albanian. Nonetheless, the municipal assembly was fragmented with eight political entities sharing the fifteen seats of the assembly and thus offering different options to establish an absolute majority during the mandate.[182] In 2017, the dominance of the SL was also confirmed in Novo Brdo/Novobërdë by winning seven out of fifteen council seats and by re-electing Mr Ivanović.[183]

Municipality of Shtërpcë/Štrpce

Štrpce/Shtërpcë is located in the southern part of Kosovo on the border with FYR of Macedonia and it is one of the key Serb enclaves in Kosovo. Its territory covers an area of approximately 247 km² that includes the Štrpce/Shtërpcë town and sixteen villages, making it the largest Serb municipality South of Ibar.[184] The 2011 census results for Štrpce/Shtërpcë were also influenced by the boycott from the Serb population and indicated a total number of 6,949 residents in the municipality, while the more accurate numbers given by the municipal office for communities and returns approximate a total population of 13,630 with the following ethnic composition:

1. Kosovo Serbs: 9,100 residing (67 per cent)
2. Kosovo Albanians: 4,500
3. Kosovo Roma: 30.[185]

As regards the local economy, the municipality of Štrpce/Shtërpcë relies mainly on agriculture, tourism and small-trade businesses. The Sharri/Šara National Park and the ski resort of Brezovica have a great potential to attract tourists and provide jobs for local population as they are two areas which present some of Kosovo's prime real estate potential.[186] However, the privatization of the Brezovica ski resort has been long delayed and blocked by the contest between Serbian parallel structures and the official local government respecting Kosovan laws.[187] If local leaders dealt with these issues, Štrpce/Shtërpcë could have a great opportunity to unite representatives of different ethnic communities under a common economic project and decrease 'the salience of ethnicity in political decision-making'.[188] But the municipality has had two local governments operating at the same time, which is a clear personification of the division among Serbs on accepting or not the authority of Kosovo in the post-independence context. The Serbian assembly of the municipality has had a staff of almost 200 employees and has been convened in the same building as that of the official assembly working under the Kosovo law.[189] At the same time, the parallel healthcare and education institutions have had a significant presence in Štrpce/Shtërpcë as it has hired approximately 300 employees paid by the Serbian Ministry of Health.[190] Altogether, after 2008 more than 1,300 residents of Štrpce/Shtërpcë were receiving Serbian salaries and another 1,245 people with minimal paychecks from the same source.[191]

Political representation

Štrpce/Shtërpcë has also had a complicated post-independence political context that reconfirmed the necessity to improve participation of Kosovo Serbs within local politics as well as higher turnout rates in elections. The boycott of the 2009 local elections by Serbs affected their political representation in the Kosovo-based institutions. The overall turnout rate was 48.87 per cent and even though SLS gained most votes (42.10 per cent), three Albanian parties (PDK, PSK and LDK) managed to win altogether ten of the total nineteen seats in the municipal assembly seats, leaving Serbs in minority with only nine seats.[192] However, in the mayoral runoff in December 2009, 6,343 voters turned out (54.3 per cent), out of which 4,345 Serbs, helping the SLS candidate Bratislav Nikolić to win the position with 65 per cent of votes.[193] The Serb turnout was superior to any previous elections and much higher than in the 2008 parallel elections organized by Serbia, probably prompted by the fact that employees of the parallel structures participated too and confirmed 'a silent consensus among the

Serbs in Shtërpce/Štrpce to support the SLS, given the upcoming privatisation of the ski resort and the supporting facilities. Also, the Serbs are aware of the importance of the new municipality and the benefits it will provide to them'.[194] Moreover, the deputy mayor after 2009, Rodoljub Mladenović (SLS), was also Serb, while the deputy mayor for communities in Shtërpce/Štrpce has been an Albanian representative, Beqir Fejzullahu (PDK). Therefore, unlike the situation in Novo Brdo/Novobërdë, this nomination of an Albanian is in accordance with the requirements of the Law on Local Governance.[195]

In the context of SLS' control over Shtërpce/Štrpce as one of the key Serb municipalities in South Kosovo, the November 2013 municipals were going to draw much attention here too because of the participation of the newly formed G.I. Srpska. The turnout was higher than in previous elections here too,[196] but the SLS mayor Bratislav Nikolić was re-elected with a 56.25 per cent score in front of the G.I. Srpska representative.[197] Shtërpce/Štrpce was thus the only Serb-majority municipality to re-elect its mayor in the context of the emergence of G.I. Srpska. However, in the municipal assembly contest G.I. Srpska secured six seats, one more than SLS, meaning that the SLS mayor had to offer 'a coalition to Albanian parties PDK and LDK to reach an absolute majority in the assembly'.[198] The new supremacy of the SL was however going to be also confirmed in the 2017 elections in Shtërpce/Štrpce, which resulted in the SL winning 74 per cent of the votes and eleven council seats, as well as the mayoral position after co-opting the re-elected Mr Nikolić.[199] Overall, the SL managed to secure the victory in all ten majority Serb municipalities (70 per cent of all votes), both in the elections for mayors and in the elections for municipal assemblies.

Therefore, the Serb List (SL) 'has cemented its position as the largest party of Kosovo Serbs, and the elections at the same time represent the "symbolic death" of the opposition'. There is no doubt then that this new position of a unitary strong voice for the Serb community in Kosovo is going to play a key role in the future dynamics of Kosovo politics, in the interaction with the Albanian parties/leaders/community, as well as in the volatile international context of Kosovo-Serbia relations.

The Turkish-minority new municipality of Mamuşa/Mamushë/Mamuša

Mamuşa/Mamushë/Mamuša is a Turkish-majority municipality and represents the only municipality where the majority of the population belongs to a non-

Serb community in Kosovo. Mamuşa/Mamushë/Mamuša obtained its status of fully fledged municipality in October 2008 after a period of three years in which it had existed as one of the pilot municipalities in Kosovo. Out of the five initial proposed pilot municipal units, only three functioned before 2008 (Mamuşa/Mamushë/Mamuša, Junik and Hani Elezit/Đeneral Janković), while the two Serb pilot municipal units of Gračanica/Graçanicë and Parteš/Partesh were never functional,[200] although they later became municipalities as a result of decentralization. The municipality of Mamuşa/Mamushë/Mamuša is located in the south of Kosovo in the Prizren region bordering Gjakovë/Đakovica and Suharekë/Suva Reka municipalities, and prior to its foundation it was part of Prizren municipality. Mamuşa/Mamushë/Mamuša covers an area of approximately 11 km^2, making it by far the smallest municipality in Kosovo with only one cadastral zone. According to the 2011 census in Kosovo, its population is of 5,507 inhabitants in total, of which

1. Kosovo Turks: 5,128
2. Kosovo Albanians: 327
3. Kosovo Roma: 39
4. Kosovo Ashkali: 12
5. Kosovo Bosniaks: 1.[201]

These figures thus indicate that Mamuşa/Mamushë/Mamuša is a very homogeneous municipality with over 90 per cent of the population belonging to the Turkish community. As a pilot and thereafter as one of the new municipal units in Kosovo, Mamuşa/Mamushë/Mamuša has been successful in building its administrative and economic capacities.[202] Mamuşa/Mamushë/Mamuša has been taking over the competencies from the mother municipality of Prizren in the fields of administration of education, financial management, health services and urbanism, and it has been 'promoted as a model of local government reform, when it comes to non-majority communities being given equal opportunities for participation in local government administration'.[203] The economy of Mamuşa/Mamushë/Mamuša is based on small-scale farming and trade activities with about seventy registered private businesses operating in the municipality.[204] A very important indicator of the positive economic situation here was the placement of the municipality as the clear top performer in the 2011 'Municipalities Competitiveness Index' (MCI) report of USAID,[205] which evaluated data on the business environment in all municipalities of Kosovo, 'based upon the direct experiences and circumstances facing local businesses'.[206] In this sense, Mamuşa/Mamushë/Mamuša has been receiving 'financial and technical assistance from Turkey that similarly may also impact the business environment'.[207] However, it should also be mentioned that subsequent reports have suggested a significant drop in the score, 'warranting a deeper investigation into the reasons for this sudden change in perceptions by local businesses'.[208] This negative development thus indicates a potential problem of sustainability even in one of the most successful examples of new municipalities formed during the process of decentralization.

As mentioned before in the chapter on the situation of non-dominant minorities in Kosovo, the Turkish community in Kosovo is generally not only better represented but also with a better economic situation than the other minorities. One of the key factors contributing to this is the support and role of Turkey in Kosovo, which has contributed to the establishment of Mamuşa/Mamushë/Mamuša in addition to the significant representation of the community within central governance in Kosovo.[209]

Political representation

In the 2009 local elections, Mamuşa/Mamushë/Mamuša had a total of 2,835 voters registered and the turnout was very good as it reached 65.1 per cent (1,759 voters).[210] The domination of the KDTP party within the Turkish community was reflected by the results as it managed to win 73 per cent of votes and secure eleven of the total fifteen seats in the municipal assembly.[211] As consequence, the assembly consisted of fourteen Kosovo Turks and only one Kosovo Albanian representative. The first mayor of Mamuşa/Mamushë/Mamuša was Arif Bütüç (KDTP), one of the key political leaders of the Kosovo Turkish community and a rival of other Turkish politicians with positions at the central level.[212] Nonetheless, despite not being a municipality with more than 10 per cent of residents belonging to communities, the municipal assembly has appointed an Albanian representative as the deputy chairperson for communities.[213]

The 2013 local elections marked the entrance of a new influential Turkish party in the political life of Kosovo, the KTAP, which threatened the dominance of KDTP and the political unity of the Turkish community in Kosovo. In Mamuşa/Mamushë/Mamuša, KTAP was victorious in both the assembly and the mayoral elections as the incumbent mayor Arif Bütüç, who moved from KDTP to KTAP, was re-elected after the first round on 3 November.[214] At the same time, KTAP secured the absolute majority within the municipal assembly with eight seats, while KDTP won five seats, the Kosova Türk Birligi (KTB) one seat, and the Albanian PDK one seat.[215] Despite this victory of KTAP, it should be mentioned that KDTP won more seats across Kosovo in the 2013 local elections. More recently, in the 2017 local elections Mamuşa/Mamushë/Mamuša voted for a new mayor, Abdulhadi Krasniq (KDTP), while KDTP and KTAP gained seven seats each after an almost equal share of the total votes.[216] Overall, despite the initial strong and unified input of the Turkish community within Kosovo politics, the 2013 and 2017 local elections suggest more division as regards its political representation and participation. In this regard, the fragility of the de jure provisions for non-dominant minorities and the incentive for political infighting may also be contributing to the unintended fragmentation of the community.

Municipality of Prizren

Multiethnicity in an Albanian-majority setting:
[Prizren] has a long history and tradition of ethnic diversity. It is culturally rich, not least because of the diversity and the ethnic heterogeneity of its population. It has a long tradition of co-operation and tolerance among its different communities.[217]

The municipality of Prizren is located in southeastern Kosovo and its territory covers an area of approximately 284.2 km² and has seventy-five cadastral zones, including the second largest town in Kosovo, Prizren, and seventy-four villages.[218] Although Prizren has an Albanian majority population, it represents the most culturally and ethnically heterogeneous municipality of Kosovo with significant population from seven minority communities. According to the 2011 census, Prizren municipality was reported with a total population of 177,781 citizens with the following ethnic composition:

1. Kosovo Albanians: 145,718
2. Kosovo Bosniaks: 16,896
3. Kosovo Turks: 9,091
4. Kosovo Roma: 2,899
5. Kosovo Ashkali: 1,350
6. Kosovo Gorani: 655
7. Kosovo Serbs: 237
8. Kosovo Egyptians: 168
9. Other: 386
10. Not specified: 381.[219]

One key element that must be highlighted is the very low number of Kosovo Serbs who reside in Prizren, in contrast with the situation before the 1999 conflict when around 10,000 Serbs were living here.[220] A similar situation has been reported within the Roma community, who, like the Serbs, 'are since displaced and there is no available exact data on their whereabouts'.[221] An effective way of illustrating the distinctive character of this municipality is looking at the special provision for Prizren within the Law on the Use of Languages. While minority languages have the status of languages in official use at the local level only when they constitute at least 5 per cent of the total population, Prizren represents an exception by including Turkish as an official language despite the fact that the Turkish community does not pass the 5 per cent threshold.[222] As a result, Prizren is the only municipality in Kosovo with four languages in official use: Albanian, Serbian, Bosnian and Turkish.

The Prizren logo case

One particular situation that has drawn attention to Prizren as an example of multiethnicity in Kosovo has been regarding the debate around the municipality's official emblem, which ended with one of the most significant cases decided by the Kosovo Constitutional Court. The case *Cemailj Kurtisi v. Municipal Assembly of Prizren* involved a referral by Mr Kurtisi, the deputy chairperson of the Prizren Assembly for Communities, meant to challenge the official emblem for the municipality that was established with the adoption of the Prizren municipality statute in October 2008.[223] The problem reported was that the emblem of Prizren ('The House of the League of Prizren' circled by the following wording '1878 – Prizren') highlighted and reflected the identity of only one community in Prizren, the Albanians. It was 1878 when the League of Prizren was founded as an assembly of Albanian leaders aiming to establish an autonomous Albanian state.[224] This was contested for not reflecting the multiethnicity of Prizren and, thus, violating the constitutional rights for the protection and promotion of minority rights in Kosovo: 'the Municipal emblem should symbolise and transmit the message of co-existence of communities and community members and the presence of multi-ethnicity, multiculturalism, multireligiousness and multilingualism'.[225]

Based on the non-multiethnic character of the year 1878 and by also emphasizing the privileged position of the Albanian community (clear majority in the Prizren Assembly that approved the emblem), the court unanimously ruled in favour of the applicant and struck down the statute of the municipality for having violated the Constitution. The court noted the significance of emblems and symbols within a multiethnic society and not only took into consideration the far-reaching Kosovo legislation in terms of minority rights protection but also invoked international human rights standards and instruments like the Council of Europe Framework Convention for the Protection of National Minorities, which is, nonetheless, incorporated in the Constitution.[226]

> The Constitutional Court considers that a prerequisite for a pluralist and genuinely democratic multiethnic society, be it a country, region, municipality or other territorial unit, is non-majority Community participation in the political, social, economic and cultural life in order to develop a sense of belonging to and having a stake in that society. Such participation cannot be achieved if the common symbol of that society does not represent the rights of all communities, but, instead, ignores the rights of non-majority Communities.[227]

The decision and the statement above endorse the central role of the Constitution to protect minorities and rule against discriminatory situations. Furthermore, the Prizren logo case represented a key test for the court given that a voting divided among ethnic lines 'would have sent a troubling signal that politics would trump law in the Court's deliberations'.[228] In the end, the case has become a symbol of the excellent opportunities for minorities to exercise their rights and the decision 'was widely reported and received immediate praise from the international community'.[229] The municipality of Prizren did not challenge the decision and took the necessary steps to implement it. Even though the outcome of this case has been celebrated, its occurrence in what it represents a truly multiethnic and multicultural city of Kosovo still highlights the troublesome active promotion of group differentiation.

Political representation

As regards political representation of non-Albanian communities in Prizren, the 2009 municipal elections resulted with a few minority seats in the municipal assembly: three seats for the Turkish community represented by the KDTP party (7 per cent of votes) and three seats for the Bosniak community. In addition, there was also a Roma representative within the municipal assembly, although as candidate for an Albanian party. Therefore, out of the total forty-one seats, the municipal assembly of Prizren formed after 2009 had seven seats belonging to minority communities. Interestingly, the distribution of assembly seats among minorities in Prizren reflected the situation from the central level, given that the Turkish community managed to secure the same number of representatives as the Bosniaks, who have a population almost double the size of that of the Turks in Prizren. Nonetheless, the municipal assembly deputy chairperson for communities in Prizren belonged after 2009 to a Bosniak representative.[230] The political division among the Bosniaks and, inversely, the political unity characterizing the Turkish community in the first years after independence are factors that have been affecting the capacity of these minorities to gain a better representation and benefit of their rights at the local level of governance. In addition, it was not surprising to discover that, in a similar fashion to other municipalities in Kosovo, there are key capacity problems in Prizren and, often, civil society organizations are expected to provide more assistance than official institutions to minority communities:

> Our role as civil society is to contribute but this needs to be project-based. We cannot play the role of the local government, it is not our mandate to replace institutions.[231]

The Kosovo 2013 municipal elections indicated a change within the political representation of minorities in Prizren. As mentioned before, the emergence of new important Turkish party, KTAP, meant that the political representation of this minority became more fragmented. In Prizren, KTAP obtained one seat while KDTP won two seats, one less than during the previous mandate.[232] While the Turkish community maintained their three seats in the Prizren assembly, more interesting was the fact that the Bosniak community obtained five seats this time (two more than after the 2009 elections), meaning 'that minority communities obtained nearly 20 per cent of the seats in this municipality'.[233] After the 2017 elections, KDTP remained the only Turkish party in the Prizren assembly (three seats) while Bosniaks were left with four seats in the current legislature.[234]

As regards the representation of minorities in key public institutions in Prizren, the situation has not been very positive. For instance, within the judiciary, out of thirty-six judges working for Prizren basic court, there were reported five non-Albanian judges representing two minority communities (Bosniaks with four judges and Roma with one judge).[235] Moreover, Prizren basic prosecutor's office has had only one minority representative (Turkish) out of seventeen prosecutors in total.[236] A more positive example is the police station in Prizren that has had 191 police officers, including 35 Bosniaks, 23 Turks, 33 Gorani, 2 Roma and 1 Ashkali.[237]

On the one hand, Prizren represents a heterogeneous municipality where the minority communities participate in the political process and cooperate with the Albanian majority. Moreover, they have also been able to advance some of their fundamental interests in debates about policies of local identity (municipal symbols, official languages) or about the distribution of funds for general projects such as modernization of the infrastructure.[238] On the other hand, it continues 'to be an ethnicised bargain between the communities over available funds and positions of influence',[239] highlighting that ethnic affiliation has remained of vital importance for political participation with a lack of multiethnic parties or cross-ethnic coalitions on the local level in Prizren, similar to all other municipalities in Kosovo.

Conclusion: The Struggle Continues

This book has addressed the difficult and controversial topic of the efforts to build a multiethnic liberal democratic state in Kosovo with a twofold challenge to secure unity at the same time with managing and protecting diversity. In the post-independence context, this has involved the adoption of an extensive framework for integrating, accommodating and protecting minorities. Firstly, this book reveals that there is a significant gap between de jure minority provisions and de facto levels of integration of minorities in Kosovo, depending mainly on the will and capacity of each community to assume their rights and on their socioeconomic, demographic and political particularities. Secondly, the mixture of intended and unintended consequences highlights the volatility of the levels of integration and the lack of social cohesion in Kosovo despite the existence of a far-reaching minority rights framework. Thirdly, the legitimacy and domestic sovereignty of Kosovo have been conditioned by the accommodation of all its constituent communities and remain fragile because of the enhanced risk of segregation and marginalization. In its quest to build sustainable plural democratic governance, Kosovo needs more than defining itself as a multiethnic republic; it also needs to function like one.

More specifically, the analysis of the post-2008 context shows that even if political integration and representation have developed quickly at the elite level, minorities continue to be highly segregated at the community level. In the case of Serbs, this has been a consequence of the lack of willingness within the community to accept the authority of Prishtinë/Priština and of the rights and privileges at central and local levels of governance that discourage cross-ethnic relations. In contrast with the aim to secure the obedience of the Serb minority after empowering them, some have actually assumed their political rights and have developed local self-governance in line with the policy of anti-establishment and non-recognition of the central authority of Kosovo. At the same time, the smaller non-dominant minorities have also been affected by the post-conflict power-sharing arrangements and similar measures, despite the fact that they have been designed to mainly address the particular situation of Kosovo Serbs. As a result of their (ethno-) political mobilization and aspirations to fully benefit of their unanticipated rights, Bosniaks, Turks, Gorani, RAE and even the smallest communities have become more differentiated and segregated from the rest of the society. Therefore, these findings confirmed my argument that extensive formal provisions for minorities do not necessarily translate into effective integration or accommodation and may become instead tools for resistance and unintended marginalization.

The case studies analysed in the second part of this book demonstrate the inconsistent results of the efforts to implement the rights and provision for minorities in Kosovo. Therefore, unintended consequences can destabilize the situation of minorities and their relationship with the majority and between them. In other words, it can emphasize the perception of minority rights as the right to differentiation. Moreover, ethnic politics can weaken the political environment at both central and local levels of governance, and the new Kosovan civic (national) identity is too fragile to act as an overarching cross-ethnic bond between the state and its citizens. As a result, the state-society relationship and the legitimacy of the plural democratic Kosovo continue to be heavily undermined by social fragmentation and the politicization of ethnic identity. The application of the multiethnic framework in Kosovo has a double problem. Not only is the functionality of minority provisions dependent on the actual capacities of each community, but their lack of appropriateness in relation to the particular circumstances of minorities can make them counterproductive. Instead of stimulating interethnic cooperation and addressing the needs of each community, the multiethnic institutional and legal setting in post-2008 Kosovo has induced differentiation and insecurity by putting emphasis on group differences.

Serb community

Given that Serbs are the largest and most difficult community to integrate in Kosovo, this book looked at the institutional setup and some of the key policies developed for their protection while also examining some of the integration challenges deriving from within the Serbian community. As revealed, some of these are the lack of unity and cooperation, different views on how to help the community (participation or support the parallel system), lack of commitment from self-interested actors and representatives, contested support from Albanian parties and limited capacity to develop a self-sustainable strong position of the entire Serb community in Kosovo. Furthermore, the Serb community has been rather sceptical about their new status in post-conflict and post-independence Kosovo and the idea of integration has not truly penetrated beyond the elite-level institutional forms of representation and participation. In the context of the twofold objective to provide post-conflict reconciliation and post-independence integration, another challenge for Kosovo Serbs has been to find and secure the genuine support of governmental institutions at both central and local levels of governance. Besides adopting the current constitutional framework, the Kosovo Government also needs to prove long-term commitment and build capacity to sustain its minorities.

Another challenge is the sustainability of the cooperation between Serbs and Albanians at both elite and community levels, particularly because the political cooperation built so far has been contested not only by the Albanian opposition and civil society but also by the Serb community itself. The rather sudden and abrupt change for Serb representation within Kosovo politics (from pro-cooperation to Belgrade-sponsored politicians) has also exposed the fragile and volatile situation of Kosovo Serbs. In this sense, this book analysed the effectiveness of the political representation of Serbs within central and local institutions and showed how their activity has been affected by factors like the lack of trust and contestation within the community, limited legitimacy given the small turnouts in the elections, capacity problems and Serbia's policy to encourage the boycott of Prishtinë/Priština institutions. Another essential factor has been the presence of the Serbian parallel institutions, which have been providing real support for Serbs but have also undermined the authority of Prishtinë/Priština and the task of integrating the community. Furthermore, pragmatic policies have been effective at the higher level of representation and participation of Serbs, but they have not been properly expanded at the community level in order to motivate and create sustainable opportunities for all members of the Serb minority. While there have been concrete results with the integration of Kosovo Serbs, the legislative framework and the formal provisions for protecting minority rights cannot fully compensate for practical needs. The recent discussions between Serbian and Kosovar representatives to potentially correct borders and swap land based on ethnic criteria confirm some of the main risks identified in this book as regards the territorial and social enclavization of Serbs.

Bosniak community

As the largest non-Serb minority group in Kosovo, Kosovo Bosniaks have generally managed to live peacefully alongside both the majority of Albanians (religious ties) and Kosovo Serb community (linguistic ties). However, even though the Bosniak community has been among the well-integrated minorities, the post-conflict and post-independence measures and legislation have been challenging their position and situation within Kosovo. For instance, the incentives for political participation and mobilization have created much division among Bosniak elites and have resulted in a fragmented Bosniak political community. In consequence, the representation and power of Bosniaks at both central and local levels of governance have been fragile and bellow its potential to play a significant role in decision-making. From the bottom-up perspective on statebuilding, the community has not been feeling advantaged by the new political and social context. This highlights that the focus on Serb-integration and particular challenges like the lack of a strong kin-state and its geographical spread undermine the Bosniaks' opportunities to make use of their constitutional rights. In addition, the community has had limited capacity to exercise their language and education rights, meaning that Bosniaks continue to partially rely on services provided by the Serbian parallel institutions and study in Serbian language without learning Albanian. These issues are in the detriment of integration and limit the socioeconomic opportunities of the community. Lastly, the fact that Bosniaks have not benefited from the decentralization process as much as other communities also illustrates that de jure rights have limited effectiveness without capacity and external support.

Turkish community

The examination of the Kosovo Turkish community, on the other hand, confirmed the benefits of being helped by a strong kin-state (Turkey), historical legacy, territorial concentration of the population, economic capacity, political unity and backing by majority elites. These are all key positive factors that have helped Turks to secure a strong position as a minority in a diverse society. Nevertheless, the changing and unstable political environment in Kosovo has shown that the political unity of Turks is fragile and that their representation and participation might not be sustainable. Moreover, the better conditions for exercising their language and education rights at the local level also have the downside of facilitating protection of rights without integration. Like in the case of Serbs and Bosniaks, Kosovo Turks, in particular the younger generations, are becoming linguistically segregated from the majority population. A similar situation is indicated by the impact of ethnic decentralization, which despite allowing Turks to create their own municipality, it might also determine territorial segregation and new problems given the lack of self-sustainability.

Roma, Ashkali and Egyptian communities

By contrast, the Roma, Ashkali and Egyptian minorities remain the most vulnerable, disadvantaged and discriminated groups in Kosovo. This is mainly due to the lack of social and political cohesion within the communities, their troublesome official recognition, their limited socioeconomic resources, the highest unemployment rates in Kosovo, the lack of education and their continued marginalization by the majority and other communities in Kosovo. It has been very difficult to correct this situation given the implications of the war and post-conflict context (accused for taking the side of one party or the other), but also given that one of the only ways of differentiating between them is through their capacity to speak one of the two official languages (Albanian or Serbian) and rarely both. Moreover, the lack of education (high levels of illiteracy) and professional training, their geographical spread, movement of the population and high numbers of refugees and the absence of competent elites have excluded RAE communities from decision-making and from meaningful participation in the civic and political life of Kosovo. Another important yet largely ignored factor is related to their condition as a stateless nation in the wider European political context. The situation of these minority groups shows that the constitutional provisions be expected to have the same impact as seen in the example of communities with more capacity and more support from institutions and the majority population. In actual fact, there are clear indicators that the legislation can be counterproductive and segregate vulnerable communities like the RAE as it has stimulated and institutionalized group differentiation. The rationale behind protecting minorities should be to directly address the issues that make such communities politically and socially vulnerable in diverse societies. Conversely, the legal provisions for minorities in Kosovo have actually become attributes for those considered a political priority (Serbs) and for those with more capacity to employ their rights. This has consequently been creating a hierarchical order of communities in Kosovo that, in the circumstances presented by this book, places the RAE minorities at the lower end of the list.

Gorani community

The examination of the situation of the Gorani community in Kosovo revealed further issues with the protection and integration of minority groups who not only must face common challenges for non-majority small communities but must also struggle to preserve and promote a generally accepted notion of their identity. The main problems facing Gorani in terms of social, economic and political conditions are the lack of qualifications, the lack of information regarding job opportunities and professional development, assimilation, language issues, territorial segregation as well as the poor state of the economy as a whole. What is particularly challenging for Goranis is their assimilation not by the majority group in this case, but by other minority communities (mainly Bosniaks, but Serbs too) as well as by external national groups (Bulgarians, Macedonians). Consequently, the community is generally divided between those who identify themselves as either Gorani or Bosniaks, a split that is also caused by their different political affiliation rather than having distinct cultural and ethnic features. Kosovo has a very difficult task to achieve a sustainable integration of the Goranis given the worrying levels of fragmentation within the community itself. Furthermore, the example of the Gorani community reveals how the focus on political representation and participation can undermine the development of rights and measures meant to address the preservation and promotion of cultural identity as well as the socioeconomic needs of a small minority. Unsurprisingly, the strong provisions for empowering minorities in Kosovo have stimulated the political mobilization of Goranis. However, the subsequent signs of fragmentation and segregation, as well as the fragility of their ethnic/cultural identity, represent worrying unintended consequences of statebuilding. The case of the Gorani community suggests that the interdependence between the cultural identity of a minority group per se and their political status has been counterproductive in post-conflict and post-independence Kosovo.

Montenegrins and Croat communities

The Croats and the Montenegrins were the last two minority communities discussed in this book. While the minorities in Kosovo represent overall a small percentage of the population, the tiny size of these two communities has a particular significance. More precisely, their continuous marginalization has been clearly confirmed by the fact that they were not even recognized initially by the Kosovo legislation and they have continued to be denied the political rights offered to all other minorities (reserved seats in the parliaments, most visibly). In this context, Croats and Montenegrins exemplify almost all challenges, limitations and problems derived from the design and implementation of the multiethnic institutional and legal framework in Kosovo. The capacity and willingness variables explain why they were excluded from the list of official non-majority communities or, in other words, not even included in the hierarchical structure of Kosovo communities. The lack of interest in their situation and their limited capability to militate for their rights and to develop a 'voice' next to the other communities confirm the ineffectiveness of far-reaching minority rights in the absence of de facto conditions to facilitate their implementation.

Overall, the exclusion by non-recognition and the marginalization of Croats and Montenegrins reveal the inconsistent and unequal application of minority rights. Moreover, it also highlights the discrepancy between the objectives behind the design of the multiethnic framework of governance and the genuine needs of minority groups. The emphasis on political provisions and elite-level forms of participation might actually indicate a counterproductive effect in terms of misperception of minority rights and neglect of factual problems. The Montenegrins have been partially assimilated by Serbs and remain dependent on the parallel institutions, while the less than 300 remaining Croats live isolated in a remote village and are very likely to become extinct. Such small and vulnerable communities should have probably been a priority of the system for safeguarding minority rights because they have almost no capacity to protect, preserve and promote their identity and their particular requirements. By contrast, they were not recognized initially in the post-independence Kosovo and continue to be a victim of the promotion and use of minority rights merely as political rights rather than as an interconnected plethora of cultural, social, economic and civic rights.

Other research findings

At a broader level, this book demonstrates the vital role of endogenous factors in challenging the applicability of an externally generated model of plural democracy and management of diversity. My research findings vis-à-vis the case of Kosovo underline the difficulties of trying to build a multiethnic liberal democratic state and present sufficient evidence to show that the exogenous and imposing character of statebuilding has been overemphasized in relation to identifying the main causes of its shortcomings. This observation challenges the extensively studied diagnoses of 'state weakness' and 'state failure' in Kosovo and similar cases of contemporary liberal interventionism and post-conflict statebuilding. The objection to this line of thought is that it mainly draws on an ideal (Western) liberal democratic model of state in order to evaluate the results of statebuilding. Instead, this book has examined Kosovo based on the idea that gaining legitimacy is at the heart of statebuilding and has adopted the *limited state*[1] approach to highlight the transformative nature of state-society relations and their inevitable impact on shaping the actual form of the state.

In this respect, I argue that the effectiveness and the actual negative or positive impact of contemporary practices of post-conflict statebuilding are dictated by local realities to a larger extent than the existing state-centric literature affirms. Therefore, policymakers and scholars should engage in more balanced and accurate work on whether the failures of contemporary statebuilding derive from the lack of more case-specific solutions and mechanisms or they are intrinsically embedded in the peculiar Western-centric nature of the liberal democratic state. Furthermore, while it is not always easy to measure the actual impact of diversity on the process of statebuilding, my evaluation of Kosovo suggests that, depending on the case, it transforms and challenges the adoption of a legitimate and functional liberal democratic state model. The actual circumstances and results of the system developed to manage diversity reflect the mutual influence between exogenous and endogenous factors. Likewise, as the study of Kosovo has illustrated, the actual form and character of newly built states are the result of the permanent multiple tension between liberal democratic norms of governance and the conditions of plurality, between the need of social cohesion and the management of diversity, between intended and unintended consequences of implementation, between local and international understanding of authority, between national and subnational forms of identity and, more broadly, between the state's *image* as a unitary and coherent political entity and the *practices* of different social actors and agencies.

This book also suggests that the mechanisms aiming to integrate and accommodate minorities in Kosovo have been developed based on an assumption rather than an indisputable claim that these groups are not integrated and, thus, will be equally helped by the adoption of political, social, economic and cultural minority rights. Given the priority to integrate the Serb community, the overall assumption has been that specific post-ethnic conflict tools for reconciliation through power-sharing arrangements would be appropriate for all communities. Therefore, the multiethnic framework of governance in Kosovo has not only been based on a generalizing view of minority integration as a uniform problem, but it has also been developed in response to the situation of one particular group, the Kosovo Serbs. This indicates another important implication of my research findings concerning the effectiveness of consociational arrangements for post-conflict statebuilding. Consociational power-sharing measures have been seen as necessary and useful for addressing the delicate situation of Kosovo Serbs given their new post-conflict status detached from the authority of Serbia and their relationship with the Albanians constituting the new majority community. To this end, it has enabled elite-level representation, participation and cooperation with the majority and other minority communities and has become a source of legitimacy in Kosovo.

However, in the long run these restrictive mechanisms for the protection of minorities may lead to the new forms of ethnic politics instead of facilitating cross-ethnic cooperation and integration. This is visible among non-Serb minorities when evaluating how the adoption of extensive rights has stimulated political mobilization of even the smallest communities and has become a source of competition and differentiation within all aspects of life beyond cultural identity, namely politics, education, social relations and economic development. Moreover, the power-sharing arrangements in Kosovo have also illustrated the problematic dependency on the willingness and ability of elites to represent the interests of their communities and reach a consensus with other groups. The ineffectiveness of minority consultative bodies and municipal human rights units in Kosovo indicates the volatility of minority representatives and their preference to secure a more direct access to power. Overall, some of my key findings subscribe to the integrationist critique of the divisive risks associated with extensive accommodation of minorities or consociational arrangements that disregard the long-term necessity of integration.

Furthermore, my empirical findings as regards decentralization as a tool for power-sharing in Kosovo revealed three main unintended consequences. Firstly, the effectiveness of the devolution of power to minority municipalities has been inconsistent and impractical. Secondly, the self-governance facilities have been misused to extend control at the local level and, thirdly, there is an increasing risk of fostering territorial segregation of some communities in the detriment of local multiethnicity. My case studies showed that establishing micro-municipalities based on ethnic decentralization is impractical and undermines other generic objectives of statebuilding such as good governance and better provision of public services at the local level. Moreover, the examination of Serb-majority municipalities confirmed that they have limited capacity for sustainable self-governance and are almost exclusively disconnected from Kosovo given the presence of the Serbian parallel institutions. These circumstances, in combination with the growing obedience towards pro-Belgrade parties, have important implications for my study as they exemplify how de jure provisions and models of accommodating diversity can paradoxically become de facto tools for segregation. In this context, the simulated participation and representation of Serbs within Kosovo's political and administrative system has not been an act of legitimization but a latent form of segregation.

Another unforeseen consequence of the far-reaching provisions for minorities is in relation to language rights. While the full-stretched protection of one of the fundamental rights of minorities has been an intended consequence, language rights may also isolate and segregate communities linguistically. This book has also shown how the language barrier is an additional obstacle for the integration of ethnic groups as it aggravates the already critical issues of poverty, unemployment, limited access to public services and lack of education and professional credentials. Overall, these issues draw attention to a clear example of how policies designed to protect minorities can be misinterpreted and misused when they are put into practice. This study claims that the right to preserve and use minority languages should not be considered an exclusive right to differentiation just as learning the language of the majority community should not be perceived as forced assimilation but as necessary and beneficial integration.

Overall, the shortcomings regarding the legislation-implementation gap and the series of unintended consequences discussed in this research cannot be neglected. They indicate the serious risks that derive from policies and strategies of statebuilding vis-à-vis the management of diversity that are based on assumptions rather than factual evaluation of the local circumstances. This is even more problematic in the context where similar solutions have been adopted in neighbouring statebuilding cases like Bosnia-Herzegovina and Macedonia, which nonetheless have been struggling to synchronize liberal democratic norms with conditions of diversity. The externally led and externally designed solutions for managing ethnic diversity in Kosovo, and possibly in most other contemporary post-conflict statebuilding cases, have disregarded a fundamental issue deriving from the impact of endogenous factors: *variation*. As Kosovo's case study has demonstrated, the multidimensional differences between groups and the changing nature of interethnic relations may require fully customized solutions and tools for management of diversity, be they in support of integration, accommodation, protection, representation or participation. Whether or not these tensions can be overcome through practices more concerned with the impact of endogenous factors and the inclusion of local agency in the design and practice of statebuilding remains open for investigation.

Statebuilding in Kosovo has required the extensive accommodation of ethnic diversity under the umbrella of an ethnically neutral civic Kosovan identity. However, in the absence of a strong emotional attachment to the Kosovan identity, political homogenization through the construction of a civic nation on a predominantly rational basis becomes much more challenging.[2] Despite the presence of an overwhelming majority population belonging to the Albanian community, Kosovo has not been designed to become a homogeneous nation state, but a hybrid multiethnic polity with an overarching civic national identity. The mechanisms to accommodate diversity have been established, but the newborn state has yet to develop a generally accepted, strong and genuine common Kosovan national civic identity. Classical statebuilding and nation-building aspired to develop national cohesion through the promotion of an assimilating overarching identity. Conversely, contemporary processes of statebuilding like the one in Kosovo have become extremely concerned with the accommodation of diversity. However, even though assimilation and accommodation have been contrasting responses to diversity, they have both been challenged by the lack of social cohesion. While assimilating statebuilding has not always managed to deny diversity and contain the inevitable fracture of the society, accommodating statebuilding has been struggling to secure unity because of its (over-)emphasis on distinctiveness. Therefore, as the findings revealed in this book suggest, in contexts like Kosovo that also lack a civic identity, this deficit of accommodating diversity is more problematic for the relationship between state and society and between state and nation.

While the post-conflict standards before status approach in Kosovo made statebuilding without statehood possible by developing a de facto state with domestic sovereignty in the absence of international recognition, the post-independence context seems to have turned this situation upside down. Despite the still limited recognition of its statehood, Kosovo has established its status as a new independent democratic, secular and multiethnic republic, but in practical terms, Kosovo does not meet the presumed standards: the society is largely ethnically homogeneous with little diversity per se but cannot pursue an Albanian-based national project of statehood, the small but existing different groups remain divided in the absence of social cohesion and a common civic link, and Kosovo has yet to create the nation. Consequently, the relationship between state and society in Kosovo remains largely undefined.

As this book illustrates, the causes and consequences of the continuing struggle for a state in Kosovo reach far beyond the interests and actions of the key political actors engaged in the post-conflict and post-independence context. With or without recognition, the lives of old and new communities in Kosovo have been affected on a daily basis by the actions or lack of action of local, regional, national and international actors. Be it the struggle for independence, for a state, for a nation or for survival altogether, the people constitute the bearers of politics with all its triumphs and wrongdoings. And this is why this book has offered a bottom-up perspective in trying to challenge the state-centric views and practices affecting international statebuilding in Kosovo. As in many other parts of the world, the remaining problem for Kosovo is to what extent and in what ways the voices of all its people and communities will continue to be heard and listened to. Despite the postcolonial, post-communist and post-conflict experiences, the formation of states disconnected from their societies is an old yet still central dilemma of our contemporary international politics.

Notes

Introduction

1 Sammy Smooha, 'Types of Democracy and Modes of Conflict Management in Ethnically Divided Societies', *Nations and Nationalism* 8(4) (2002), pp. 423–431.
2 David Roberts, *Liberal Peacebuilding and Global Governance: Beyond the Metropolis* (London: Routledge, 2011), p. 16.
3 To this date, Kosovo has been recognized by 110 UN member states (57 per cent), but it lacks UN membership as the UNSC remains divided on this issue, with Russia and China not recognizing the declaration of independence. The EU member states are also divided as only twenty-three out of twenty-eight members (82 per cent) have recognized Kosovo.
4 For a detailed recent analysis of this see Gëzim Visoka, *Acting Like a State Kosovo and the Everyday Making of Statehood* (Oxon: Routledge, 2018).
5 Robert Egnell and Peter Halden, 'Introduction: The Need for New Agendas in Statebuilding' in R. Egnell and P. Halden (eds), *New Agendas in Statebuilding: Hybridity, Contingency, and History* (London: Routledge, 2013), p. 1.
6 Joseph S. Migdal, *State in Society. Studying How States and Societies Transform and Constitute One Another* (Cambridge: Cambridge University Press, 2001).
7 Ibid., p. 18.
8 Stephen D. Krasner, *Sovereignty: Organized Hypocrisy* (Princeton, NJ: Princeton University Press, 1999).
9 Richard J. Ponzio, *Democratic Peacebuilding: Aiding Afghanistan* (Oxford: Oxford University Press, 2011), p. 35.
10 Ibid., p. 9.
11 Juan J. Linz and Alfred Stepan, *Problems of Democratic Transition and Consolidation: Southern Europe, South America, and Post-communist Europe* (Baltimore: Johns Hopkins University Press, 1996). Ibid., p. 429.
12 Franke Wilmer, 'Minority Rights and Charles Tilly's "Stateness"', *Constitutionalism Web-papers*, ConWEB No 3. (2006), p. 16.
13 See Richard Caplan, *International Governance of War-torn Territories: Rule and Reconstruction* (Oxford: Oxford University Press, 2005); David Chandler, 'The Problems of "Nation-building": Imposing Bureaucratic "Rule from Above"', *Cambridge Review of International Affairs* 17(3) (2004), pp. 577–591; D. Chandler, *Empire in Denial: The Politics of State-building* (London: Pluto, 2006); D. Chandler,

International Statebuilding. The Rise of Post-liberal Governance (Oxon: Routledge, 2010); Christopher Clapham, *Africa and the International System: The Politics of State Survival* (New York: Cambridge University Press, 1996); Aidan Hehir, *Kosovo, Intervention and Statebuilding: The International Community and the Transition to Independence* (London: Routledge, 2010); Michael Ignatieff, *Empire Lite: Nation Building in Bosnia, Kosovo and Afghanistan* (London: Vintage, 2003); Robert Jackson, *Quasi-states: Sovereignty, International Relations and the Third Word* (Cambridge: Cambridge University Press, 1990); Roland Paris, 'Peacebuilding and the Limits of Liberal Internationalism', *International Security* 22(2) (1997), pp. 54–89; Oliver P. Richmond and Jason Franks, *Liberal Peace Transitions: Between Statebuilding and Peacebuilding* (Edinburgh: Edinburgh University Press, 2009); Dominik Zaum, *The Sovereignty Paradox: The Norms and Politics of International Statebuilding* (Oxford: Oxford University Press, 2007).

14 Oisın Tansey, 'Democratization without a State: Democratic Regime-building in Kosovo', *Democratization* 14(1) (2007), pp. 129–150; See also Nina Caspersen, *Unrecognized States: The Struggle for Sovereignty in the Modern International System* (Cambridge: Polity, 2012) and Bridget Coggins, *Power Politics and State Formation in the Twentieth Century: The Dynamics of Recognition* (New York: Cambridge University Press, 2014).

15 See Denisa Kostovicova, *Kosovo: The Politics of Identity and Space* (London: Routledge, 2005); Denisa Kostovicova and Vesna Bojicic-Dzelilovic (eds), *Persistent State Weakness in the Global Age* (London: Ashgate, 2009).

16 See James Ker-Lindsay, *Kosovo: The Path to Contested Statehood in the Balkans* (London: I.B. Tauris, 2009); Aidan Hehir, 'Introduction: Kosovo and the International Community' in A. Hehir (ed), *Kosovo, Intervention and Statebuilding: The International Community and the Transition to Independence* (London: Routledge, 2010), pp. 1–16 and Marc Weller, *Contested Statehood: Kosovo's Struggle for Independence* (Oxford: Oxford University Press, 2009).

17 See Vesna Bojicic-Dzelilovic, James Ker-Lindsay and Denisa Kostovicova, 'Introduction: Civil Society and Multiple Transitions – Meanings, Actors and Effects' in D. Kostovicova and V. Bojicic-Dzelilovic (eds), *Civil Society and Transitions in the Western Balkans. New Perspectives on South-east Europe* (Basingstoke: Palgrave Macmillan, 2013), pp. 1–25.

18 Ibid., p. 13.

Chapter 1

1 Sebastian Von Einsiedel, 'Policy Responses to State Failure' in S. Chesterman et al. (eds), *Making States Work* (Tokyo: United Nations University Press, 2005), p. 15.

2. Robert H. Jackson and Carl G. Rosberg, 'Why Africa's Weak States Persist: The Empirical and the Juridical in Statehood', *World Politics* 35(1) (1982), pp. 1–24.
3. Charles Tilly, 'State Formation as Organized Crime' in P. Evans, D. Rueschemeyer and T. Skocpol (eds), *Bringing the State Back In* (Cambridge: Cambridge University Press, 1985), pp.169–191.
4. Jennifer Milliken and Keith Krause, 'State Failure, State Collapse, and State Reconstruction: Concepts, Lessons and Strategies', *Development and Change* 33(5) (2002), p. 756.
5. Felix Gerdes, *Civil War and State Formation – The Political Economy of War and Peace in Liberia* (Frankfurt: Campus Verlag, 2013), p. 5.
6. Natasha Ezrow and Erica Frantz, *Failed States and Institutional Decay: Understanding Instability and Poverty in the Developing World* (New York: Bloomsbury Academic, 2013), p. 16.
7. Kristina Roepstorff, *The Politics of Self-determination: Beyond the Decolonisation Process* (Abingdon: Routledge, 2013), p. 47.
8. David Lake, 'The New Sovereignty in International Relations', *International Studies Review* 5(1) (2003), p. 304.
9. Roepstorff, *The Politics of Self-determination*, p. 47.
10. Stephen Krasner suggested a concentration of the meanings of sovereignty in four categories: Westphalian, domestic, international and interdependence. Domestic sovereignty 'involves both authority and control, both specification of legitimate authority within a polity and the extent to which that authority can be effectively exercised' (In Krasner, *Sovereignty*, p. 4).
11. Timothy Mitchell, 'The Limits of the State: Beyond Statist Approaches and Their Critics', *American Political Science Review* 85(1) (1991), p. 95.
12. Migdal, *State in Society*.
13. Ibid., p. 250.
14. See Talcott Parson, *The Social System* (London: Routledge & Kegan Paul, 1951).
15. Migdal, *State in Society*, p. 8.
16. Max Weber, 'Politics as a Vocation' in H. H. Gerth and C. W. Mills (eds), *From Max Weber: Essays in Sociology* (London: Routledge & Kegan Paul, 1948), p. 82.
17. Migdal, *State in Society*, p. 14.
18. Ibid., p. 16.
19. Ibid., p. 18.
20. Ibid.
21. Michael Keating, 'So Many Nations, So Few States: Territory and Nationalism in the Global Era' in A.-G. Gagnon and J. Tully (eds), *Multinational Democracies* (Cambridge: Cambridge University Press, 2001), p. 55.
22. Hideaki Shinoda, *Re-examining Sovereignty: From Classical Theory to the Global Age* (Houndmills: Macmillan Press, 2000), p. 49.

23 Montserrat Guibernau, 'Between Autonomy and Secession: The Accommodation of Minority Nationalism' in A.-G. Gagnon, M. Guibernau and F. Rocher (eds), *The Conditions of Diversity in Multinational Democracies* (Montreal: IRPP-McGill University Press, 2003), p. 116.
24 Dominique Arel, 'Political Stability in Multinational Democracies Comparing Language Dynamics in Brussels, Montreal and Barcelona' in A.-G. Gagnon and J. Tully (eds), *Multinational Democracies*, p. 69.
25 Ibid., p. 77.
26 Jackson, *Quasi-states*, p. 79.
27 Guibernau, 'Between Autonomy and Secession', p. 116.
28 Ibid.
29 Ted Robert Gurr, 'Minorities, Nationalists, and Islamists' in Crocker et al. (eds), *Leashing the Dogs of War: Conflict Management in a Divided World* (Washington, DC: United States Institute of Peace Press, 2007), p. 133.
30 Ibid., p. 100.
31 Mersiha Gadzo, 'Are Ethnic Borders Being Drawn for a "Greater Serbia"?', *Al Jazeera News*, 10 August 2018.
32 Volker Boege, M. Anne Brown, Kevin P. Clements and Anna Nolan, 'On Hybrid Political Orders and Emerging States: State Formation in the Context of "Fragility"' in *Berghof Handbook Dialogue* (8) (Berlin: Berghof Research Center for Constructive Conflict Management, 2008), p. 19.
33 Jack S. Levy, 'International Sources of Interstate and Intrastate War' in Crocker et al. (eds), *Leashing the Dogs of War*, p. 29.
34 See Christopher Clapham, *Africa and the International System: The Politics of State Survival* (Cambridge: Cambridge University Press, 1996); Siba N. Grovogui, *Sovereigns, Quasi-sovereigns, and Africans: Race and Self-determination in International Law* (Minneapolis: University of Minnesota Press, 1996); Sankaran Krishna, 'The Importance of Being Ironic: A Postcolonial View on Critical International Relations Theory', *Alternatives* 18(3) (1993), pp. 385–417 and Ali A. Mazrui, 'The Blood of Experience: The Failed State and Political Collapse in Africa', *World Policy Journal* 12(1) (1995), pp. 28–34.
35 Christopher Bickerton, 'State-building: Exporting State Failure' in C. Bickerton, P. Cunliffe and A. Gourevitch (eds), *Politics without Sovereignty. A Critique of Contemporary International Relations* (London: UCL Press, 2007), p. 102.
36 Mostafa Rejai and Cynthia H. Enloe, 'Nation-states and State-nations', *International Studies Quarterly* 13(2) (1969), p. 155.
37 Jackson, *Quasi-states*, p. 21.
38 Migdal, *State in Society*, p. 263.
39 Cunliffe, *Politics without Sovereignty*, p. 51.
40 Edmond J. Keller and Donald Rothschild, *Africa in New International Order: Rethinking. State Sovereignty and Regional Security* (Boulder, CO: Lynne Rienner, 1996), p. 230.

41 Bickerton, 'State-building: Exporting State Failure', p. 101.
42 Levy, 'International Sources and Intrastate War', p. 29.
43 Ibid.
44 There is a vast literature on the critique of liberal statebuilding and interventionism, also mentioned in the Introduction (p. 6).
45 John P. Lederach, *Building Peace: Sustainable Reconciliation in Divided Societies* (Washington, DC: United States Institute of Peace, 1997), p. 84.
46 Michael Barnett, 'Building a Republican Peace: Stabilizing States after War', *International Security* 30(4) (2006), pp. 87–112.
47 Ibid.
48 Bruce Russet, 'The Fact of Democratic Peace' in M. Brown et al. (eds), *Debating the Democratic Peace* (Cambridge, MA: MIT Press, 1996), p. 97.
49 Ibid., p. 97.
50 Edward D. Mansfield and Jack Snyder, 'Democratization and the Danger of War', *International Security* 20(1) (1995), p. 33.
51 Michael Barnett, Hunjoon Kim, Madalene O'Donnell and Laura Sitea, 'Peacebuilding: What Is in a Name?', *Global Governance* 13(1) (2007), p. 49.
52 Ibid.
53 Thomas Carothers, 'The End of the Transition Paradigm', *Journal of Democracy* 13(1) (2002), pp. 5–21.
54 Roland Paris, *At War's End: Building Peace after Civil Conflict* (Cambridge: Cambridge University Press, 2004).
55 Barnett et al., *Global Governance*, p. 51.
56 David Chandler, 'What Do We Do When We Critique Liberalism? The Uncritical Critique of Liberal Peace', *Review of International Studies* 36(1) (2009), pp. 137–155; Toby Dodge, 'Iraq: The Contradictions of Exogenous State-building in Historical Perspective', *Third World Quarterly* 27(1) (2006), pp. 187–200; Roger Mac Ginty, 'Hybrid Peace: The Interaction between Top-down and Bottom-up Peace', *Security Dialogue* 41(4) (2010), pp. 391–412; Paris, 'Peacebuilding and the Limits of Liberal Internationalism'; Roland Paris, 'Understanding the "Co-ordination Problem" in Post-war Statebuilding', Draft paper for the *Research Partnership on Postwar Statebuilding* (RPPS) (2006); Oliver Richmond, 'Resistance and the Post-liberal Peace', *Millennium: Journal of International Studies* 38(3) (2010), pp. 665–692; David Roberts, 'Saving Liberal Peacebuilding from Itself', *Peace Review: A Journal of Social Justice* 24(3) (2012), pp. 366–373.
57 Paris, *At War's End*, p. 185.
58 Ibid., p. 188.
59 Susan L. Woodward, 'Is Democracy Possible in the Balkans? On Preconditions and Conditions in Bosnia, Kosovo, and Serbia', *Working Paper Series* (Washington, DC, and Seattle, WA: National Council for Eurasian and East European Research, 2007), p. 25.
60 Paris, *At War's End*, p. 189.

61 Ibid., pp. 194–198.
62 Ibid., p. 207.
63 David Chandler, *International Statebuilding: The Rise of Post-liberal Governance* (London: Routledge, 2010).
64 Ibid., p. 95.
65 Ibid.
66 Richmond and Franks, *Liberal Peace Transitions*, p. 140.
67 Marlies Glasius and Denisa Kostovicova, 'The European Union as a State-builder: Policies towards Serbia and Sri Lanka', *Südosteuropa* 56(1) (2008), p. 87.
68 Robert I. Rotberg, 'The Challenge of Weak, Failing, and Collapsed States' in Crocker et al. (eds), *Leashing the Dogs of War*, pp. 83–94.
69 Ibid., p. 85.
70 Ramesh Kumar, 'Corruption and Transparency in Governance and Development: Reinventing Sovereignty for Promoting Good Governance' in T. Jacobsen, C. Sampford and R. Thakur (eds), *Re-envisioning Sovereignty: The End of Westphalia?* (Aldershot: Ashgate, 2008), p. 253.
71 Rotberg, 'The Challenge of Weak', p. 86.
72 Ashraf Ghani and Clare Lockhart, *Fixing Failed States: A Framework for Rebuilding a Fractured World* (Oxford: Oxford University Press, 2008); Robert I. Rotberg, 'The Failure and Collapse of Nation-states: Breakdown, Prevention and Repair' in R. I. Rotberg (ed), *When States Fail: Causes and Consequences* (Princeton, NJ: Princeton University Press, 2004), pp. 1–45.
73 Chandler, *International Statebuilding: The Rise of Post-liberal Governance*, p. 5.
74 Migdal, *State in Society*, p. 12.
75 Barry Buzan, *People, States, and Fear: An Agenda for International Security Studies in the Post–Cold War Era*, 2nd ed. (Colchester: ECPR Press, 2007), p. 94.
76 Guibernau, 'Between Autonomy and Secession', pp. 116–117.
77 Ibid.
78 Linz and Stepan, *Problems of Democratic Transition*.
79 Smooha, 'Types of Democracy'.
80 Ibid., p. 424.
81 Sammy Smooha, 'The Model of Ethnic Democracy: Israel as a Jewish and Democratic State', *Nations and Nationalism* 8(4) (2002), p. 475.
82 Ibid., p. 476.
83 Arendt Lijphart, *Democracy in Plural Societies: A Comparative Exploration* (New Haven, CT: Yale University Press, 1977).
84 Smooha, 'Types of Democracy', p. 425.
85 Smooha, 'The Model of Ethnic Democracy', p. 476.
86 Linz and Stepan, *Problems of Democratic Transition*, p. 31.
87 Smooha, 'Types of Democracy', p. 425.

88 Smooha, 'The Model of Ethnic Democracy', p. 476.
89 Ibid., p. 478.
90 John McGarry and Brendan O'Leary, 'Introduction' in J. McGarry and B. O'Leary (eds), *The Politics of Ethnic Conflict Regulation: Case Studies of Protracted Ethnic Conflicts* (New York: Routledge, 1993), p. 4.
91 Ibid., p. 6.
92 Ibid., p. 27.
93 Ibid., p. 24.
94 Ibid., p. 25.
95 John McGarry, Brendan O'Leary and Richard Simeon, 'Integration of Accommodation? The Enduring Debate in Conflict Regulation' in S. Choudhry (ed), *Constitutional Design for Divided Societies. Integration of Accommodation?* (Oxford: Oxford University Press, 2008), p. 50.
96 McGarry and O'Leary, 'Introduction', p. 18.
97 Jacques Bertrand and Oded Haklai, 'Democratization and Ethnic Minorities' in J. Bertrand and O. Haklai (eds), *Democratization and Ethnic Minorities: Conflict or Compromise?* (New York: Routledge, 2014), p. 8.
98 Will Kymlicka, *Politics in the Vernacular: Nationalism, Multiculturalism, and Citizenship* (Oxford: Oxford University Press, 2001).
99 Ibid., p. 101.
100 McGarry and O'Leary, 'Introduction', p. 35.
101 Sujit Choudhry, 'Bridging Comparative Politics and Comparative Constitutional Law: Constitutional Design in Divided Societies' in S. Choudhry (ed), *Constitutional Design for Divided Societies*, p. 18.
102 Ian S. Lustick, 'Lijphart, Lakatos, and Consociationalism', *World Politics* 50(1) (1997), p. 92.
103 Donald L. Horowitz, 'Democracy in Divided Societies', *Journal of Democracy* 4(4) (1993), p. 36.
104 Arendt Lijphart, 'Consociational Democracy', *World Politics* 21(2) (1969), p. 216.
105 Lijphart, *Democracy in Plural Societies*, p. 24.
106 Ben Spiecker and Jan Steutel, 'Multiculturalism, Pillarization and Liberal Civic Education in the Netherlands', *International Journal of Educational Research* 35(3) (2001), p. 295.
107 Lijphart, *Democracy in Plural Societies*, p. 41.
108 Ibid., p. 38.
109 Ibid., p. 39.
110 Ibid., p. 41.
111 Arendt Lijphart, 'Constitutional Design for Divided Societies', *Journal of Democracy* 15(2) (2004), p. 97.
112 McGarry et al., 'Integration of Accommodation?', p. 53.

113 Donald L. Horowitz, *A Democratic South Africa? Constitutional. Engineering in a Divided Society* (Berkeley: University of California Press, 1991), pp. 137–145.
114 Ibid., p. 196.
115 Ibid., p. 184.
116 Ibid., p. 195.
117 Ibid., p. 196.
118 Ibid.
119 John McGarry and Brendan O'Leary, 'Federation as a Method of Ethnic Conflict Regulation' in S. Noel (ed), *From Power-sharing to Democracy: Post Conflict Institutions in Ethnically Divided Societies* (Montreal: McGill Queens University Press, 2005), p. 263.
120 Horowitz, *A Democratic South Africa*, p. 217.
121 Ibid., p. 226.
122 Paris, 'Peacebuilding and the Limits of Liberal Internationalism', p. 84.
123 Florian Bieber, 'Power sharing after Yugoslavia. Functionality and Dysfunctionality of Power Sharing Institutions in Post-war Bosnia, Macedonia and Kosovo' in S. Noel (ed), *From Power-sharing to Democracy: Post-conflict Institutions*, p. 101.
124 Jack Snyder, *From Voting to Violence: Democratization and Nationalist Conflict* (London: W. W. Norton, 2000).
125 Allison McCulloch, *Power-sharing and Political Stability in Deeply Divided Societies* (New York: Routledge, 2014), p. 10.
126 Bieber, 'Power Sharing after Yugoslavia', p. 85.
127 Will Kymlicka, 'The Internationalization of Minority Rights' in S. Choudhry (ed), *Constitutional Design for Divided Societies*, p. 111.
128 See McGarry, O'Leary and Simeon, 'Integration of Accommodation?'.
129 Kymlicka, 'The Internationalization of Minority Rights', p. 138.
130 Barry Buzan, 'The Consociational Model and Its Dangers', *European Journal for Political Research* 3(4) (1975), pp. 393–412; Kanchan Chandra, 'Ethnic Parties and Democratic Stability', *Perspectives on Politics* 3(2) (2005), pp. 235–252; Donald L. Horowitz, *Ethnic Groups in Conflict* (Berkeley: University of California Press, 1985) and Donald L. Horowitz, 'Constitutional Design: Proposals versus Processes' in A. Reynolds (ed), *The Architecture of Democracy: Constitutional Design, Conflict Management and Democracy* (Oxford: Oxford University Press, 2002), pp. 15–36 and Donald Rothchild, *Sustainable Peace: Power and Democracy after Civil Wars* (New York: Cornell University Press, 2005).
131 Joel Sawat Selway and Kharis Templeman, 'The Myth of Consociationalism? Conflict Reduction in Divided Societies', *Comparative Political Studies* 45(12) (2012), p. 1552.
132 Arendt Lijphart, 'The Alternative Vote: A Realistic Alternative for South Africa?', *Politikon* 18(2) (1991), pp. 9–101; Arendt Lijphart, 'The Wave of Power-sharing

Democracy' in A. Reynolds (ed), *The Architecture of Democracy*, pp. 37–54 and Arendt Lijphart, *Thinking about Democracy: Power Sharing and Majority Rule in Theory and Practice* (London: Routledge, 2008).
133 Matthijs Bogaards, 'Electoral Choices for Divided Societies: Moderation through Constituency Pooling and Vote Pooling', ECPR Joint Sessions Institute of Political Studies (Grenoble 6–11 April 2001), p. 10.
134 Patrick J. O'Halloran, 'Post-conflict Reconstruction: Bosnia and Kosovo' in S. Noel (ed), *From Power-sharing to Democracy*, p. 116.
135 Richard H. Pildes, 'Ethnic Identity and Democratic Institutions: A Dynamic Perspective' in S. Choudhry (ed), *Constitutional Design for Divided Societies*, p. 201.
136 Ibid.

Chapter 2

1 Denisa Kostovicova, 'State Weakness in the Western Balkans as a Security Threat: The European Union Approach and a Global Perspective', *Western Balkans Security Observer* 2(7–8) (2007), p. 12.
2 Richmond and Franks, *Liberal Peace Transitions*, p. 140.
3 Zaum, *The Sovereignty Paradox*, p. 129.
4 Ibid., p. 130.
5 Noel Malcolm, *Kosovo: A Short History*, 2nd ed. (London: Pan, 2002).
6 Ker-Lindsay, *Kosovo: The Path to Contested Statehood in the Balkans*, p. 9.
7 Ibid., p. 10.
8 Malcolm, *Kosovo: A Short History*.
9 Timothy W. Crawford, 'Pivotal Deterrence and the Kosovo War: Why the Holbrooke Agreement Failed', *Political Science Quarterly* 116(4) (2001), pp. 499–523.
10 Ibid.
11 Hehir, 'Introduction: Kosovo and the International Community'.
12 Neil Tweedie, 'Kosovo War: Thousands Killed as Serb Forces Tried to Keep Control of Province', *The Telegraph*, 31 March 2009.
13 Milka Domanovic, 'List of Kosovo War Victims Published', *BIRN*, 4 December 2014.
14 NATO, 'NATO's Role in Kosovo'. Available at https://www.nato.int/cps/en/natolive/topics_48818.htm (accessed 1 September 2018).
15 Ponzio, *Democratic Peacebuilding*, p. 35.
16 Kumar, 'Corruption and Transparency', p. 253.
17 Trutz von Trotha, 'The "Andersen Principle": On the Difficulty of Truly Moving beyond State-centrism' in M. Fischer and B. Schmelzle (eds), *Building Peace in*

the Absence of States: Challenging the Discourse on State Failure (Berlin: Berghof Research Centre, 2009), p. 41.
18 Ibid.
19 Ibid.
20 Tobias Hagmann and Markus V. Hoehne, 'Failures of the State Failure Debate: Evidence from the Somali Territories', *Journal of International Development* 21(1) (2009), p. 52.
21 UNSCR 1244 (1999).
22 M. L. Arastey Sahún and Pilar R. Vallejo, 'The Legal Construction of the Social Security System of the Republic of Kosovo', *International Social Security Review* 62(1) (2009), p. 67.
23 Tansey, 'Democratization without a State', p. 134.
24 Ibid., p. 5.
25 Spyros Economides, 'Kosovo' in M. Berdal and S. Economides (eds), *United Nations Interventionism, 1991–2004* (Cambridge: Cambridge University Press, 2007), p. 239.
26 UNMIK/European Union Pillar, *European Union Pillar: The 10 Key Achievements. End of Mission Report (1999–2008)* (Pristina: EU Pillar IV, 2008), p. 4.
27 Ibid., p. 8.
28 Ibid., p. 31.
29 Tansey, 'Democratization without a State', p. 136.
30 Ibid., p. 8.
31 European Commission, *Communication from the European Commission on the Subject of the Enlargement Strategy* (Brussels: EU Commission, 2007), p. 52.
32 Ibid., p. 53.
33 Hehir, 'Introduction: Kosovo and the International Community'.
34 Economides, 'Kosovo', p. 244.
35 Ibid.
36 'The Audit of War', *The Economist*, 9 September 2004.
37 International Crisis Group (ICG), 'Collapse in Kosovo', *Europe Report No. 155*, April 2004.
38 Ibid.
39 For more information, see European Roma Rights Centre (ERRC), 'Abandoned Minority: Roma Rights History in Kosovo', December 2011. Available at http://www.errc.org/cms/upload/file/abandoned-minority-roma-rights-history-in-kosovo-dec-2011.pdf (accessed 1 September 2018). The same report specifies: 'The mass return of displaced Kosovo Albanians was immediately followed by the expulsion or flight of non-Albanians, including Roma, Ashkali and Egyptians from and within Kosovo. Every Romani, Ashkali and Egyptian community visited by the ERRC during the mid-1999 field mission had half or fewer of its pre-war inhabitants. According to some sources, more than 100,000 Roma, Ashkali and

Egyptians left the province prior to the conflict, during the conflict and after the NATO intervention.'
40 Zaum, *The Sovereignty Paradox*, p. 131.
41 Ignatieff, *Empire Lite*, p. 70.
42 Charles T. Call, 'The Fallacy of the "Failed State"', *Third World Quarterly* 29(8) (2008), p. 1503.
43 Zaum, *The Sovereignty Paradox*, p. 135.
44 Richmond and Franks, *Liberal Peace Transitions*, p. 131.
45 Boege et al., 'On Hybrid Political Orders', p. 21.
46 Ibid.
47 Ibid.
48 Ibid.
49 Ibid., p. 10.
50 The Comprehensive Proposal for Kosovo Status Settlement (CSP), UNSC, 26 March 2007.
51 Tim Judah, *Kosovo: War and Revenge*, 2nd ed. (New Haven, CT: Yale University Press, 2002), p. 113.
52 ICG, 'Kosovo: No Good Alternatives to the Ahtisaari Plan', *Europe Report No. 182*, May 2007.
53 Ibid., p. 8.
54 Ibid., p. 2.
55 Elizabeth Pond, 'The EU's Test in Kosovo', *The Washington Quarterly* 31(4) (2008), p. 98.
56 Letter to UNSC, December 2007, pp. 11–12. Available at http://www.kosovocompromise.com/admin/download/files/_id_236/The-14-working-points-chart.pdf (accessed 1 September 2018).
57 ICG, 'Kosovo: No Good Alternatives to the Ahtisaari Plan'.
58 For up-to-date information, visit http://www.kosovothanksyou.com (accessed 1 September 2018).
59 Tansey, 'Democratization without a State', p. 134.
60 EC, *Kosovo (under UNSCR 1244/99) 2008 Progress Report* (Brussels: EC, 2008), p. 5.
61 Tansey, 'Democratization without a State'.
62 Ibid., p. 11.
63 Veton Surroi, 'The Unfinished State(s) in the Balkans and the EU: The Next Wave' in J. Rupnik (ed), *The Western Balkans and the EU: 'The Hour of Europe'*, Chaillot Papers (Paris: Institute for Security Studies, 2011), pp. 111–120.
64 Pond, 'The EU's Test in Kosovo'.
65 James Ker-Lindsay and Spyros Economides, 'Standards before Status before Accession: Kosovo's EU Perspective', *Journal of Balkan and Near Eastern Studies* 14(1) (2012), p. 87.

66 From the *Declaration of Independence* adopted by the Assembly of Kosovo on 17 February 2008. Available at: http://news.bbc.co.uk/1/hi/world/europe/7249677.stm (accessed 1 September 2018).
67 Constitution of the Republic of Kosovo, Article 3(1), p. 1.
68 Kosovo Agency of Statistics. Available at http://esk.rks-gov.net/rekos2011/?cid=2,1 (accessed 1 September 2018).
69 In the context of the boycott of the census by Serbs in northern Kosovo, the data has not been seen as reliable. However, all estimates indicate the Albanian population at about 90 per cent.
70 Gëzim Krasniqi, 'Equal Citizens, Uneven Communities: Differentiated and Hierarchical Citizenship in Kosovo', *Ethnopolitics* 14(2) (2015), pp. 197–217.
71 Law No. 03/L-047 'On the Protection and Promotion of the Rights of Communities and Their Members in Kosovo' (Law on Communities), 13 March 2008.
72 Constitution of the Republic of Kosovo, Chapter III, Article 57(1).
73 Personal interview with Suzana Andelkovic, advisor Ministry of Communities and Returns, Fushe Kosove, 29 May 2012.
74 Kosovar Institute for Policy Research and Development (KIPRED), *Integration of Minority Communities in the Post-status Kosovo* (Pristina: KIPRED, 2006), p. 6.
75 Ibid.
76 Faith Bailey, 'Kosovo to Recognize Montenegrin Minority', *Balkan Insight*, 2 November 2012.
77 Law No. 04/L-020 'On Amending and supplementing of the Law No. 03/L-047 on the protection and promotion of the rights of communities and their members in Republic of Kosovo'.
78 CCC website. Available at http://www.ccc-president-ksgov.net (accessed 1 September 2018).
79 Ibid.
80 Constitution of the Republic of Kosovo, Article 22:
(1) Universal Declaration of Human Rights;
(2) European Convention for the Protection of Human Rights and Fundamental Freedoms and Its Protocols;
(3) International Covenant on Civil and Political Rights and Its Protocols;
(4) Council of Europe Framework Convention for the Protection of National Minorities;
(5) Convention on the Elimination of All Forms of Racial Discrimination;
(6) Convention on the Elimination of All Forms of Discrimination against Women;
(7) Convention on the Rights of the Child;
(8) Convention against Torture and Other Cruel, Inhumane or Degrading Treatment or Punishment.

81 Ibid., Chapter III, Article 58(2).
82 Ibid., Article 58(6).
83 'The Comprehensive Proposal for Kosovo Status Settlement', UNSC, 26 March 2007.
84 The European Centre for Minority Issues Kosovo (ECMI Kosovo), *Strengthening the Institutional System for Communities in Post-independence Kosovo* (Pristina: ECMI, January 2009), p. 16.
85 Personal interviews with Serb, Bosniak, RAE, Turkish politicians and civil society members, Pristina, Prizren, February–June 2012 and 2013.
86 KIPRED, 'Kosovo Serbs after the Declaration of Independence: The Right Momentum for Confidence Building Measures', July 2008, p. 5.
87 Personal interview with Lutfi Haziri, PDK MP, and ex-minister of Culture and Local Self-Governance, Head of the Negotiation Team for Kosovo, 8 May 2012, Pristina, Kosovo.
88 European Commission, *Kosovo Analytical Report* (Brussels: EC, 2012), p. 13.
89 OSCE, 'Kosovo Serbs Profile' in *2010 Kosovo Communities Profiles* (Pristina: OSCE, February 2011), p. 33.
90 Article 1.2. 'The exercise of public authority in Kosovo shall be based upon the equality of all citizens and respect for the highest level of internationally recognized human rights and fundamental freedoms, as well as the promotion and protection of the rights and contributions of all its Communities and their members', 'The Comprehensive Proposal for Kosovo Status Settlement', *UNSC*, 26 March 2007.
91 International Foundation for Electoral Systems (IFES), *Post-elections Public Opinion in Kosovo* (Pristina: IFES, 2011), p. 13.
92 Constitution of the Republic of Kosovo, Article 58(1–7):
    [1] ensure appropriate conditions enabling communities, and their members to preserve, protect, and develop their identities ...
    [2] promote a spirit of tolerance, dialogue and support reconciliation among communities ...
    [3] take all necessary measures to protect persons who may be subject to threats or acts of discrimination, hostility or violence as a result of their national, ethnic, cultural or religious identity ...
    [4] adopt adequate measures as may be necessary to promote, in all areas of economic, social, political and cultural life, full and effective equality among members of communities ...
    [5] promote the preservation of the cultural and religious heritage of all communities as an integral part of the heritage of Kosovo ...
    [6] take effective actions against all those undermining the enjoyment of the rights of members of communities ...

[7] The Republic of Kosovo ensures, on a non-discriminatory basis, that all communities and their members may exercise their rights specified in this Constitution.

93 Law No. 03/L-047.
94 Law No. 02/L-37 'On the Use of Languages', as promulgated by UNMIK Regulation No. 2006/51.
95 Law on Communities, Article 4(1).
96 Kosovo Agency of Statistics (ASK), Kosovo 2011 Census. Available at http://ask.rks-gov.net/media/2129/estimation-of-kosovo-population-2011.pdf (accessed 1 September 2018).
97 Law on Communities, Article 8(1).
98 Law No. 03/L-068 'On Education in the Municipalities of the Republic of Kosovo', Chapter V, Article 12.
99 Ibid., Article 13.
100 Ibid.
101 Ibid., Article 14(d).
102 Ibid., Article 14(f).
103 Law on Communities, Article 6(5).
104 Law No. 04/L-046 'On Radio Television of Kosovo', Article 8(3).
105 Law on Communities, Article 7(6).
106 Kosovo Constitution, Article 103, p. 36, and UNMIK Regulation 2006/25, 27 April 2006.
107 Kosovo Constitution, Article 108(10), p. 39.
108 Ministry for Community and Return website. Available at http://mzp-rks.org/en/mission-and-vision.html (accessed 1 September 2018).
109 Office for Community Affairs website. Available at http://kryeministri-ks.net/zyra-e-kryeministrit/zyrat/zyra-per-ceshtje-te-komuniteteve (accessed 1 September 2018).
110 Article 4 of OPM AI No. 2005/08 and Article 3(4) of MLGA AI No. 2011/04.
111 Administrative Instruction – MLGA- No. 2008/02.
112 Constitution of the Republic of Kosovo, Article 63, p. 20.
113 Article 148 [Transitional Provisions for the Assembly of Kosovo]: 'Any seats gained through elections shall be in addition to the ten (10) reserved seats allocated to the Kosovo Serb Community and other Communities respectively', Constitution of the Republic of Kosovo, p. 57.
114 KIPRED, 'Kosovo National Elections 2010: Overview and Trends', April 2011.
115 ECMI, *Special Report: Community Political Parties and Government Formation* (Pristina: ECMI, February 2011).
116 1. Laws changing municipal boundaries, establishing or abolishing municipalities, defining the scope of powers of municipalities and their participation in intermunicipal and cross-border relations;

2. Laws implementing the rights of Communities and their members, other than those set forth in the Constitution;

3. Laws on the use of language;

4. Laws on local elections;

5. Laws on protection of cultural heritage;

6. Laws on religious freedom or on agreements with religious communities;

7. Laws on education;

8. Laws on the use of symbols, including Community symbols and on public holidays.

117 Fisnik Korenica and Dren Doli, 'Constitutional Rigidity in Kosovo: Relevance, Outcomes and Rationale', *Pace International Law Review* 2(6) (2011), p. 12.

118 Gëzim Visoka and Adem Beha, 'Minority Consultative Bodies in Kosovo: A Quest for Effective Emancipation or Elusive Participation?', *Journal on Ethnopolitics and Minority Issues in Europe* 10(1) (2011), p. 2.

119 Law on Communities [03/L-047], Article 12.

120 Ibid.

121 Law on Communities [03/L-047], Article 12(6).

122 Humanitarian Law Center (HLC), 'The Beginning of Implementation of the Law on the Promotion and Protection of Rights of Communities and Their Members in the Republic of Kosovo', December 2012, pp. 90–97.

123 'The Constitutional Framework on Provisional Self-Government in Kosovo', Article 9.

124 Visoka and Beha, 'Minority Consultative Bodies in Kosovo', p. 15.

125 Constitution of the Republic of Kosovo, Article 78.

126 Cabinet Decision on the creation of the Office, No. 06/34, 3 September 2008.

127 Office for Community Affairs website. Available at http://kryeministri-ks.net/zyra-e-kryeministrit/zyrat/zyra-per-ceshtje-te-komuniteteve (accessed 1 September 2018).

128 HLC, 'The Beginning of Implementation of the Law', p. 98.

129 Personal interviews with Suzana Novoberdali, LDK MP, 15 May 2012, Pristina, Kosovo and with Albert Kinolli, Roma MP, 14 May 2012.

Chapter 3

1 Richmond and Franks, *Liberal Peace Transitions*, p. 140.

2 Personal interviews with Kosovo Albanian and Serb politicians and civil society representatives, February–June 2012, Pristina, Kosovo.

3 Henry H. Perritt, *The Road to Independence for Kosovo: A Chronicle of the Ahtisaari Plan* (Cambridge: Cambridge University Press, 2009), p. 75.

4 Ibid.

5 Small Serbian parties in Kosovo: The Serbian Democratic Party of Kosovo and Metohija, the Serb People's Party, the New Democracy Party, the Serb Kosovo-Metohija Party and the New Democratic Initiative of Kosovo.
See ECMI, *Special Report: Community Political Parties and Government Formation*.
6 ICG, 'Setting Kosovo Free: Remaining Challenges', *Report No. 218*, September 2012, p. 7.
7 Personal interviews with SLS politicians, February–June 2012.
8 Personal interview with Jasmina Živković, Serb Community, MP for SLS, Pristina, 4 April 2013.
9 Personal interviews with Serb politicians and civil society representatives, February–June 2012 & February–June 2013.
10 Ibid.
11 Kosovo Central Electoral Commission (CEC). Available at http://www.kqz-ks.org (accessed 1 September 2018).
12 '2007 Kosovo Assembly Elections Results – Detailed Results by Parties and Candidates', July 2007. Available at http://www.osce.org/kosovo/38258, and 2007 Kosovo Assembly Elections Results – Seats allocation. Available at http://www.osce.org/kosovo/38259 (accessed 1 September 2018).
13 Ibid.
14 Ibid. The Turk and Bosniak representatives with the lowest number of votes were Mufera Sinik (1,040 votes) from KDTP party and Spresa Murati (1,061 votes) from VAKAT party.
15 KIPRED, 'Decentralization in Kosovo I: Municipal Elections and the Serb Participation', December 2009, p. 11.
16 Ibid., p. 9.
17 Ibid., p. 7.
18 Personal interview with Dragana Milutinovic (Serb minority), Forum ZFD, 5 April 2012, Pristina, Kosovo.
19 European Union Election Expert Mission (EU EEM), 'Final Report of the European Union Election Expert Mission to Kosovo', 25 January 2011, p. 41.
20 Ibid., p. 41.
21 Ibid., p. 8, and Personal interviews with Kosovo Serb representatives between February and June 2012.
22 Personal interviews with JSL and SLS members, February–June 2012, Pristina, Kosovo.
23 See Alvin Rabushka and Kenneth A. Shepsle, *Politics in Plural Societies: A Theory of Democratic Instability* (Columbus, OH: Charles E. Merrill, 1972) and Horowitz, *Ethnic Groups in Conflict*.
24 Brian Shoup, *Conflict and Cooperation in Multi-ethnic States: Institutional Incentives, Myths, and Counterbalancing* (Oxon: Routledge, 2008), p. 35.

25　Paul Mitchell, Geoffrey Evans and Brendan O'Leary, 'Extremist Outbidding in Ethnic Party Systems Is Not Inevitable: Tribune Parties in Northern Ireland', *Political Studies* 57(2) (2009), p. 416.
26　Ibid., p. 417.
27　Personal interview with Jasmina Živković, Serb Community, MP for SLS, Pristina, 4 April 2013.
28　ECMI, *Special Report: Community Political Parties and Government Formation*.
29　KIPRED, 'Kosovo National Elections 2010: Overview and Trends', p. 20.
30　Ibid., p. 23.
31　Muhamet Brajshori and Granit Tërnava, *The Republic of Kosovo's 2013 Local Elections Handbook* (Berlin: Konrad-Adenauer-Stiftung, 2013), p. 8.
32　ECMI, Information Bulletin, 'Kosovo Local Elections – Which Self-government for Minority Communities?' (Pristina: ECMI, November 2013).
33　Ilir Deda, *Kosovo after the Brussels Agreement: From Status Quo to an Internally Ethnically Divided State* (Pristina: Konrad-Adenauer-Stiftung, 2013), p. 3.
34　ECMI, *Kosovo Local Elections 2013: Lessons Learnt for Minority Communities. A Short Analysis* (Pristina: ECMI, December 2013).
35　Granit Tërnava, *Local Elections in Kosovo Final Results* (Pristina: Konrad-Adenauer-Stiftung Policy Brief, 2014), p. 8.
36　Deda, *Kosovo after the Brussels Agreement*, p. 3.
37　ECMI, *Kosovo Local Elections 2013*.
38　Ibid.
39　Dejan Guzina and Branka Marijan, 'A Fine Balance: The EU and the Process of Normalizing Kosovo-Serbia Relations', CIGI papers, no. 23, January 2014.
40　ECMI, *Minority Communities' Political Parties in Kosovo's Changing Political Landscape: The General Elections of June 2014 and Their Aftermath* (Pristina: ECMI, July 2014), p. 10.
41　The 2014 elections introduced the Guaranteed Seats System for the representation of minorities in the Assembly, replacing the Reserved Seats System, which was applied in previous national elections.
42　Other former SLS MPs who changed to Srpska are Saša Milosavljevic, Jasmina Živkovic and Jelena Bontic (ECMI, *Information Bulletin*, July 2014).
43　National Democratic Institute (NDI), 'Kosovo's June 2017 Parliamentary Elections', 12 July 2017.
44　TANJUG, 'Serb List Won't Join Cabinet with Self-determination', *B92 News*, 17 September 2014. Available at http://www.b92.net/eng/news/politics.php?yyyy=2014&mm=09&dd=17&nav_id=91640 (accessed 1 September 2018).
45　BIRN, 'Kosovo Forms New Government', *Prishtina Insight*, 9 September 2017.
46　Personal interview with Andrea Najvirtova, ECMI Kosovo, Pristina, Kosovo, 10 May 2012.

47 Florian Bieber, 'Power Sharing and Democracy in Southeast Europe', *Taiwan Journal of Democracy*, Special Issue (2013), p. 138.
48 UNDP, Public Pulse Reports for Kosovo, I–VII, 2010–2014.
49 Personal interview with Nenad Maksimovic, Center for Peace and Tolerance, Gracanica, Kosovo, 6 March 2012.
50 Personal interviews with political representatives of Serb, RAE, Bosniak communities in Kosovo, Pristina, Kosovo, February–June 2012.
51 This behaviour was confirmed by most NGOs working with minority rights protection in Kosovo (ECMI, KFOS, CIVIKOS, Balkan Sunflower, YIHR, HLC), Personal interviews, Pristina, Kosovo, February–June 2012.
52 ICG, 'Setting Kosovo Free: Remaining Challenges', p. 8.
53 UNDP, Pulse Report 4, August 2012, p. 24.
54 Personal interview with Nenad Rasic, minister of Labour and Social Welfare, Pristina, Kosovo, 18 May 2012.
55 Council for Inclusive Governance, 'Serbs in Kosovo's Institutions', February 2012.
56 Personal interview with Suzana Andelkovic, advisor of the Ministry of Communities and Returns, Fushe Kosova, 29 May 2012.
57 Ivan Briscoe and Megan Price, *Kosovo's New Map of Power: Governance and Crime in the Wake of Independence*, Clingendael Institute, 3 May 2011, p. 33.
58 Personal interview with Nenad Maksimovic.
59 OSCE, 'Kosovo Serb Profile', *2010 Communities Profiles*, p. 33.
60 Anna Matveeva and Wolf-Christian Paes, 'The Kosovo Serbs. An Ethnic Minority between Collaboration and Defiance', Bonn International Center for Conversion, Friedrich Naumann Foundation and Saferworld, June 2003, p. 18.
61 Ibid., p. 19.
62 ICG, 'Serb Integration in Kosovo: Taking the Plunge', *Report No. 200*, 12 May 2009, p. 9.
63 OSCE, *2010 Kosovo Communities Profiles*, p. 3.
64 ICG, 'Setting Kosovo Free: Remaining Challenges', p. 1.
65 The Office for Community Affairs (OCA) website.
66 The Kosovo Agency of Statistics (ASK), 'Kosovo Population and Housing Census 2011. Final Results. Main Data', September 2012, p. 143.
67 GAP Institute for Advanced Studies, 'Population Census Data and Their Impact on Public Policies', October 2012.
68 OSCE, *2010 Kosovo Communities Profiles*, p. 3.
69 ICG, 'Serb Integration in Kosovo: Taking the Plunge', p. 16.
70 Personal interviews with Albanian and Serb civil society representatives, February–June 2012.
71 Personal interview with Nenad Maksimovic.
72 International Foundation for Electoral Systems (IFES), *Post-elections Public Opinion in Kosovo* (Pristina: IFES, 2011), p. 10.

73 Florian Bieber and Sören Keil, 'Power-sharing Revisited: Lessons Learned in the Balkans', *Review of Central and East European Law* 34(4) (2009), pp. 337–360.
74 Personal interview with Sami Kurteshi, Kosovo Ombudsperson, Pristina, Kosovo, 18 May 2012.
75 UNDP Public Pulse Report 4, August 2012, p. 15.
76 Ibid.
77 Ibid., p. 16.
78 Personal interview with Slaviša Mladenović, Serb Community, Language Commissioner, Pristina, 30 May 2013.
79 KIPRED, 'Kosovo Serbs after the Declaration of Independence: The Right Momentum for Confidence Building Measures', July 2008.
80 Roland Gjoni, Anna Wetterberg and David Dunbar, 'Decentralization as a Conflict Transformation Tool: The Challenge in Kosovo', *Public Administration and Development* 30(5) (2010), p. 299.
81 OSCE, *2010 Kosovo Communities Profiles*, p. 21.
82 Ibid., p. 22.
83 Personal interviews with Serb political and civil society representatives, Kosovo, February–June 2012 and March–June 2013.
84 Ibid.
85 Personal interview with Dušan Radaković, Serb Community, Project Officer, NDI, Mitrovica/Mitrovicë North, 5 June 2013
86 IFES, *Post-election Public Opinion in Kosovo*, p. 2.
87 Ibid., p. 3.
88 ICG, 'Serb Integration in Kosovo: Taking the Plunge', p. 14.
89 ICG, 'Setting Kosovo Free: Remaining Challenges', p. 13.
90 Project on Ethnic Relations-Kosovo (PER-K) and Democracy for Development (D4D), 'Boosting Prospects for Young Kosovo Serbs/Urban Life in Kosovo Serb Communities', March 2012.
91 ICG, 'Setting Kosovo Free: Remaining Challenges', p. 1.
92 PER-K and D4D, 'Boosting Prospects for Young Kosovo Serbs', March 2012, p. 17.
93 Personal interview with Nenad Maksimovic.
94 OCA, 'Policy Study No.1: Employment of Members of Non-majority Communities within Kosovo Civil Service and Publicly Owned Enterprises', May 2010, p. 73.
95 Law on the Civil Service of the Republic of Kosovo. Law No. 03/L-149, Article 11.3.
96 ICG, 'Setting Kosovo Free: Remaining Challenges', pp. 13–14.
97 Personal interviews with Kosovo Albanian and Serbian civil society representatives, February–June 2012; Personal interview with Patrick Schmelzer, Policy Office, EU Office, Pristina, Kosovo, 10 May 2012; Personal interview with Chris Decker, Programme Coordinator, UNDP, Pristina, Kosovo, 18 May 2012.
98 IFES, *Post-election Public Opinion in Kosovo*, p. 16.

99 Personal interview with Refik Saciri, deputy minister for the Ministry of European Integration, 28 May 2012.
100 Personal interview with Gjuljeta Mushkolaj, judge at the Constitutional Court and former member of the Constitutional Commission in Kosovo, 25 May 2012.
101 United Nations (UN), 'Lessons Learned in Post-conflict State Capacity: Reconstructing Governance and Public Administration Capacities in Post Conflict Countries', United Nations Department of Economic and Social Affairs, 2007, p. 21.
102 See also UN Department of Economic and Social Development, 'Building Capacities for Public Service in Post-conflict Countries', 2007 and UN, 'United Nations Policy for Post-conflict Employment Creation, Income Generation and Reintegration', 2009.
103 OCA, 'Policy Study No.1', p. 35.
104 Kosovo Government, 'Answers to the Questionnaire on the Preparation of the Feasibility Study for a Stabilisation and Association Agreement', June 2012, p. 42.
105 OCA, 'Policy Study No.1', p. 36.
106 Ibid., p. 36.
107 Forty-four Serbs in the Ministry of Internal Affairs (MIA), twenty-six in the Ministry of Justice, seventeen in the Ministry of Public Administration (MPA), 1.8 per cent in the Ministry of Economy and Finance (MEF), two Serbs in the Ministry of Education, Science and Technology (MEST), only one Serb working in the Ministry of Local Government Administration (MLGA) and one for the Ministry of Environment and Spatial Planning (MESP), no Serbs in the Ministry of Trade and Industry (MTI), the Ministry of Energy and Mining (MEM) or the Ministry of Foreign Affairs (MFA).
108 OCA, 'Policy Study No.1', p. 55.
109 Ibid., p. 60.
110 Ibid., p. 73.
111 Kosovo Government, 'Answers to the Questionnaire', p. 223.
112 PER-K and D4D, 'Boosting Prospects for Young Kosovo Serbs', March 2012, p. 12.
113 UNMIK/REG/2001/19, Section 4(2), September 2001, p. 4.
114 OCA, 'Policy Study No.1', p. 97.
115 Law on the Civil Service of the Republic of Kosovo. Law No. 03/L-149, Article 11(3).
116 See OSCE, 'Community Rights Assessment Report on Kosovo', July 2012; and ECMI Kosovo, 'Perspectives on Local Economic Development in Kosovo's Decentralised Municipalities', June 2012, Pristina, Kosovo.
117 OSCE, *2010 Kosovo Communities Profiles*, pp. 6–8.
118 Ibid.
119 Ibid.
120 Ibid., p. 26.

121 Suzana Andelkovic, advisor Ministry of Communities and Returns, Fushe Kosove, 29 May 2012.
122 PER-K and D4D, 'Boosting Prospects for Young Kosovo Serbs', March 2012.
123 Ibid. and Personal interviews with Kosovo civil society representatives, February–June 2012.
124 Real GDP growth: 2009 (2.9 per cent), 2010 (3.9 per cent), 2011 (5 per cent), 2012 (3.8 per cent est.) and projections: 2013 (4.1 per cent) 2014 (4.6 per cent) – International Monetary Fund (IMF), 'World Economic Outlook: Growth Resuming, Dangers Remain', April 2012, p. 182.
125 World Bank, 'Kosovo's Energy Crisis', World Bank Publications, 1 February 2012.
126 Bertelsmann Stiftung, *BTI 2012- Kosovo Country Report* (Gütersloh: Bertelsmann Stiftung, 2012), p. 15.
127 European Commission, *Kosovo Analytical Report 2012* (Brussels: European Commission, 2012), p. 16,
128 Kosovo Ministry of Culture, Youth and Sports (MCYS), 'Kosovo Youth Strategy and Action Plan 2010–2012', September 2009. Available at http://www.youthpolicy.org/national/Kosovo_2009_Youth_Strategy_Action_Plan.pdf (accessed 1 September 2018).
129 IFES, *Post-election Public Opinion in Kosovo*, p. 7.
130 Central Bank of Kosovo (CBK), 'Annual Report 2011', August 2012.
131 European Commission, EU Enlargement Strategy and Progress Annual Reports (2008–2012).
132 See also UNDOC, 'Corruption in the Western Balkans', Vienna, 2011; USAID, 'Kosovo Strategic Plan 2010–2014', 20 May, 'Setting Kosovo Free: Remaining Challenges', *ICG Report No. 218*, 10 September 2012, Bertelsmann Stiftung, BTI 2012 – Kosovo Country Report.
133 Despite their decline from 17.5 per cent of GDP in 2004 to 13 per cent of GDP in 2010, remittances are vital for Kosovo's economy and thousands of livelihoods. KRHS 2011 data shows that a quarter, 25 per cent of Kosovan households, receives remittances. From UNDP, 'Kosovo Remittance Study', July 2012.
134 OSCE, 'Community Rights Assessment Report on Kosovo'.
135 Office of the Prime Minister, 'Action Plan of the Economic Vision of Kosovo 2011–2014', July 2011.
136 OSCE, 'Community Rights Assessment Report on Kosovo', p. 32.
137 Kosovo Ministry of Labour and Social Welfare, 'Labour and Employment in Kosovo. Annual Report 2011', May 2012.
138 Ibid., p. 15.
139 IFES, *Post-election Public Opinion in Kosovo*, p. 7.
140 Personal interviews with Kosovo MPs, February–June 2012, Pristina, Kosovo.
141 UN, *Lessons Learned in Post-conflict State Capacity: Reconstructing Governance and Public Administration Capacities in Post Conflict Countries* (UN, 2009), p. 21.

142 European Commission, *Feasibility Study on a Stabilisation and Association Agreement between the EU and Kosovo** (Brussels: European Commission, 2012).
143 Council for Inclusive Governance, *The Serb Community in Kosovo. Challenges and Opportunities* (New York: CIG, 2010) and Personal interviews with Serb and Albanian civil society representatives, February–June 2012.
144 Marius-Ionut Calu, 'Unintended Consequences of State-building and the Management of Diversity in Post-conflict Kosovo', *Nationalities Papers* 46(1) (2018), pp. 86–104.

Chapter 4

1 Constitution of the Republic of Kosovo, Chapter IV, Assembly of the Republic of Kosovo, Article 64(2) [Structure of the Assembly].
2 Ibid., Article 148 [Transitional Provisions for the Assembly of Kosovo]: 'Any seats gained through elections shall be in addition to the ten (10) reserved seats allocated to the Kosovo Serb Community and other Communities respectively.'
3 Personal interviews with Serb, Bosniak and Turkish MPs, Pristina, Kosovo, February–June 2013.
4 Constitution of the Republic of Kosovo, Article 96(3) (4) [Ministries and Representation of Communities].
5 Ibid.
6 CCC website.
7 Its chairperson was Goran Marinković, one of the four Serb members in the committee, which had only three other minority representatives: one Roma representative (Albert Kinolli), one Turkish (Müfera Şinik) and one Bosniak (Rasim Demiri).
8 Constitution of the Republic of Kosovo, Article 108(2).
9 Ibid.
10 Personal interviews with Andrea Najvirtova, Project manager at ECMI Kosovo, 10 May 2012. And Suzana Andelkovic, Advisor Ministry of Communities and Return, Fushe Kosove, 29 May 2012.
11 Constitution of the Republic of Kosovo, Article 128(4).
12 Ibid., Article 133(2).
13 Ibid., Article 139(4).
14 ASK, 'Kosovo Population and Housing Census 2011. Final Results. Main Data', p. 143.
15 Ibid.
16 ECMI, *Minority Communities in the 2011 Kosovo Census Results: Analysis and Recommendations* (Pristina: ECMI, December 2012), p. 4.
17 Ibid., p. 5.
18 Ibid.

19   Previous estimates: 1,650.
20   Office for Community Affairs (OCA), 'Overview of Kosovo Communities'.
21   OSCE, 'Kosovo Bosniaks', *2010 Kosovo Communities Profiles*, 2010, p. 3.
22   OCA, 'Overview of Kosovo Communities'.
23   Ibid.
24   OSCE, *2010 Kosovo Communities Profiles*, p. 3.
25   Georgina Stevens, 'Filling the Vacuum: Ensuring Protection and Legal Remedies for Minorities in Kosovo', Minority Rights Group International (MRG), 15 April 2009, p. 8.
26   Clive Baldwin, 'Minority Rights in Kosovo under International Rule', MRG, July 2006, p. 9.
27   OSCE, *2010 Kosovo Communities Profiles*, p. 3.
28   Personal interview with Ćerim Bajrami, Bosniak community.
29   Personal interview with Refik Saciri, Deputy Minister of European Integration, 28 May 2012.
30   Personal interviews with Bosniak representatives, February–June 2012 and March–June 2013.
31   ECMI, *Informational Bulletin*, p. 12: The two VAKAT deputies in the Kosovo Assembly have been Rasim Demiri, who in 2010 won 1,574 votes and Duda Balje with a lower score of 748 votes. The two MPs regained their seats in the 2014 elections, which brought an increase for VAKAT total number of votes to 6,476 (0.89 per cent) in line with the overall increase among for the Bosniak community.
32   Ibid.
33   CEC, 2010 Results of all candidates.
34   CEC, 2010 General results.
35   Personal interview with Ilir Deda, Director of KIPRED, Pristina, 16 March 2012 and Ćerim Bajrami, Bosniak Community, Deputy Minister, Pristina, 28 March 2013.
36   Ibid.
37   Personal interview with Duda Balje, Bosniak Community, MP for VAKAT, Pristina, 5 April 2013.
38   OSCE, *2010 Kosovo Communities Profiles*, p. 7.
39   CEC, 2009 Local elections results.
40   Personal interview with Duda Balje.
41   Personal interview with Mustafa Balje, Bosniak Community, Journalist for RTK, Prizren, 11 April 2013.
42   OSCE, *2010 Kosovo Communities Profiles*, p. 4.
43   Ibid.
44   The Law on the Use of Languages, Law No. 02/L-37, Article 2(4), specifies that in municipalities inhabited by a community whose mother tongue is not one of the official languages of Kosovo and which represents above 3 (three) per cent of

the total population of the municipality, the language of the community shall have the status of a language in official use.
45 Personal interview with Ćerim Bajrami, Bosniak community.
46 Personal interviews with Bosniak representatives, February–June 2012 and March–June 2013.
47 OCA, 'Overview of Kosovo Communities'.
48 Personal interview with Duda Balje, Bosniak Community.
49 UNDP, 'Public Pulse', 2012, p. 31.
50 OSCE, *2010 Kosovo Communities Profiles*, p. 6: According to the numbers provided by the regional employment office in 2010, out of 58,605 persons registered as job seekers, 3,651 were Bosniaks from Prizren, and 1,322 were Bosniaks from Dragash/Dragaš. Furthermore, all Kosovo Bosniaks over 65 years of age receive pensions from Kosovo institutions, while some also receive pensions from parallel institutions financed by Serbia.
51 Ibid., p. 5.
52 OCA, 'Policy Study No.1', p. 70.
53 OSCE, Municipal Profiles, 'Prizren'.
54 Ibid.
55 Ibid.
56 Ibid., p. 10.
57 MRGI website, 'Minorities and Indigenous Peoples in Kosovo' – Bosniaks, March 2018. Available at https://minorityrights.org/minorities/bosniaks-5/ (accessed 1 September 2018).
58 Ibid., p. 8.
59 ASK, Kosovo 2011 Census.
60 OSCE, 'Kosovo Turks', *2010 Kosovo Communities Profiles*, p. 3.
61 Personal interview with Tahir Luma, Turkish Community, Member of CCC, Prizren, 6 April 2013.
62 OSCE, *2010 Kosovo Communities Profiles*, p. 3.
63 Ibid.
64 OCA, 'Overview of Kosovo Communities'.
65 KIPRED, 'Kosovo National Elections 2010: Overview and Trends', p. 8.
66 KDTP website. Available at http://www.kdtp.org/?page_id=5 (accessed 1 September 2018).
67 Ibid.
68 Ibid. and OSCE, 'The Political Entity Brochure', October 2004. Available at www.osce.org/kosovo/38329 (accessed 1 September 2018).
69 CEC, General results 2007.
70 OSCE, 2007 Election results. Available at http://www.osce.org/kosovo/38257 (accessed 1 September 2018).
71 Personal interview with Mahir Yağcilar, Turkish Community, Minister of Public Administration, Pristina, 5 April 2013.

72 ECMI, *Informational Bulletin*, p. 11.
73 OSCE, Municipal Profiles, September 2015. Available at https://www.osce.org/kosovo/66047 (accessed 1 September 2018).
74 Ibid.
75 CEC, 2009 Local elections results.
76 Ibid.
77 OSCE Municipal Profiles.
78 Personal interview with Tahir Luma, Turkish Community, Member of CCC, Prizren, 6 April 2013.
79 Personal interview with Turkish representative, Pristina, 15 May 2012.
80 Personal interview with Tahir Luma.
81 Nazif Mandaci, 'The Turks of Kosovo and the Protection of Minority Culture at the Local Level', *Perceptions* 9(2) (2004), p. 65.
82 OSCE, *2010 Kosovo Communities Profiles*, p. 12.
83 Ibid., p. 8.
84 Personal interviews with Turkish and Albanian civil society representatives, May–June 2013, Prizren, Kosovo.
85 Ibid., p. 4.
86 UNDP, 'Public Pulse Report', 2011, p. 31.
87 Personal interview with Nora Ahmetaj, Director of Centre for Research, Documentation and Publication (CRDP), Pristina, 19 March 2012.
88 OSCE, *2010 Kosovo Communities Profiles*, p. 6.
89 Ibid.
90 Ibid., p. 98.
91 OSCE, *2010 Kosovo Communities Profiles*, p. 6.
92 OSCE, 'Disclaimer for the Sections on Roma, Ashkali and Egyptian communities'.
93 KIPRED, 'Integration of Minority Communities in the Post Status Kosovo', p. 6.
94 Law on Communities, Article 9(2).
95 Constitution of Kosovo, Article 57(3).
96 UNMIK Regulation No. 2001/19 on the Executive Branch of the Provisional Institutions of Self-government in Kosovo.
97 See European Roma Rights Centre, 'Abandoned Minority: Roma Rights History in Kosovo', December 2011, p. 44; Gerlachus Duijzings, *Religion and the Politics of Identity in Kosovo* (London: Hurst & Co., 2000) and the Norwegian Helsinki Committee (NHC), 'Second-class Minorities: The Continued Marginalization of RAE Communities in Kosovo' (NHC, 2007).
98 Ibid.
99 Council of Europe, 'Information Fact Sheets on the History of Ashkali and Egyptians' (CoE, 2010), p. 2. Available at http://www.coe.int/t/dg4/education/ibp/source/FS_1_10.5.pdf (accessed 1 September 2018).
100 NHC, 'Second-class Minorities', p. 7.
101 ERRC, 'Abandoned Minority: Roma Rights History in Kosovo', p. 9.

102 Ibid.
103 Nicolae Gheorghe and Josephine Verspaget, 'Report on the Joint OSCE/ODIHR – Council of Europe Field Mission on the Situation of the Roma in Kosovo' (CoE, 1999). Available at http://www.bndlg.de/~wplarre/na990818b.htm (accessed 1 September 2018).
104 ERRC, 'Abandoned Minority: Roma Rights History in Kosovo', p. 14.
105 ECMI, *Minority Communities in the 2011 Kosovo Census Results*, p. 5.
106 Personal interview with Muhamet Arifi, Ashkali member of CCC, Pristina, 6 March 2012.
107 NHC, 'Second-class Minorities', p. 6.
108 OSCE, *2010 Kosovo Communities Profiles* and OCA, 'Overview of Kosovo Communities'.
109 Personal interview with Lutfi Haziri, LDK MP, Pristina, 8 May 2012.
110 ECMI, *Minority Communities in the 2011 Kosovo Census Results*, p. 5.
111 Ibid.
112 Ibid.
113 OSCE, 'Kosovo Roma', *2010 Kosovo Communities Profiles*, p. 3.
114 OCA, 'Overview of Kosovo Communities'.
115 OSCE, *2010 Kosovo Communities Profiles*, p. 24.
116 Personal interview with Kutjim Pacaku, Roma Community, Member of CCC, Pristina, 3 April 2013.
117 OSCE, *2010 Kosovo Communities Profiles*, p. 16.
118 Kosovo Foundation for Open Society (KFOS), 'The Position of Roma, Ashkali and Egyptian Communities in Kosovo. Baseline Survey' (KFOS, 2009), p. 35.
119 OSCE, 'Implementation of the Action Plan on the Strategy for the Integration of the Roma, Ashkali and Egyptian Communities in Kosovo', 2011.
120 Kosovo Government, Office of the Prime Minister, 'Strategy for the Integration of Roma, Ashkali and Egyptian Communities in the Republic of Kosovo 2009–2015', December 2008. Available at http://kfos.org/wp-content/uploads/2011/10/Strategy-for-the-Integration-of-Roma_-Ashkali-and-Egyptian-Communities-in-the-Republic-of-Kosovo-2009-2015.pdf (accessed 1 September 2018).
121 ERRC, 'Abandoned Minority: Roma Rights History in Kosovo', p. 92.
122 CEC, 2010 General results.
123 ECMI, *Informational Bulletin*, p. 12.
124 CEC, 2009 General results.
125 Personal interview with Daut Qulangjiu, Roma Community, Member of CCC, Prizren, 6 April 2013.
126 OSCE, *2010 Kosovo Communities Profiles*, p. 21.
127 Personal interviews with Kosovo civil society members and Roma representatives, February–June 2012, Pristina, Kosovo; & OSCE Communities Profiles, 'Kosovo Roma'.

128 OSCE, *2010 Kosovo Communities Profiles*, p. 21.
129 ERRC, 'Abandoned Minority: Roma Rights History in Kosovo', p. 44.
130 Personal interview with Albert Kinolli, Roma MP, Pristina, 14 May 2012.
131 OSCE, *2010 Kosovo Communities Profiles*, p. 21
132 The plan introduces concrete measures to improve the representation and participation of the Roma, Ashkali and Egyptian communities in Kosovo society.
133 Personal interview with Besnik Advosoj, Roma Community, Project Coordinator 'Iniciativa 6', Prizren, 10 April 2013.
134 OSCE, *2010 Kosovo Communities Profiles*, p. 5.
135 Ibid., p. 15.
136 OSCE, *2010 Kosovo Communities Profiles*, p. 13.
137 Ibid., p. 5.
138 UNDP, 'Public Pulse Report', 2012, p. 31.
139 OCA, 'Policy Study No.1'.
140 Ibid., p. 85.
141 OSCE, *2010 Kosovo Communities Profiles*, p. 8.
142 ERRC, 'Abandoned Minority: Roma Rights History in Kosovo', p. 67.
143 OSCE, 'Kosovo Ashkali', *2010 Kosovo Communities Profiles*, p. 3.
144 NHC, 'Second-class Minorities', p. 6.
145 OSCE, *2010 Kosovo Communities Profiles*, p. 17.
146 Ibid., p. 19.
147 Ibid., p. 13.
148 Personal interview with Muhamet Arifi.
149 UNDP, 'Public Pulse Report', 2012, p. 31.
150 Ibid., p. 4.
151 Ibid., p. 12.
152 OSCE, *2010 Kosovo Communities Profiles*, p. 7.
153 Ibid.
154 UN, 'Kosovo Statistical Overview' (UNHCR, September 2012), p. 4.
155 OSCE, *2010 Kosovo Communities Profiles*, p. 7.
156 Personal interview with Muhamet Arifi, Ashkali community.
157 'Ashkali community in Ferizaj/Uroševac demands release of Sabit Rrahmani', *Kosova Press*, 22 June 2007.
158 According to the rules of procedure, if a member of the Assembly throughout a period of six months attends none of the sessions of the Assembly or of a committee, of which he/she is a member, and cannot show good cause to the satisfaction of the president of the Assembly, the president shall propose to the Assembly that the member concerned cease to be a member. OSCE, 'Assessment of the work of the Assembly of Kosovo. Compilation of the Monitoring Reports 1 December 2007–31 December 2008', April 2009.
159 CEC, 2010 General results.

160 Ibid.
161 ECMI, *Informational Bulletin*, p. 13.
162 OSCE, Municipal Profiles, 'Ferizaj/Uroševac'.
163 OSCE, Municipal Profiles, 'Fushë Kosovë/Kosovo Polje'.
164 Personal interview with Muhamet Arifi, Ashkali member of CCC, Pristina, 6 March 2012 and OSCE, Communities Profiles, 'Kosovo Ashkali', p. 16.
165 ECMI, *Minority Communities in the 2011 Kosovo Census Results*, p. 6.
166 Elena Marushiakova and Vesselin Popov, 'New Ethnic Identities in the Balkans: The Case of the Egyptians', *Philosophy and Sociology* 2(8) (2001), p. 474.
167 OSCE, 'Kosovo Egyptians', *2010 Kosovo Communities Profiles*, p. 3.
168 Ibid., p. 15.
169 Ibid., p. 11.
170 Ibid., p. 4.
171 UNDP, 'Public Pulse Report', 2012, p. 31.
172 OSCE, *2010 Kosovo Communities Profiles*, p. 3.
173 OCA, 'Policy Study No.1'.
174 OSCE, *2010 Kosovo Communities Profiles*, p. 7.
175 Ibid., p. 8.
176 Kosovo Stability Initiative (IKS), *A Power Primer: A Handbook to Politics, People and Parties in Kosovo* (Pristina, December 2011), p. 83.
177 CEC, 2010 General results.
178 ECMI, *Informational Bulletin*, p. 13.
179 Personal interview with Muhamet Arifi (Ashkali member of CCC), Pristina, 6 March 2012.
180 OSCE, Municipal Profiles, 'Istog/Istok/Istok' and 'Gjakovë/Đakovica'.
181 OSCE, *2010 Kosovo Communities Profiles*, p. 13.
182 ASK, Kosovo 2011 Census.
183 OCA, Communities Profiles.
184 ECMI, *Policy Brief* (December 2012), p. 6.
185 OSCE, 'Kosovo Gorani', *2010 Kosovo Communities Profiles*, p. 3.
186 OCA, Communities Profiles.
187 Ibid.
188 ECMI, *Policy Brief*, p. 6.
189 Personal interview with Murselj Halili, Gorani Community, MP for GIG, Pristina, 4 April 2013.
190 Personal interview with Gazmen Salijevic, Roma community, ECMI Kosovo, Pristina, 29 February 2012.
191 OSCE, *2010 Kosovo Communities Profiles*, p. 3.
192 Personal interview with Murselj Halili.
193 Ibid., p. 10.
194 Ibid., p. 4.

195 UNDP, 'Public Pulse Report', 2012, p. 31.
196 OSCE, *2010 Kosovo Communities Profiles*, p. 4.
197 Ibid.
198 OCA, 'Policy Study No.1', pp. 37–60.
199 OSCE, *2010 Kosovo Communities Profiles*, p. 6.
200 OCA, Communities Profiles.
201 OSCE, 'The Political Entity Brochure', p. 23.
202 CEC, 2010 Elections, General results.
203 Personal interview with Murselj Halili.
204 IKS, *A Power Primer*, p. 66.
205 Ibid., p. 67.
206 ECMI, *Informational Bulletin*, p. 13.
207 OSCE, *2010 Kosovo Communities Profiles*, p. 13.
208 Personal interview with Snežana Karadžić, Montenegrin Community, Political Adviser, Ministry of Local Government Administration (MLGA) and former Member of CCC, Pristina, 3 April 2013.
209 Law No. 04/L-020, December 2011.
210 Personal interviews with Kosovo civil society representatives, Pristina, February–June 2012.
211 ECMI, *Policy Brief*, p. 6.
212 OSCE, Communities Profiles, 'Kosovo Montenegrins', p. 15.
213 Ibid., p. 14.
214 Ibid., p. 3.
215 Ibid.
216 Personal interview with Snežana Karadžić.
217 OSCE, 'Kosovo Montenegrins', *2010 Kosovo Communities Profiles*.
218 Ibid., p. 5.
219 Personal interview with Snežana Karadžić.
220 OSCE, Communities Profiles, 'Kosovo Montenegrins', p. 9.
221 IKS, *A Power Primer*, p. 83.
222 OSCE, Municipalities Profiles, 'Fushë Kosovë/Kosovo Polje'.
223 CEC, 2010 Elections, General results.
224 Ibid.
225 OSCE, 'Kosovo Croats', *2010 Kosovo Communities Profiles*, p. 14.
226 OSCE, *The Kosovo Croats of Viti/Vitina Municipality: A. Vulnerable Community* (OSCE, October 2011), p. 3. Available at http://www.osce.org/kosovo/83789 (accessed 1 September 2018).
227 OSCE, *2010 Kosovo Communities Profiles*, p. 14.
228 Ibid., p. 4.
229 Ibid., p. 10.
230 Ibid., p. 4.

231 OSCE, *The Kosovo Croats*, p. 4.
232 OSCE, *2010 Kosovo Communities Profiles*, p. 5.
233 OSCE, *The Kosovo Croats*, p. 13.
234 OSCE, *2010 Kosovo Communities Profiles*, p. 10.
235 Ibid.

Chapter 5

1   For a recent review of the literature see Dawn Walsh, *Territorial Self-government as a Conflict Management Tool* (Basingstoke: Palgrave Macmillan, 2018) and Soeren Keil and Paul Anderson, 'Decentralization as a Tool of Conflict Resolution' in E. Hepburn and K. Detterbeck (eds), *Handbook of Territorial Politics* (Cheltenham: Edward Elgar, 2018), pp. 89–106.
2   Carothers, 'The End of the Transition Paradigm'.
3   Minority municipalities represent municipalities where the majority of the local population belongs to one of the minority communities.
4   Constitution of Kosovo, 'Local Government and Territorial Organization', Article 123(4).
5   Personal interview with Gjuljeta Mushkolaj, judge at the Constitutional Court and former member of the Constitutional Commission in Kosovo, Pristina, 25 May 2012.
6   Personal interviews with Bosniak representatives.
7   HLC Kosovo, *Decentralization. A Challenging Process* (Pristina: HLC Kosovo, 2011), p. 76.
8   Stacey White, *Government Decentralization in the 21st Century* (Washington: Centre for Strategic and International Studies, December 2011), p. 4.
9   Andrés Rodriguez-Rose and Nicholas Gill, 'The Global Trend towards Devolution and Its Implications', *Environment and Planning C: Government and Policy* 21(3) (2003), p. 337.
10 Ronan Paddison, *The Fragmented State: The Political Geography of Power* (Oxford: Basil Blackwell, 1985), p. 127.
11 See Harry Blair, 'Participation and Accountability at the Periphery: Democratic Local Governance in Six Countries', *World Development* 28(1) (2000), pp. 21–39; Richard C. Crook and James Manor, *Democracy and Decentralization in South Asia and West Africa: Participation, Accountability and Performance* (Cambridge: Cambridge University Press, 1998); William F. Fox, *Fiscal Decentralization in Post-conflict Countries* (Washington, DC: USAID, December 2007); and Christiane Loquai and Sonia Le Bay, 'Building Capacities for Monitoring and Evaluating Decentralization and Local Governance' in *In Brief*, no. 19 (The European Centre for Development Policy Management (ECDPM), December 2007).

12 David Loew, 'Decentralization as a Model of Conflict Transformation: The Case of Kosovo', *CCS Working Papers*, No. 16 (Marburg, 2013), p. 10.
13 Ibid., p. 11.
14 Ibid.
15 Dawn Brancati, *Peace by Design: Managing Intrastate Conflict through Decentralization* (Oxford: Oxford University Press, 2008) and Carrie Manning, 'Local Level Challenges to Post-conflict Peacebuilding', *International Peacekeeping* 10(3) (2003), pp. 25–43.
16 Ibid.
17 Dawn Brancati, 'Decentralization: Fueling the Fire or Dampening the Flames of Ethnic. Conflict and Secessionism?', *International Organization* 60(3) (2006), p. 656.
18 Loew, 'Decentralization as a Model of Conflict Transformation', p. 11.
19 Jean-Pierre Tranchant, 'Decentralization and Ethnic Conflict: The Role of Empowerment' (HAL, 2011), p. 2.
20 Lars Burema, 'Decentralisation in Kosovo: Furthering National Unity of Ethnic Isolation?' in W. Bartlett, S. Maleković and V. Monastiriotis (eds), *Decentralization and Local Development in South East Europe* (Basingstoke: Palgrave Macmillan, 2013), p. 102.
21 György Hajnal and Gábor Péteri, *Local Reform in Kosovo. Final Report* (Forum 2015, 2010), p. 23.
22 Ilija G. Vujacic, 'The Challenges of Ethnic Federalism: Experiences and Lessons of the Former Yugoslavia' in J. Rose and J. Ch. Traut (eds), *Federalism and Decentralization. Perspectives for the Transformation Process in Eastern and Central Europe* (Basingstoke: Palgrave Macmillan, 2002), p. 261.
23 Hajnal and Péteri, *Local Reform in Kosovo. Final Report*, p. 102.
24 Burema, 'Decentralisation in Kosovo', p. 103.
25 Loew, 'Decentralization as a Model of Conflict Transformation', p. 14.
26 Ibid.
27 ICG, 'Kosovo: No Good Alternatives to the Ahtisaari Plan', *Europe Report No. 182*, May 2007, p. 9.
28 Ahtisaari Plan, Annex III. Article 1(1).
29 Personal interviews with Serb political and civil society representatives, February–June 2012 and March–June 2013.
30 Ahtisaari Plan.
31 Ibid., Article 7.
32 Ibid., Article 10(1).
33 Ibid., Article 11.
34 Ibid., Article 12(4).
35 Ibid., Article 123(4).
36 Law on Local Self-government, Chapter II, Article 4(1).
37 Ibid., Article 4(3).

38 Loew, 'Decentralization as a Model of Conflict Transformation', p. 15.
39 Law on Local Self-government, Article 17.
40 Ibid., Article 18(1).
41 Ibid., Article 18(3).
42 Ibid., Article 19(1).
43 Ibid., Article 19(2).
44 Ibid., Article 20–21.
45 Ibid., Article 22(1).
46 Ibid., Article 30.
47 Personal interviews with Serb representatives from Gracanica, Shtërpce/Štrpce and Serb MPs, Pristina, March–June 2013.
48 Law No. 03/L- 049 'On Local Government Finances', Article 2(1).
49 Ibid., Article 6.
50 Ibid., Article 7(1).
51 Law on Local Self-government, Article 54(1), 'In municipalities where at least ten per cent (10 per cent) of the citizens belong to Communities not in the majority in those municipalities, a post of the Chairperson of the Municipal Assembly for Communities shall be reserved for a representative of these communities.'
52 Ibid., Article 55.
53 Ibid., Article 61(4).
54 Ibid., Article 53(2).
55 OSCE, *Protection and Promotion of the Rights of Communities in Kosovo: Local-level Participation Mechanisms* (OSCE, December 2010), p. 30.
56 Loew, 'Decentralization as a Model of Conflict Transformation', p. 19.
57 Ibid.
58 Law No. 03/L-041, 'On Administrative Municipal Borders'.
59 Law, 'On Administrative Municipal Borders', Article 12.
60 Loew, 'Decentralization as a Model of Conflict Transformation', p. 15.
61 Ibid., p. 16, and Personal interviews with representatives of non-Serb minorities, Kosovo, February–June 2012 and March–June 2013.
62 Loew, 'Decentralization as a Model of Conflict Transformation', p. 16.
63 Misha Savic, 'EU Urged to Back Serbia and Kosovo as They Mull Border Change', *Bloomberg*, 26 August 2018.
64 Loew, 'Decentralization as a Model of Conflict Transformation', p. 16.
65 HLC, *Decentralization. A Challenging Process*, pp. 73–75 and personal interviews with political and civil society representatives from both minority and majority communities, Kosovo, February–June 2012 and March–June 2013.
66 Ibid., p. 75.
67 Loew, 'Decentralization as a Model of Conflict Transformation', p. 18.
68 Ibid., p. 22.

69 Ibid.
70 Besnik Tahiri, *Decentralization a Heavy Weight to Be Carried Out* (Pristina: Friedrich-Ebert-Stiftung, July 2011), p. 31.
71 Loew, 'Decentralization as a Model of Conflict Transformation', p. 16 and personal interviews with representatives of all minority communities.
72 Ibid.
73 Hajnal and Péteri, *Local Reform in Kosovo. Final Report*, p. 55.
74 Personal interviews with civil society representatives from both minority and majority communities, Kosovo, February–June 2012 and March–June 2013.
75 Loew, 'Decentralization as a Model of Conflict Transformation', p. 17.
76 HLC, *Decentralization. A Challenging Process*, p. 80, and OSCE, Municipal Profiles, 'Gračanica/Graçanicë'.
77 ASK, Kosovo 2011 Census.
78 OSCE, Municipal Profiles, 'Gračanica/Graçanicë'.
79 Ministry of Local Government Administration (MLGA), *Progress Report on Implementation of Decentralization in the Republic of Kosovo* (Pristina: MLGA, 2012), p. 28.
80 Tahiri, *Decentralization a Heavy Weight to Be Carried Out*, p. 11; MLGA, *Progress Report*; KIPRED, 'Decentralization in Kosovo I: Municipal Elections and the Serb Participation', July 2009.
81 HLC, *Decentralization. A Challenging Process*, p. 80.
82 Graçanicë/Gracanica municipality official website. Available at https://kk.rks-gov.net/gracanice/en/ (accessed 1 September 2018).
83 MLGA, *Progress Report*, p. 28.
84 HLC, *Decentralization. A Challenging Process*, p. 81.
85 MLGA, *Progress Report*, p. 30.
86 Tahiri, *Decentralization a Heavy Weight to Be Carried Out*, p. 11.
87 OSCE, Municipal Profiles, 'Gračanica/Graçanicë'.
88 HLC, *Decentralization. A Challenging Process*, p. 82.
89 OSCE, Municipal Profiles, 'Gračanica/Graçanicë'.
90 Tahiri, *Decentralization a Heavy Weight to Be Carried Out*, p. 11.
91 HLC, *Decentralization. A Challenging Process*, p. 83.
92 Ibid.
93 Ibid.
94 HLC, *Decentralization. A Challenging Process*, p. 83.
95 Personal interviews with Serb political and civil society representatives, Kosovo, February–June 2012 and March–June 2013.
96 OSCE, Municipal Profiles, 'Gračanica/Graçanicë'.
97 Ibid.
98 CEC, Local Elections 2013, Statistics based on Municipalities for Mayors.

99 Ibid.
100 Kosovo Local Government Institute (KLGI), *Municipalities from Elections to Solutions* (Pristina: KLGI, February 2018).
101 OSCE, Municipal Profiles, 'Ranilug/Ranillug'.
102 HLC, *Decentralization. A Challenging Process*, p. 86.
103 OSCE, Municipal Profiles, 'Ranilug/Ranillug'.
104 Ibid.
105 Tahiri, *Decentralization a Heavy Weight to Be Carried Out* and HLC, *Decentralization. A Challenging Process* and MLGA, *Progress Report*.
106 Tahiri, *Decentralization a Heavy Weight to Be Carried Out*, p. 12.
107 Loew, 'Decentralization as a Model of Conflict Transformation', p. 19.
108 Tahiri, *Decentralization a Heavy Weight to Be Carried Out*, p. 12.
109 MLGA, *Progress Report*, p. 32.
110 Personal interviews with political and civil society representatives from both minority and majority communities, Kosovo, February–June 2012 and March–June 2013.
111 HLC, *Decentralization. A Challenging Process*, p. 87.
112 OSCE, Municipal Profiles, 'Ranilug/Ranillug'.
113 Balkan Policy Institute (IPOL), *Building New Municipalities* (Pristina: IPOL, November 2011), p. 11.
114 Tahiri, *Decentralization a Heavy Weight to Be Carried Out*, p. 13.
115 HLC, *Decentralization. A Challenging Process*, p. 86.
116 IPOL, *Building New Municipalities*, p. 10.
117 OSCE, Municipal Profiles, 'Ranilug/Ranillug'.
118 Ibid.
119 Ibid.
120 HLC, *Decentralization. A Challenging Process*, p. 88.
121 Tahiri, *Decentralization a Heavy Weight to Be Carried Out*, p. 13.
122 CEC, Local Elections 2013, Statistics based on Municipalities for Mayors.
123 Ibid.
124 ECMI, *Kosovo Local Elections 2013*.
125 KLGI, *Municipalities from Elections to Solutions*.
126 OSCE, Municipal Profiles, 'Klokot/Kllokot'.
127 Tahiri, *Decentralization a Heavy Weight to Be Carried Out*.
128 OSCE, Municipal Profiles, 'Klokot/Kllkot'.
129 Tahiri, *Decentralization a Heavy Weight to be Carried Out*, p. 13.
130 HLC, *Decentralization. A Challenging Process*, p. 90.
131 Loew, 'Decentralization as a Model of Conflict Transformation', p. 19.
132 HLC, *Decentralization. A Challenging Process*, p. 91.
133 Ibid., p. 92.

134 OSCE, Municipal Profiles, 'Klokot/Kllokot'.
135 Ibid.
136 HLC, *Decentralization. A Challenging Process*, p. 93.
137 OSCE, Municipal Profiles, 'Klokot/Kllokot'.
138 MLGA, *Progress Report*, p. 34.
139 HLC, *Decentralization. A Challenging Process*, p. 91.
140 Tahiri, *Decentralization a Heavy Weight to Be Carried Out*, p. 14.
141 Ibid., p. 15.
142 HLC, *Decentralization. A Challenging Process*, p. 90.
143 OSCE, Municipal Profiles, 'Klokot/Kllokot'.
144 Ibid.
145 Ibid.
146 CEC, Local Elections 2013, Statistics based on Municipalities for Mayors.
147 Ibid.
148 ECMI, *Kosovo Local Elections 2013*, p. 6.
149 New Social Initiative (NSI), *Report on Local Elections 2017* (NSI, June 2018).
150 OSCE, Municipal Profiles, 'Parteš/Partesh'.
151 Ibid and MLGA, *Progress Report*, p. 34.
152 OSCE, Municipal Profiles, 'Parteš/Partesh'.
153 Tahiri, *Decentralization a Heavy Weight to Be Carried Out*, p. 15.
154 Helsinki Committee for Human Rights (HCHR) in Serbia, *Serb Community in Kosovo* (Helsinki Committee, June 2012), p. 34.
155 Ibid.
156 OSCE, Municipal Profiles, 'Parteš/Partesh'.
157 MLGA, *Progress Report*, p. 35.
158 Ibid.
159 OSCE, Municipal Profiles, 'Parteš/Partesh'.
160 Ibid.
161 Ibid.
162 ECMI, *Kosovo Local Elections 2013*.
163 CEC, Local Elections 2013, Statistics based on Municipalities for Mayors.
164 Ibid.
165 ECMI, *Kosovo Local Elections 2013*.
166 Ibid.
167 NSI, *Report on Local Elections 2017*.
168 Ibid.
169 Helsinki Committee, *Serb Community in Kosovo*, p. 60.
170 OSCE, Municipal Profiles, 'Novo Brdo/Novobërdë'.
171 Ibid.
172 Tahiri, *Decentralization a Heavy Weight to Be Carried Out*, p. 16.

173 Ibid., p. 15.
174 OSCE, Municipal Profiles, 'Novo Brdo/Novobërdë'.
175 Helsinki Committee, *Serb Community in Kosovo*, p. 62.
176 Ibid., p. 61.
177 OSCE, Municipal Profiles, 'Novo Brdo/Novobërdë'.
178 Tahiri, *Decentralization a Heavy Weight to Be Carried Out*, p. 16.
179 OSCE, Municipal Profiles, 'Novo Brdo/Novobërdë'.
180 CEC, Local Elections 2013, Statistics based on Municipalities for Mayors.
181 Ibid.
182 ECMI, *Kosovo Local Elections 2013*.
183 NSI, *Report on Local Elections 2017*.
184 OSCE, Municipal Profiles, 'Štrpce/Shtërpcë'.
185 Ibid.
186 ICG, *Kosovo: Štrpce, a Model Serb Enclave?* (Pristina/Brussels: ICG, October 2009), p. 2.
187 Ibid., p. 1.
188 Loew, 'Decentralization as a Model of Conflict Transformation', p. 19.
189 Helsinki Committee, *Serb Community in Kosovo*, p. 51.
190 OSCE, Municipal Profiles, 'Štrpce/Shtërpcë'.
191 Helsinki Committee, *Serb Community in Kosovo*, p. 51.
192 OSCE, Municipal Profiles, 'Štrpce/Shtërpcë'.
193 KIPRED, 'Decentralization in Kosovo I', p. 11.
194 Ibid.
195 Ibid.
196 CEC, Local Elections 2013, Statistics based on Municipalities for Mayors.
197 Ibid.
198 ECMI, *Kosovo Local Elections 2013*.
199 NSI, *Report on Local Elections 2017*.
200 OSCE, *From Pilot Municipal Units to Fully Fledged Municipalities: First Year Review* (OSCE, March 2010), p. 5.
201 OSCE, Municipal Profiles, 'Mamuşa/Mamushë/Mamuša'.
202 OSCE, *From Pilot Municipal Units to Fully Fledged Municipalities* and USAID, *Kosovo Municipalities Competitiveness Index Reports* (USAID, 2011 and 2012).
203 OSCE, *From Pilot Municipal Units to Fully Fledged Municipalities*, p. 16.
204 OSCE, Municipal Profiles, 'Mamuşa/Mamushë/Mamuša'.
205 USAID, *Kosovo Municipalities Competitiveness Index Report* (2011), p. 20.
206 Ibid., p. 7.
207 Ibid., p. 12.
208 USAID, *Kosovo Municipalities Competitiveness Index Report* (2012), p. 41.

209 Personal interviews with civil society representatives from both minority and majority communities *and* with representatives of international actors from the EU Office, UNDP, OSCE, Kosovo, February–June 2012 and March–June 2013.
210 OSCE, Municipal Profiles, 'Mamuşa/Mamushë/Mamuša'.
211 Ibid.
212 Personal interviews with civil society representatives from the Turkish community, Kosovo, April–June 2013.
213 Ibid.
214 ECMI, *Kosovo Local Elections 2013*.
215 Ibid.
216 KLGI, *Municipalities from Elections to Solutions*.
217 The Constitutional Court of the Republic of Kosovo, Judgment Case No. KO 01/09, 'Cemailj Kurtisi and the Municipal Assembly of Prizren', Pristina, 18 March 2010. Available at http://eudo-citizenship.eu/caselawDB/docs/KOS per cent2001 per cent2009 per cent20vendimi per cent20(English).pdf (accessed 1 September 2018).
218 OSCE, Municipal Profiles, 'Prizren'
219 Ibid.
220 Ibid.
221 Ibid.
222 Article 2(3) of the Law on the Use of Languages.
223 Judgment Case No. KO 01/09.
224 Nicolas Mansfield, *Creating a Constitutional Court: Lessons from Kosovo* (East–West Management Institute, 2013), p. 9.
225 Judgment Case No. KO 01/09, p. 4.
226 Ibid., p. 13.
227 Ibid., p. 14.
228 Mansfield, *Creating a Constitutional Court*, p. 10.
229 Ibid., p. 10.
230 OSCE, Municipal Profiles, 'Prizren'.
231 Personal interview with Bariu Zenelaj, Executive Director, Academy for Trainings and Technical Assistance (ATTA), Prizren, 8 June 2013.
232 ECMI, *Kosovo Local Elections 2013*.
233 Ibid.
234 KLGI, *Municipalities from Elections to Solutions*.
235 OSCE, Municipal Profiles, 'Prizren'.
236 Ibid.
237 Ibid.
238 Loew, 'Decentralization as a Model of Conflict Transformation', p. 18 and Personal interviews with minority representatives, Prizren, April–June 2013.
239 Ibid., p. 19.

Conclusion

1 Migdal, *State in Society*, p. 250.
2 Montserrat Guibernau, *Belonging: Solidarity and Division in Modern Societies* (Cambridge: Polity Press, 2013), p. 6.

Bibliography

Arel, Dominique, 'Political Stability in Multinational Democracies Comparing Language Dynamics in Brussels, Montreal and Barcelona' in A.-G Gagnon and J. Tully (eds), *Multinational Democracies* (Cambridge: Cambridge University Press, 2001), pp. 65–89.

Bailey, Faith, 'Kosovo Forms New Government', *Prishtina Insight*, 9 September 2017.

Baldwin, Clive, 'Minority Rights in Kosovo under International Rule', MRG, July 2006.

Barnett, Michael, 'Building a Republican Peace: Stabilizing States after War', *International Security* 30(4) (2006), pp. 87–112.

Barnett, Michael, Kim, Hunjoon, O'Donnell, Madalene and Sitea, Laura, 'Peacebuilding: What Is in a Name?', *Global Governance* 13(1) (2007), pp. 35–58.

Bertelsmann Stiftung, *BTI 2012 – Kosovo Country Report* (Gütersloh: Bertelsmann Stiftung, 2012).

Bertrand, Jacques and Haklai, Oded, 'Democratization and Ethnic Minorities' in J. Bertrand and O. Haklai (eds), *Democratization and Ethnic Minorities: Conflict or Compromise?* (New York: Routledge, 2014), pp. 103–129.

Bickerton, Christopher, 'State-building: Exporting State Failure' in C. Bickerton, P. Cunliffe and A. Gourevitch (eds), *Politics without Sovereignty. A Critique of Contemporary International Relations* (London: UCL Press, 2007), pp. 93–111.

Bieber, Florian, 'Power Sharing after Yugoslavia. Functionality and Dysfunctionality of Power Sharing Institutions in Post-war Bosnia, Macedonia and Kosovo' in S. Noel (ed), *From Power-sharing to Democracy: Post Conflict Institutions in Ethnically Divided Societies* (Montreal: McGill Queens University Press, 2005), pp. 85–103.

Bieber, Florian, 'Power Sharing and Democracy in Southeast Europe', *Taiwan Journal of Democracy*, Special Issue (2013), pp. 129–148.

Bieber, Florian and Keil, Sören, 'Power-sharing Revisited: Lessons Learned in the Balkans', *Review of Central and East European Law* 34(4) (2009), pp. 337–360.

BIRN, 'Kosovo to Recognize Montenegrin Minority', *Balkan Insight*, 2 November 2012.

Blair, Harry, 'Participation and Accountability at the Periphery: Democratic Local Governance in Six Countries', *World Development* 28(1) (2000), pp. 21–39.

Boege, Volker, Brown, M. Anne, Clements, Kevin P. and Nolan, Anna, 'On Hybrid Political Orders and Emerging States: State Formation in the Context of "Fragility"', in *Berghof Handbook Dialogue* (8) (Berlin: Berghof Research Center for Constructive Conflict Management, 2008), pp. 15–35.

Bogaards, Matthijs, 'Electoral Choices for Divided Societies: Moderation through Constituency Pooling and Vote Pooling', *ECPR Joint Sessions Institute of Political Studies* (Grenoble 6–11 April 2001).

Bojicic-Dzelilovic, Vesna, Ker-Lindsay, James and Kostovicova, Denisa, 'Introduction: Civil Society and Multiple Transitions – Meanings, Actors and Effects' in D. Kostovicova and V. Bojicic-Dzelilovic (eds), *Civil Society and Transitions in the Western Balkans. New Perspectives on South-east Europe* (Basingstoke: Palgrave Macmillan, 2013), pp. 1–25.

Brajshori, Muhamet and Tërnava, Granit, *The Republic of Kosovo's 2013 Local Elections Handbook* (Berlin: Konrad-Adenauer-Stiftung, 2013).

Brancati, Dawn, 'Decentralization: Fueling the Fire or Dampening the Flames of Ethnic. Conflict and Secessionism?', *International Organization* 60(3) (2006), pp. 651–685.

Brancati, Dawn, *Peace by Design: Managing Intrastate Conflict through Decentralization* (Oxford: Oxford University Press, 2008).

Briscoe, Ivan and Price, Megan, *Kosovo's New Map of Power: Governance and Crime in the Wake of Independence*, Clingendael Institute, 3 May 2011.

Burema, Lars, 'Decentralisation in Kosovo: Furthering National Unity of Ethnic Isolation?' in W. Bartlett, S. Maleković and V. Monastiriotis (eds), *Decentralization and Local Development in South East Europe* (Basingstoke: Palgrave Macmillan, 2013), pp. 100–117.

Buzan, Barry, 'The Consociational Model and Its Dangers', *European Journal for Political Research* 3(4) (1975), pp. 393–412.

Buzan, Barry, *People, States, and Fear: An Agenda for International Security Studies in the Post–Cold War Era*, 2nd ed. (Colchester: ECPR Press, 2007).

Call, Charles T., 'The Fallacy of the "Failed State"', *Third World Quarterly* 29(8) (2008), pp. 1491–1507.

Calu, Marius, 'Unintended Consequences of State-building and the Management of Diversity in Post-conflict Kosovo', *Nationalities Papers* 46(1) (2018), pp. 86–104.

Caplan, Richard, *International Governance of War-torn Territories: Rule and Reconstruction* (Oxford: Oxford University Press, 2005).

Carothers, Thomas, 'The End of the Transition Paradigm', *Journal of Democracy* 13(1) (2002), pp. 5–21.

Caspersen, Nina, *Unrecognized States: The Struggle for Sovereignty in the Modern International System* (Cambridge: Polity, 2012).

Central Bank of Kosovo (CBK), 'Annual Report 2011', August 2012.

Chandler, David, 'The Problems of "Nation-building": Imposing Bureaucratic "Rule from Above"', *Cambridge Review of International Affairs* 17(3) (2004), pp. 577–591.

Chandler, David, *Empire in Denial: The Politics of State-building* (London: Pluto 2006).

Chandler, David, 'What Do We Do When We Critique Liberalism? The Uncritical Critique of Liberal Peace', *Review of International Studies* 36(1) (2009), pp. 137–155.

Chandler, David, *International Statebuilding. The Rise of Post-liberal Governance* (Oxon: Routledge, 2010).

Chandra, Kanchan, 'Ethnic Parties and Democratic Stability', *Perspectives on Politics* 3(2) (2005), pp. 235–252.

Choudhry, Sujit, 'Bridging Comparative Politics and Comparative Constitutional Law: Constitutional Design in Divided Societies' in S. Choudhry (ed), *Constitutional Design for Divided Societies. Integration of Accommodation?* (Oxford: Oxford University Press, 2008), pp. 3–41.

Christiane, Loquai and Le Bay, Sonia, 'Building Capacities for Monitoring and Evaluating Decentralization and Local Governance' in *In Brief*, no. 19 (The European Centre for Development Policy Management (ECDPM), December 2007).

Clapham, Christopher, *Africa and the International System: The Politics of State Survival* (New York: Cambridge University Press, 1996).

Coggins, Bridget, *Power Politics and State Formation in the Twentieth Century: The Dynamics of Recognition* (New York: Cambridge University Press, 2014).

Council for Inclusive Governance, *The Serb Community in Kosovo. Challenges and Opportunities* (New York: CIG, 2010).

Council for Inclusive Governance, 'Serbs in Kosovo's Institutions', February 2012.

Council of Europe, 'Information Fact Sheets on the History of Ashkali and Egyptians' (CoE, 2010). Available at http://www.coe.int/t/dg4/education/ibp/source/FS_1_10.5.pdf (accessed 1 September 2018).

Crawford, Timothy W., 'Pivotal Deterrence and the Kosovo War: Why the Holbrooke Agreement Failed', *Political Science Quarterly* 116(4) (2001), pp. 499–523.

Crook, Richard C. and Manor, James, *Democracy and Decentralization in South Asia and West Africa: Participation, Accountability and Performance* (Cambridge: Cambridge University Press, 1998).

Deda, Ilir, *Kosovo after the Brussels Agreement: From Status Quo to an Internally Ethnically Divided State* (Pristina: Konrad-Adenauer-Stiftung, 2013).

Democracy for Development (D4D), 'Boosting Prospects for Young Kosovo Serbs/ Urban Life in Kosovo Serb Communities', March 2012.

Dodge, Toby, 'Iraq: The Contradictions of Exogenous State-building in Historical Perspective', *Third World Quarterly* 27(1) (2006), pp. 187–200.

Domanovic, Milka, 'List of Kosovo War Victims Published', *BIRN*, 4 December 2014.

Duijzings, Gerlachus, *Religion and the Politics of Identity in Kosovo* (London: Hurst & Co., 2000).

ECMI, *Special Report: Community Political Parties and Government Formation* (Pristina: ECMI, February 2011).

ECMI, *Perspectives on Local Economic Development in Kosovo's Decentralised Municipalities* (Pristina: ECMI, June 2012).

ECMI, *Minority Communities in the 2011 Kosovo Census Results: Analysis and Recommendations* (Pristina: ECMI, December 2012).

ECMI, *Kosovo Local Elections – Which Self-government for Minority Communities?* (Pristina: ECMI, November 2013).

ECMI, *Kosovo Local Elections 2013: Lessons Learnt for Minority Communities. A Short Analysis* (Pristina: ECMI, December 2013).

ECMI, *Minority Communities' Political Parties in Kosovo's Changing Political Landscape: the General Elections of June 2014 and Their Aftermath* (Pristina: ECMI, July 2014).

Economides, Spyros, 'Kosovo' in M. Berdal and S. Economides (eds), *United Nations Interventionism, 1991–2004* (Cambridge: Cambridge University Press, 2007), pp. 217–245.

Egnell, Robert and Halden, Peter, 'Introduction: The Need for New Agendas in Statebuilding' in R. Egnell and P. Halden (eds), *New Agendas in Statebuilding: Hybridity, Contingency, and History* (London: Routledge, 2013), pp. 1–11.

The European Centre for Minority Issues Kosovo (ECMI Kosovo), *Strengthening the Institutional System for Communities in Post-independence Kosovo* (Pristina: ECMI, January 2009).

European Commission, *Communication from the European Commission on the Subject of the Enlargement Strategy* (Brussels: EU Commission, 2007).

European Commission, *EU Enlargement Strategy and Progress Annual Reports* (2008–2012).

European Commission, *Feasibility Study on a Stabilisation and Association Agreement between the EU and Kosovo** (Brussels: European Commission, 2012).

European Commission, *Kosovo Analytical Report 2012* (Brussels: European Commission, 2012).

European Roma Rights Centre (ERRC), 'Abandoned Minority: Roma Rights History in Kosovo', December 2011. Available at http://www.errc.org/cms/upload/file/abandoned-minority-roma-rights-history-in-kosovo-dec-2011.pdf (accessed 1 September 2018).

European Union Election Expert Mission (EU EEM), 'Final Report of the European Union Election Expert Mission to Kosovo', 25 January 2011.

Ezrow, Natasha and Frantz, Erica, *Failed States and Institutional Decay: Understanding Instability and Poverty in the Developing World* (New York: Bloomsbury Academic, 2013).

Fox, William F., *Fiscal Decentralization in Post-conflict Countries* (Washington, DC: USAID, December 2007).

Gadzo, Mersiha 'Are Ethnic Borders Being Drawn for a "Greater Serbia"?', *Al Jazeera News*, 10 August 2018.

GAP Institute for Advanced Studies, 'Population Census Data and Their Impact on Public Policies', October 2012.

Gerdes, Felix, *Civil War and State Formation – The Political Economy of War and Peace in Liberia* (Frankfurt: Campus Verlag, 2013).

Ghani, Ashraf and Lockhart, Clare, *Fixing Failed States: A Framework for Rebuilding a Fractured World* (Oxford: Oxford University Press, 2008).

Gheorghe, Nicolae and Verspaget, Josephine, 'Report on the Joint OSCE/ODIHR – Council of Europe Field Mission on the Situation of the Roma in Kosovo' (CoE, 1999). Available at http://www.bndlg.de/~wplarre/na990818b.htm (accessed 1 September 2018).

Gjoni, Roland, Wetterberg, Anna and Dunbar, David, 'Decentralization as a Conflict Transformation Tool: The Challenge in Kosovo', *Public Administration and Development* 30(5) (2010), pp. 291–312.

Glasius, Marlies and Kostovicova, Denisa, 'The European Union as a State-builder: Policies towards Serbia and Sri Lanka', *Südosteuropa* 56(1) (2008), pp. 84–114.

Grovogui, Siba N., *Sovereigns, Quasi-sovereigns, and Africans: Race and Self-determination in International Law* (Minneapolis: University of Minnesota Press, 1996).

Guibernau, Montserrat, 'Between Autonomy and Secession: The Accommodation of Minority Nationalism' in A.-G. Gagnon, M. Guibernau and F. Rocher (eds), *The Conditions of Diversity in Multinational Democracies* (Montreal: IRPP-McGill University Press, 2003), pp. 115–134.

Guibernau, Montserrat, *Belonging: Solidarity and Division in Modern Societies* (Cambridge: Polity Press, 2013).

Gurr, Ted Robert, 'Minorities, Nationalists, and Islamists' in Crocker et al. (eds), *Leashing the Dogs of War: Conflict Management in a Divided World* (Washington, DC: United States Institute of Peace Press, 2007), pp. 131–160.

Guzina, Dejan and Marijan, Branka, 'A Fine Balance: The EU and the Process of Normalizing Kosovo-Serbia Relations', CIGI papers, no. 23 January 2014.

Hagmann, Tobias and Hoehne, Markus V., 'Failures of the State Failure Debate: Evidence from the Somali Territories', *Journal of International Development* 21(1) (2009), pp. 42–57.

Hajnal, György and Péteri, Gábor, *Local Reform in Kosovo. Final Report* (Forum 2015, 2010).

Hehir, Aidan, 'Introduction: Kosovo and the International Community' in A. Hehir (ed), *Kosovo, Intervention and Statebuilding: The International Community and the Transition to Independence* (London: Routledge, 2010), pp. 1–16.

Hehir, Aidan, *Kosovo, Intervention and Statebuilding: The International Community and the Transition to Independence* (London: Routledge, 2010).

Helsinki Committee for Human Rights (HCHR) in Serbia, *Serb Community in Kosovo* (Helsinki Committee, June 2012).

Horowitz, Donald L., *Ethnic Groups in Conflict* (Berkeley: University of California Press, 1985).

Horowitz, Donald L., *A Democratic South Africa? Constitutional. Engineering in a Divided Society* (Berkeley: University of California Press, 1991), pp. 137–145.

Horowitz, Donald L., 'Democracy in Divided Societies', *Journal of Democracy* 4(4) (1993), pp. 18–38.

Horowitz, Donald L., 'Constitutional Design: Proposals versus Processes' in A. Reynolds (ed), *The Architecture of Democracy: Constitutional Design, Conflict Management and Democracy* (Oxford: Oxford University Press, 2002), pp. 15–36.

Humanitarian Law Center (HLC), *Decentralization. A Challenging Process* (Pristina: HLC Kosovo, 2011).

Humanitarian Law Center (HLC), 'The Beginning of Implementation of the Law on the Promotion and Protection of Rights of Communities and Their Members in the Republic of Kosovo', December 2012.

Ignatieff, Michael, *Empire Lite: Nation Building in Bosnia, Kosovo and Afghanistan* (London: Vintage, 2003).

International Crisis Group (ICG), 'Collapse in Kosovo', *Europe Report No. 155*, April 2004.

International Crisis Group (ICG), 'Kosovo: No Good Alternatives to the Ahtisaari Plan', *Europe Report No. 182*, May 2007.

International Crisis Group (ICG), 'Serb Integration in Kosovo: Taking the Plunge', *Report No. 200*, 12 May 2009.

International Crisis Group (ICG), *Kosovo: Štrpce, a Model Serb Enclave?* (Pristina/Brussels: ICG, October 2009).

International Crisis Group (ICG), 'Setting Kosovo Free: Remaining Challenges', *Report No. 218*, 10 September 2012.

International Foundation for Electoral Systems (IFES), *Post-elections Public Opinion in Kosovo* (Pristina: IFES, 2011).

International Monetary Fund (IMF), 'World Economic Outlook: Growth Resuming, Dangers Remain', April 2012.

Jackson, Robert H. and Rosberg, Carl G., 'Why Africa's Weak States Persist: The Empirical and the Juridical in Statehood', *World Politics* 35(1) (1982), pp. 1–24.

Jackson, Robert H. and Rosberg, Carl G., *Quasi-states: Sovereignty, International Relations and the Third Word* (Cambridge: Cambridge University Press, 1990).

Judah, Tim, *Kosovo: War and Revenge*, 2nd ed. (New Haven, CT: Yale University Press, 2002).

KDTP website. Available at http://www.kdtp.org/?page_id=5 (accessed 1 September 2018).

Keating, Michael, 'So Many Nations, So Few States: Territory and Nationalism in the Global Era' in A.-G. Gagnon and J. Tully (eds), *Multinational Democracies* (Cambridge: Cambridge University Press, 2001), pp. 39–64.

Keil, Soeren and Paul, Anderson, 'Decentralization as a Tool of Conflict Resolution' in E. Hepburn and K. Detterbeck (eds), *Handbook of Territorial Politics* (Cheltenham: Edward Elgar, 2018), pp. 89–107.

Keller, Edmond J. and Rothschild, Donald, *Africa in New International Order: Rethinking. State Sovereignty and Regional Security* (Boulder, CO: Lynne Rienner, 1996).

Ker-Lindsay, James, *Kosovo: The Path to Contested Statehood in the Balkans* (London: I.B.Tauris, 2009).

Ker-Lindsay, James and Economides, Spyros, 'Standards before Status before Accession: Kosovo's EU Perspective', *Journal of Balkan and Near Eastern Studies* 14(1) (2012), pp. 77–92.

Korenica, Fisnik and Doli, Dren, 'Constitutional Rigidity in Kosovo: Relevance, Outcomes and Rationale', *Pace International Law Review* 2(6) (2011), pp. 4–22.

Kosovar Institute for Policy Research and Development (KIPRED), *Integration of Minority Communities in the Post-status Kosovo* (Pristina: KIPRED, 2006).

Kosovar Institute for Policy Research and Development (KIPRED), 'Kosovo Serbs after the Declaration of Independence: The Right Momentum for Confidence Building Measures', July 2008.

Kosovar Institute for Policy Research and Development (KIPRED), 'Decentralization in Kosovo I: Municipal Elections and the Serb Participation', December 2009.

Kosovar Institute for Policy Research and Development (KIPRED), 'Kosovo National Elections 2010: Overview and Trends', April 2011.

The Kosovo Agency of Statistics (ASK), 'Kosovo Population and Housing Census 2011. Final Results. Main Data', September 2012.

Kosovo Agency of Statistics (ASK), Kosovo 2011 Census. Available at http://ask.rks-gov.net/media/2129/estimation-of-kosovo-population-2011.pdf (accessed 1 September 2018).

Kosovo Central Electoral Commission (CEC). Available at http://www.kqz-ks.org (accessed 1 September 2018).

Kosovo Foundation for Open Society (KFOS), 'The Position Of Roma, Ashkali And Egyptian Communities In Kosovo. Baseline Survey' (KFOS, 2009).

Kosovo Government, Office of the Prime Minister, 'Strategy for the Integration of Roma, Ashkali and Egyptian Communities in the Republic of Kosovo 2009–2015', December 2008.

Kosovo Government, Office of the Prime Minister, 'Action Plan of the Economic Vision of Kosovo 2011–2014', July 2011.

Kosovo Government, 'Answers to the Questionnaire on the Preparation of the Feasibility Study for a Stabilisation and Association Agreement', June 2012.

Kosovo Ministry of Culture, Youth and Sports (MCYS), 'Kosovo Youth Strategy and Action Plan 2010–2012', September 2009.

Kosovo Ministry of Labour and Social Welfare, 'Labour and Employment in Kosovo. Annual Report 2011', May 2012.

Kosovo Stability Initiative (IKS), *A Power Primer: A Handbook to Politics, People and Parties in Kosovo* (Pristina, December 2011).

Kostovicova, Denisa, *Kosovo: The Politics of Identity and* Space (London: Routledge, 2005).

Kostovicova, Denisa, 'State Weakness in the Western Balkans as a Security Threat: The European Union Approach and a Global Perspective', *Western Balkans Security Observer* 2(7–8) (2007), pp. 10–15.

Kostovicova, Denisa and Bojicic-Dzelilovic, Vesna (eds), *Persistent State Weakness in the Global Age* (London: Ashgate, 2009).

Krasner, Stephen D., *Sovereignty: Organized Hypocrisy* (Princeton, NJ: Princeton University Press, 1999).

Krasniqi, Gëzim, 'Equal Citizens, Uneven Communities: Differentiated and Hierarchical Citizenship in Kosovo, *Ethnopolitics* 14(2) (2015), pp. 197–217.

Krishna, Sankaran, 'The Importance of Being Ironic: A Postcolonial View on Critical International Relations Theory', *Alternatives* 18(3) (1993), pp. 385–417.

Kumar, Ramesh, 'Corruption and Transparency in Governance and Development: Reinventing Sovereignty for Promoting Good Governance' in T. Jacobsen, C. Sampford and R. Thakur (eds), *Re-envisioning Sovereignty: The End of Westphalia?* (Aldershot: Ashgate, 2008), pp. 251–265.

Kymlicka, Will, *Politics in the Vernacular: Nationalism, Multiculturalism, and Citizenship* (Oxford: Oxford University Press, 2001).

Kymlicka, Will, 'The Internationalization of Minority Rights' in S. Choudhry (ed), *Constitutional Design for Divided Societies. Integration of Accommodation?* (Oxford: Oxford University Press, 2008), pp. 111–140.

Lake, David, 'The New Sovereignty in International Relations', *International Studies Review* 5(1) (2003), pp. 303–323.

Lederach, John P., *Building Peace: Sustainable Reconciliation in Divided Societies* (Washington, DC: United States Institute of Peace, 1997).

Levy, Jack S., 'International Sources of Interstate and Intrastate War' in Crocker et al. (eds), *Leashing the Dogs of War: Conflict Management in a Divided World* (Washington, DC: United States Institute of Peace Press, 2007), pp. 17–39.

Lijphart, Arendt, 'Consociational Democracy', *World Politics* 21(2) (1969), pp. 207–225.

Lijphart, Arendt, *Democracy in Plural Societies: A Comparative Exploration* (New Haven, CT: Yale University Press, 1977).

Lijphart, Arendt, 'The Alternative Vote: A Realistic Alternative for South Africa?', *Politikon* 18(2) (1991), pp. 9–101.

Lijphart, Arendt, 'The Wave of Power-sharing Democracy' in A. Reynolds (ed), *The Architecture of Democracy: Constitutional Design, Conflict Management and Democracy* (Oxford: Oxford University Press, 2002), pp. 37–54.

Lijphart, Arendt, 'Constitutional Design for Divided Societies', *Journal of Democracy* 15(2) (2004), pp. 96–109.

Lijphart, Arendt, *Thinking about Democracy: Power Sharing and Majority Rule in Theory and Practice* (London: Routledge, 2008).

Linz, Juan J. and Stepan, Alfred, *Problems of Democratic Transition and Consolidation: Southern Europe, South America, and Post-communist Europe* (Baltimore: Johns Hopkins University Press, 1996).

Loew, David, 'Decentralization as a Model of Conflict Transformation: The Case of Kosovo', *CCS Working Papers*, No. 16 (Marburg, 2013).

Lustick, Ian S., 'Lijphart, Lakatos, and Consociationalism', *World Politics* 50(1) (1997), pp. 88–117.

Mac Ginty, Roger, 'Hybrid Peace: The Interaction between Top-down and Bottom-up Peace', *Security Dialogue* 41(4) (2010), pp. 391–412.

Malcolm, Noel, *Kosovo: A Short History*, 2nd ed. (London: Pan, 2002).

Mandaci, Nazif, 'The Turks of Kosovo and the Protection of Minority Culture at the Local Level', *Perceptions* 9(2) (2004), pp. 59–74.

Manning, Carrie, 'Local Level Challenges to Post-conflict Peacebuilding', *International Peacekeeping* 10(3) (2003), pp. 25–43.

Mansfield, Edward D. and Snyder, Jack, 'Democratization and the Danger of War', *International Security* 20(1) (1995), pp. 5–38.

Mansfield, Nicolas, *Creating a Constitutional Court: Lessons From Kosovo* (East–West Management Institute, 2013).

Marushiakova, Elena and Popov, Vesselin, 'New Ethnic Identities in the Balkans: The Case of the Egyptians', *Philosophy and Sociology* 2(8) (2001), pp. 465–477.

Matveeva, Anna and Paes, Wolf-Christian, 'The Kosovo Serbs. An Ethnic Minority between Collaboration and Defiance', Bonn International Center for Conversion, Friedrich Naumann Foundation and Saferworld, June 2003.

Mazrui, Ali A., 'The Blood of Experience: The Failed State and Political Collapse in Africa', *World Policy Journal* 12(1) (1995), pp. 28–34.

McCulloch, Allison, *Power-sharing and Political Stability in Deeply Divided Societies* (New York: Routledge, 2014).

McGarry, John and O'Leary, Brendan, 'Introduction' in J. McGarry and B. O'Leary (eds), *The Politics of Ethnic Conflict Regulation: Case Studies of Protracted Ethnic Conflicts* (New York: Routledge, 1993), pp. 1–41.

McGarry, John and O'Leary, Brendan, 'Federation as a Method of Ethnic Conflict Regulation' in S. Noel (ed), *From Power-sharing to Democracy: Post Conflict Institutions in Ethnically Divided Societies* (Montreal: McGill Queens University Press, 2005), pp. 263–296.

McGarry, John, O'Leary, Brendan and Simeon, Richard, 'Integration of Accommodation? The Enduring Debate in Conflict Regulation' in S. Choudhry (ed), *Constitutional Design for Divided Societies. Integration of Accommodation?* (Oxford: Oxford University Press, 2008), pp. 41–90.

Migdal, Joseph S., *State in Society. Studying How States and Societies Transform and Constitute One Another* (Cambridge: Cambridge University Press, 2001).

Milliken, Jennifer and Krause, Keith, 'State Failure, State Collapse, and State Reconstruction: Concepts, Lessons and Strategies', *Development and Change* 33(5) (2002), pp. 753–774.

Ministry for Community and Return website. Available at http://mzp-rks.org/en/mission-and-vision.html (accessed 1 September 2018).

Ministry of Local Government Administration (MLGA), *Progress Report on Implementation of Decentralization in the Republic of Kosovo* (Pristina: MLGA, 2012).

Mitchell, Paul, Evans, Geoffrey and O'Leary, Brendan, 'Extremist Outbidding in Ethnic Party Systems Is Not Inevitable: Tribune Parties in Northern Ireland', *Political Studies* 57(2) (2009), pp. 397–421.

Mitchell, Timothy, 'The Limits of the State: Beyond Statist Approaches and Their Critics', *American Political Science Review* 85(1) (1991), pp. 77–94.

MRGI website, 'Minorities and Indigenous Peoples in Kosovo'- Bosniaks, March 2018. Available at https://minorityrights.org/minorities/bosniaks-5/ (accessed 1 September 2018).

National Democratic Institute (NDI), 'Kosovo's June 2017 Parliamentary Elections', 12 July 2017.

NATO, 'NATO's Role in Kosovo'. 2018 Available at https://www.nato.int/cps/en/natolive/topics_48818.htm (accessed 1 September 2018).

New Social Initiative (NSI), *Report on Local Elections 2017* (NSI, June 2018).

The Norwegian Helsinki Committee (NHC), 'Second-class Minorities: The Continued Marginalization of RAE Communities in Kosovo' (NHC, 2007).

O'Halloran, Patrick J., 'Post-conflict Reconstruction: Bosnia and Kosovo' in S. Noel (ed), *From Power-sharing to Democracy: Post Conflict Institutions in Ethnically Divided Societies* (Montreal: McGill Queens University Press, 2005), pp. 104–119.

Office for Community Affairs (OCA), 'Policy Study No.1: Employment of Members of Non-majority Communities within Kosovo Civil Service and Publicly Owned Enterprises', 2010.

Office for Community Affairs website. Available at http://kryeministri-ks.net/zyra-e-kryeministrit/zyrat/zyra-per-ceshtje-te-komuniteteve (accessed 1 September 2018).

Organization for Security and Co-operation in Europe (OSCE), 'The Political Entity Brochure', October 2004. Available at www.osce.org/kosovo/38329 (accessed 1 September 2018).

Organization for Security and Co-operation in Europe (OSCE), 2007 Election Results. Available at http://www.osce.org/kosovo/38257 (accessed 1 September 2018).

Organization for Security and Co-operation in Europe (OSCE), *From Pilot Municipal Units to Fully Fledged Municipalities: First Year Review* (OSCE, March 2010).

Organization for Security and Co-operation in Europe (OSCE), *Protection and Promotion of the Rights of Communities in Kosovo: Local Level Participation Mechanisms* (OSCE, December 2010).

Organization for Security and Co-operation in Europe (OSCE), *2010 Kosovo Communities Profiles* (Pristina: OSCE, February 2011).

Organization for Security and Co-operation in Europe (OSCE), 'Implementation of the Action Plan on the Strategy for the Integration of the Roma, Ashkali and Egyptian Communities in Kosovo', 2011.

Organization for Security and Co-operation in Europe (OSCE), *The Kosovo Croats of Viti/Vitina Municipality: A. Vulnerable Community* (OSCE, October 2011).

Organization for Security and Co-operation in Europe (OSCE), 'Community Rights Assessment Report on Kosovo', July 2012.

Organization for Security and Co-operation in Europe (OSCE), 'Municipal Profiles', September 2015. Available at https://www.osce.org/kosovo/66047 (accessed 1 September 2018).

Paddison, Ronan, *The Fragmented State: The Political Geography of Power* (Oxford: Basil Blackwell, 1985).

Paris, Roland, 'Peacebuilding and the Limits of Liberal Internationalism', *Post-Communist* 22(2) (1997), pp. 54–89.

Paris, Roland, *At War's End: Building Peace after Civil Conflict* (Cambridge: Cambridge University Press, 2004).

Paris, Roland, 'Understanding the "Co-ordination Problem" in Post-war Statebuilding', Draft paper for the *Research Partnership on Postwar Statebuilding* (RPPS) (2006).

Parson, Talcott, *The Social System* (London: Routledge & Kegan Paul, 1951).

Perritt, Henry H., *The Road to Independence for Kosovo: A Chronicle of the Ahtisaari Plan* (Cambridge: Cambridge University Press, 2009).

Pildes, Richard H., 'Ethnic Identity and Democratic Institutions: A Dynamic Perspective' in S. Choudhry (ed), *Constitutional Design for Divided Societies. Integration of Accommodation?* (Oxford: Oxford University Press, 2008), pp. 173–204.

Pond, Elizabeth, 'The EU's Test in Kosovo', *The Washington Quarterly* 31(4) (2008), pp. 97–112.

Ponzio, Richard J., *Democratic Peacebuilding: Aiding Afghanistan* (Oxford: Oxford University Press, 2011).

Rabushka, Alvin and Shepsle, Kenneth A., *Politics in Plural Societies: A Theory of Democratic Instability* (Columbus, OH: Charles E. Merrill, 1972).

Rejai, Mostafa and Enloe, Cynthia H., 'Nation-states and State-nations', *International Studies Quarterly* 13(2) (1969), pp. 140–158.

Richmond, Oliver, 'Resistance and the Post-liberal Peace', *Millennium: Journal of International Studies* 38(3) (2010), pp. 665–692.

Richmond, Oliver P. and Franks, Jason, *Liberal Peace Transitions: Between Statebuilding and Peacebuilding* (Edinburgh: Edinburgh University Press, 2009).

Roberts, David, *Liberal Peacebuilding and Global Governance: Beyond the Metropolis* (London: Routledge, 2011).

Roberts, David, 'Saving Liberal Peacebuilding from Itself', *Peace Review: A Journal of Social Justice* 24(3) (2012), pp. 366–373.

Rodriguez-Rose, Andrés and Gill, Nicholas, 'The Global Trend towards Devolution and Its Implications', *Environment and Planning C: Government and Policy* 21(3) (2003), pp. 333–351.

Roepstorff, Kristina, *The Politics of Self-determination: Beyond the Decolonisation Process* (Abingdon: Routledge, 2013).

Rotberg, Robert I., 'The Failure and Collapse of Nation-states: Breakdown, Prevention and Repair' in R. I. Rotberg (ed), *When States Fail: Causes and Consequences* (Princeton, NJ: Princeton University Press, 2004), pp. 1–45.

Rotberg, Robert I., 'The Challenge of Weak, Failing, and Collapsed States' in Crocker et al. (eds), *Leashing the Dogs of War: Conflict Management in a Divided World* (Washington, DC: United States Institute of Peace Press, 2007), pp. 83–94.

Rothchild, Donald, *Sustainable Peace: Power and Democracy after Civil Wars* (New York: Cornell University Press, 2005).

Russet, Bruce, 'The Fact of Democratic Peace' in M. Brown et al. (eds), *Debating the Democratic Peace* (Cambridge, MA: MIT Press, 1996), pp. 58–81.

Sahún, M.L. Arastey and Vallejo, Pilar R., 'The Legal Construction of the Social Security System of the Republic of Kosovo', *International Social Security Review* 62(1) (2009), pp. 65–89.
Savic, Misha, 'EU Urged to Back Serbia and Kosovo as They Mull Border Change', *Bloomberg*, 26 August 2018.
Selway, Joel S. and Templeman, Kharis, 'The Myth of Consociationalism? Conflict Reduction in Divided Societies', *Comparative Political Studies* 45(12) (2012), pp. 1542–1571.
Shinoda, Hideaki, *Re-examining Sovereignty: From Classical Theory to the Global Age* (Houndmills: Macmillan Press, 2000).
Shoup, Brian, *Conflict and Cooperation in Multi-ethnic States: Institutional Incentives, Myths, and Counterbalancing* (Oxon: Routledge, 2008).
Smooha, Sammy, 'The Model of Ethnic Democracy: Israel as a Jewish and Democratic State', *Nations and Nationalism* 8(4) (2002), pp. 475–503.
Smooha, Sammy, 'Types of Democracy and Modes of Conflict Management in Ethnically Divided Societies', *Nations and Nationalism* 8(4) (2002), pp. 423–431.
Snyder, Jack, *From Voting to Violence: Democratization and Nationalist Conflict* (London: W. W. Norton, 2000).
Spiecker, Ben and Steutel, Jan, 'Multiculturalism, Pillarization and Liberal Civic Education in the Netherlands', *International Journal of Educational Research* 35(3) (2001), pp. 293–304.
Stevens, Georgina, 'Filling the Vacuum: Ensuring Protection and Legal Remedies for Minorities in Kosovo', Minority Rights Group International (MRG), 15 April 2009.
Surroi, Veton, 'The Unfinished State(s) in the Balkans and the EU: The Next Wave' in J. Rupnik (ed), *The Western Balkans and the EU: 'The Hour of Europe'*, Chaillot Papers (Paris: Institute for Security Studies, 2011), pp. 111–120.
Tahiri, Besnik, *Decentralization a Heavy Weight to Be Carried Out* (Pristina: Friedrich-Ebert-Stiftung, July 2011).
TANJUG, 'Serb List Won't Join Cabinet with Self-determination', *B92 News*, 17 September 2014.
Tansey, 'Oisın, Democratization without a State: Democratic Regime-building in Kosovo', *Democratization* 14(1) (2007), pp. 129–150.
Tërnava, Granit, *Local Elections in Kosovo Final Results* (Pristina: Konrad-Adenauer-Stiftung Policy Brief, 2014).
Tilly, Charles, 'State Formation as Organized Crime' in P. Evans, D. Rueschemeyer and T. Skocpol (eds), *Bringing the State Back In* (Cambridge: Cambridge University Press, 1985), pp. 169–191.
Tranchant, Jean-Pierre, 'Decentralization and Ethnic Conflict: The Role of Empowerment' (HAL, 2011).
Trutz von Trotha, 'The "Andersen Principle": On the Difficulty of Truly Moving Beyond State-centrism' in M. Fischer and B. Schmelzle (eds), *Building Peace in the Absence of States: Challenging the Discourse on State Failure* (Berlin: Berghof Research Centre 2009), pp. 37–46.

Tweedie, Neil, 'Kosovo War: Thousands Killed as Serb Forces Tried to Keep Control of Province', *The Telegraph*, 31 March 2009.
United Nations (UN), 'Building Capacities for Public Service in Post-conflict Countries', United Nations Department of Economic and Social Affairs, 2007.
United Nations (UN), 'Lessons Learned in Post-conflict State Capacity: Reconstructing Governance and Public Administration Capacities in Post Conflict Countries', United Nations Department of Economic and Social Affairs, 2007.
United Nations (UN), 'Lessons Learned in Post-conflict State Capacity: Reconstructing Governance and Public Administration Capacities in Post Conflict Countries', United Nations Department of Economic and Social Affairs, 2009.
United Nations (UN), 'United Nations Policy for Post-conflict Employment Creation, Income Generation and Reintegration', 2009.
UNMIK/European Union Pillar, *European Union Pillar: The 10 Key Achievements. End of Mission Report (1999–2008)* (Pristina: EU Pillar IV, 2008).
Visoka, Gëzim, *Acting Like a State Kosovo and the Everyday Making of Statehood* (Oxon: Routledge, 2018).
Visoka, Gëzim and Beha, Adem, 'Minority Consultative Bodies in Kosovo: A Quest for Effective Emancipation or Elusive Participation?', *Journal on Ethnopolitics and Minority Issues in Europe* 10(1) (2011), pp. 1–30.
Von Einsiedel, Sebastian, 'Policy Responses to State Failure' in S. Chesterman et al. (eds), *Making States Work* (Tokyo: United Nations University Press, 2005), pp. 13–35.
Vujacic, Ilija G., 'The Challenges of Ethnic Federalism: Experiences and Lessons of the Former Yugoslavia' in J. Rose and J. Ch. Traut (eds), *Federalism and Decentralization. Perspectives for the Transformation Process in Eastern and Central Europe* (Basingstoke: Palgrave Macmillan, 2002), pp. 259–270.
Walsh, Dawn, *Territorial Self-government as a Conflict Management Tool* (Basingstoke: Palgrave Macmillan, 2018).
Weber, Max, 'Politics as a Vocation' in H. H.Gerth and C. W. Mills (eds), *From Max Weber: Essays in Sociology* (London: Routledge & Kegan Paul, 1948), pp. 77–128.
Weller, Marc, *Contested Statehood: Kosovo's Struggle for Independence* (Oxford: Oxford University Press, 2009).
White, Stacey, *Government Decentralization in the 21st Century* (Washington: Centre for Strategic and International Studies, December 2011).
Wilmer, Franke, 'Minority Rights and Charles Tilly's "Stateness"', *Constitutionalism Web-papers*, ConWEB No. 3 (2006).
Woodward, Susan L., 'Is Democracy Possible in the Balkans? On Preconditions and Conditions in Bosnia, Kosovo, and Serbia', *Working Paper Series* (National Council for Eurasian and East European Research: Washington, DC, and Seattle, WA, 2007).
World Bank, 'Kosovo's Energy Crisis', World Bank Publications, 1 February 2012.
Zaum, Dominik, *The Sovereignty Paradox: The Norms and Politics of International Statebuilding* (Oxford: Oxford University Press, 2007).

Index

accommodation 4, 12, 16, 18, 19, 22, 30–3, 35, 40, 47, 49, 61, 66, 74, 76, 85, 97, 99, 147, 150, 154–5, 190, 192, 199, 203
accommodationist 20, 30, 47, 53, 62
Ahtisaari Plan 64, 66–7, 83, 149, 153–4, 157, 159, 216, 219, 236, 243
Albanians 4, 16, 60, 66, 68, 70–1, 76, 78, 93, 99–100, 108, 113–15, 116, 118, 122, 124, 125–7, 128, 164, 171, 174, 177, 181–2, 194, 196, 199, 217
assimilation 30, 33, 37, 41, 43, 113, 127, 156, 193, 201, 203
authority 6, 8, 10, 26, 28, 30, 32–6, 39, 46, 49, 59, 68, 70, 73, 85, 93, 101, 116, 120, 123, 126, 149, 153, 155, 157–9, 167, 178, 190, 194, 197, 199, 208, 211
autonomy 8, 13, 43–5, 47, 51, 53, 58–60, 70, 81, 149, 151, 153, 157, 160, 163

borders 30–5, 37, 43, 58, 73, 155, 161, 165, 171, 194
Bosnia and Herzegovina 2, 12, 41, 59, 62, 70, 71, 113, 117, 120, 201, 207, 210, 213, 215, 239, 242, 248
Bosnia-Herzegovina 2, 12, 62, 201

Catholic Slavs 143
centripetalism 53, 62
citizenship 10, 37, 39, 45, 98, 120, 236
civic 6, 16, 18, 30, 32, 35, 37, 39, 43, 66, 76, 115, 129, 191, 193, 195, 203–4
civic identity 6, 16, 35, 39, 43, 203
civil society 46, 63, 133
coexistence 32, 58, 153, 158
collective rights 32, 39, 63, 97, 114
Conflict management 39
consociational 30, 35, 37, 46–9, 51, 53–5, 58, 60, 62, 91, 97, 100, 107, 112–14, 155, 199
consociationalism 41, 49, 62
  grand coalition 51, 53, 81
  mutual veto 51, 53
  proportionality 35, 51–3
  segmental autonomy 51, 55, 81, 100, 120
constituent peoples 6, 10, 12, 30, 39, 62, 66
Constitution (of Kosovo) 70, 76, 78, 81–3, 87, 89, 91–5, 97, 103, 109, 114–18, 124, 147, 158, 184, 211–15, 228–9, 235
consultative bodies 81, 92, 108, 114, 153, 199
culture 31, 33, 35, 44–5, 48–9, 60, 83, 119, 124, 126, 131, 139, 158, 166, 175
Cyprus 62, 70

Dayton 71, 72
de facto 19, 26, 66, 68, 70, 76, 97, 116, 126, 151, 155, 190, 195, 201, 203
de jure 19, 22, 26, 61, 68, 76, 97, 115, 149, 155, 181, 190, 196, 201
decentralization
  ethnic decentralization 155, 157, 158
  territorial decentralization 155, 157, 165
decision-making 45, 49, 52, 64, 66, 81, 92, 101, 153, 161, 178, 191
democracy 2, 5, 8, 10, 32–5, 37–9, 47, 49, 51, 55, 62, 83, 89, 97, 126, 149, 153, 196
  centrifugal democracy 47
  centripetal democracy 47
democratization 4, 8, 10, 12, 37, 39, 42, 44, 46, 72, 74, 126, 128, 147, 157
demos 10, 33
devolution 47, 58, 153, 200
discrimination 7, 40, 60, 76, 83, 87, 89, 98, 118, 135, 137, 143, 167, 211

Index

diversity 2, 6, 8, 16, 18, 21, 26, 30–3, 35, 39, 49, 58, 60, 62, 66, 68, 76, 99, 101, 145, 148, 151, 155, 158, 160, 163, 167, 171, 173, 175, 178, 181, 184, 188, 190, 197, 201, 203, 209, 228, 240–1
dominant nation 10, 39

ECLO 74
education 45, 83, 85, 91, 114, 116, 120, 124, 126, 129, 131, 135, 137, 139, 141, 143, 148, 155, 157, 158, 161, 167, 172, 174, 178, 181, 196, 197, 199, 215, 226, 241
elections 39, 41–2, 55, 57, 68, 73, 89, 91, 101, 103, 105, 107, 109, 111, 115–18, 126, 128, 133, 139, 142, 143, 151, 164, 169, 171–5, 177–9, 182, 184, 194, 213, 215, 219, 228, 243
electoral system 36, 48, 51, 55, 57–8, 63, 81, 117
enclave 60–1, 105, 120–1, 151, 174, 177
endogenous 12, 18, 46, 64, 72, 74, 124, 195, 197, 202–3
equality 2, 8, 32, 33, 35, 37, 39, 53, 83, 89, 211–12
ethnic cleansing 33
ethnic majority 16
ethnic outbidding 105
ethnic politics 42, 157, 177, 192, 199
EU 2, 5, 41, 44, 46, 56–9, 64, 66, 68, 70, 72, 74, 171, 206, 211, 215, 217, 219, 224, 226, 228, 236, 243–5
EULEX 5, 8, 74
Europeanization 5, 44
EUSR 74
executive level 87, 89
exogenous 12, 37, 44, 64, 72, 74, 197

failed state 73
federalism 45, 47, 57–60, 151
France 35, 71
functionalist 74

Germany 71
good governance 2, 48, 89, 147, 149, 151, 155, 158, 200

Greece 70
group differentiation 184, 192, 191
guaranteed seats 78, 82, 89, 103, 114–16, 128, 133, 137, 147

heterogeneous 49, 58, 60, 64, 151, 161, 164–5, 181
hierarchy 22, 28, 113
homogeneity 37
homogeneous 32, 58, 157, 161, 164
homogenization 30, 32, 35, 203
Horowitz, Donald 47, 53, 55, 57, 60, 62, 213, 218, 241
human rights 35, 41, 43, 45, 74, 56, 59, 62, 83, 89, 158, 169, 184, 199, 211
hybrid 12, 37, 63–4, 72, 203

identity 6, 9, 16, 18–19, 31–2, 35, 37, 39, 41, 43, 45, 62, 64, 76, 83, 85, 101, 113, 115, 120, 125–9, 131, 135, 139, 141, 143, 145, 153, 182, 188, 192, 195, 197, 199, 203, 212
  collective identity 31, 32
illiberal 12, 41, 46, 63
implementation 16–18, 22, 41, 49, 62, 64, 66, 89, 93, 97, 99, 114, 122, 135, 139, 145, 151, 153, 155, 157, 159, 161, 163, 172–3, 195, 197, 201
independence 2, 4, 18, 20–1, 23, 26, 35, 46, 61, 62, 64, 66, 68, 70, 72, 74, 76, 78, 93, 97–100, 101, 103, 109, 111, 116, 118, 120, 122, 127–8, 145, 147–9, 151, 153, 157, 160, 164, 173, 178, 190, 194–6, 205–6
institutionalist 46, 74
institution-building 12, 37, 44, 49, 62, 74, 153
integration 4, 6, 8, 16–19, 22, 26, 28, 30, 32, 33, 40–3, 53–5, 61–2, 66, 74, 76, 95, 97, 99–101, 105, 107–8, 110, 112–15, 119, 123, 129, 131, 145, 150, 151–5, 157, 163, 167, 190, 192–4, 196, 199–201, 203
integrationist 20, 30, 43, 47, 53, 199
integrative 30, 45, 47, 53–5, 57–8, 60, 62–4, 100, 155
interethnic 4, 47, 54, 58, 70, 122, 124, 157, 161, 192, 202

international administration 12
international community 4, 8, 12, 16, 21, 26, 35, 39, 41, 61, 62, 66, 71, 73, 92, 97, 99, 124, 126, 138, 152, 184
international law 4, 28, 62
international organizations 62, 93
international relations 12, 33, 66
intervention 4, 12, 33, 39, 44, 48, 72, 219
Italy 70, 71

judiciary 30, 72, 81, 87, 118

KFOR 60, 73
kin-state 196
KLA 42, 63, 68, 70-1
Kymlicka, Will 45, 213, 246

language 35, 44-5, 81-3, 85, 87, 91, 95, 99, 108, 114, 119-21, 127, 131, 135, 137, 141, 143, 145, 148, 157, 161, 182, 196, 197, 201, 215, 223
language rights 45, 83, 85, 122, 119, 141, 201
LDK 10, 71, 91, 103, 133, 171-2, 175, 177-9, 215, 227
legal 2, 4, 8, 13, 15-18, 20, 22, 23, 26, 37, 44, 57, 62, 64, 72, 74, 78, 81, 87, 95, 97, 101, 103, 105, 112, 114, 126, 145, 147, 149, 151, 153, 157, 160, 163, 165, 192, 195
legality 8, 73, 62
legitimacy 6, 8-9, 12-13, 20, 26, 28, 30, 32, 35, 39, 44, 49, 57, 66, 74, 101, 113-16, 126, 153, 157, 167, 172-3, 190, 192, 194, 197, 199
legitimate. *See* legitimacy
liberal 2, 4-6, 8, 10, 12, 16, 18-20, 23, 26, 28, 32-5, 37, 39, 41, 42, 44, 46, 49, 60, 62, 64, 66, 68, 74, 190, 197, 201, 207, 210, 240
liberal-democratic 4-6, 10, 12, 16, 18-20, 23
liberal interventionism 12, 33, 41, 197
liberal peace 38, 40, 41, 68
Lijphart, Arendt 35, 47, 49, 51, 53, 58, 62, 211-15, 247
linguistic 12, 16, 18, 34, 48, 51, 58, 64, 77-8, 85, 113, 120-1, 127, 141, 153, 158, 196

local level 22, 58-60, 63, 85, 101, 109, 117, 118, 124, 128, 133, 137, 139, 143-7, 149, 151, 153, 155-60, 162-165, 167, 169, 172, 182, 188, 191, 200-1
local ownership 12, 35, 44, 46, 59, 62, 66, 70, 75

Macedonia 62, 70, 120, 141, 143, 177, 201, 213, 239
majority group 16, 55, 62, 193
management of diversity 2, 8, 10, 20, 22, 24, 30, 37, 60, 76, 99, 147, 196-7, 201, 203
marginal groups 39
marginalization 18, 60, 114-15, 121, 127, 129, 133, 143, 190-2, 195
marginalized 16, 111-12
media 41, 82-3, 87, 98, 139, 213, 245
Migdal, Joel 30-1, 39, 206-9, 211, 238, 248
Milosevic, Slobodan 68, 71, 73
minority groups 2, 16, 22, 35, 43, 45, 81, 112, 157-8, 165, 191, 193, 195
minority parties 89, 91, 116-17, 139, 145
minority rights 6, 17, 20, 22, 34, 45, 47, 59, 75, 81, 89, 92-5, 97-9, 108, 110, 112, 114, 124, 147, 151, 153, 155, 182, 184, 190, 192-5, 198, 221
multicultural democracy 35, 37
multiculturalism 12, 37, 182
multiethnic 2, 6, 12, 16, 18-23, 26, 31, 39, 41, 45, 49, 53, 58, 60, 66, 72, 74-6, 81, 97, 99, 114, 118, 123, 145, 162, 165, 182, 184, 188, 190, 192, 195, 196, 199, 203
multinational 6, 8, 16, 49, 33
municipal level 85, 89, 103, 129, 133, 139, 149, 151, 161, 165

nation 2, 5-6, 10, 18, 30-3, 35, 37-9, 41, 63, 68, 70, 151, 191, 203, 205
　civic nation 32, 35
　ethnic nation 32
nation state 5-6, 10, 31-3, 35, 37, 203
national identity 16, 203
nationalism 10, 30, 32, 37, 66
NATO 4, 33, 60-3, 70, 72, 73, 215, 219, 248

non-majority communities 100–3, 116, 160, 165, 184
non-state actors 63
North Macedonia 2

OECD 74
official language 45, 83–5, 124, 161, 188, 191, 222
overrepresentation 52, 118, 147

parallel institutions 46, 68–9, 71, 98, 110–14, 123, 136, 141, 144, 149, 151, 157, 159, 161, 163, 167, 169, 171–3, 178, 193–6, 201, 223
peacebuilding 2, 4, 33, 39, 41–2, 60, 68, 81
peacekeeping 12, 39
plurality 16, 30, 41, 48–9, 62, 64, 197
political participation 8, 22, 32–3, 99, 109, 115, 188, 196
postcolonial 12, 32, 35, 37, 49, 63, 205
post-communist 10, 32–3, 37, 46, 49, 74, 97, 205
post-conflict 2, 4, 6, 8, 10, 12, 16, 18, 20, 26, 32, 37, 39, 41–3, 53, 60–2, 72, 74, 97, 100, 112–15, 124, 143, 147, 153–5, 157, 191–3, 197, 199, 202, 203, 205
poverty 98, 104, 105, 131, 135, 137, 144, 153, 201
power-sharing 4, 16, 20, 30, 35, 41, 45, 47, 49, 51, 53, 60, 62, 64, 81, 97, 107, 114, 147, 151, 155, 192, 199
public companies 85, 126, 127
public goods 46

quasi-states 35

Rambouillet 73
recognition 5, 6, 8, 33, 35, 37, 68, 70, 72, 74, 101, 119, 127, 129, 141, 144, 155, 159, 191, 195, 203, 205
reconciliation 4, 12, 16, 30, 54, 55, 60, 68, 74, 88, 122, 124, 147, 157, 153, 194, 198, 211
religion 35, 81, 83, 124
religious 2, 16, 30, 46, 48, 58–9, 64, 77–8, 87, 95, 116, 122, 131, 143, 153, 155, 158–9, 196, 212, 215

Rugova, Ibrahim 69, 71, 57
rule of law 2, 41, 48, 58, 64, 74, 76, 105
Russia 66, 68, 74, 206

secession 33, 37, 41, 49, 58, 100, 98
secure unity 10, 16, 39, 49, 100, 190, 203
security 6, 28, 39, 41–3, 48, 53, 56, 59, 63, 66, 70, 74, 122, 133, 137, 143, 148, 156
Security Council 66, 70–1, 72, 74
segregation 18, 22, 26, 43, 58, 114, 120, 147, 153, 157, 167, 190–3, 200–1
self-determination 4, 8, 31, 41, 43, 59, 155, 157, 165
self-government 35, 56, 59, 66, 70, 151, 153, 155, 157, 158, 163
separatism 47, 59, 60
Serbia 4, 62, 66, 68, 73, 81, 85, 99–100, 105, 107, 109–11, 114, 120, 122, 124–7, 131, 143, 148–9, 151, 157, 160, 165, 167, 171, 173, 175, 178–9, 194, 199, 209–11, 219, 223, 237, 243–4
Slavic Muslims 113, 141
Slovakia 70
social cohesion 8, 10, 35, 39, 43, 46, 66, 101, 105, 114, 127, 190, 197, 203–4
social division 8, 48, 115
sovereignty 6–7, 10, 13, 20, 26, 28, 30, 32–7, 39, 44, 62, 66, 72, 73, 78, 101, 208
  domestic sovereignty 5, 8, 12, 13, 35, 37, 46, 48, 99, 101, 190, 203
  legal sovereignty 13
  popular sovereignty 33
  sovereignty as control 36, 39
  sovereignty as responsibility 36, 39
Spain 6, 70
Stabilisation and Association Process 57, 68, 74
standards before status 12, 73, 62, 203
state failure 39, 48–9, 74, 197
state formation 2, 6, 10, 16, 18, 20, 24, 26, 28, 33, 35
state fragility 12
state weakness 39, 46, 47, 48, 74, 63, 197
statebuilding 2, 4, 6, 8, 10, 12, 16, 18, 20,

24, 26, 28, 30–5, 37–9, 41–4, 46,
49, 56–9, 62–3, 70, 72, 74, 101,
112–15, 128, 147, 151, 153, 158,
165, 193, 197–201, 203, 205, 210
state-centric 3, 74, 197, 205
statehood 5, 27, 35, 44, 46, 57, 62, 70, 72, 74, 203
stateness 9–10
state-society relationship 6, 12, 20, 192
status issue 59
substate 8
symbols 43, 45, 82, 184, 188, 215

territorial integrity 43, 60, 66
Thaçi, Hashim 68, 127
Turkey 117, 123, 182, 197

UK 4, 6, 71
UN 2, 9, 41, 56, 62, 64, 66–8, 70–1, 72, 73, 74, 100, 206, 225, 227, 229
unemployment 98, 105, 120, 123, 129, 135–7, 141, 153, 161, 171–3, 175, 191, 201

unfinished state 73
unintended consequences 3, 16, 18, 23, 26, 49, 165, 190, 192–3, 197, 199, 201
United States 9, 35, 37, 43, 64, 66, 68, 209–10, 241, 247
UNMIK 4, 9, 16, 56–9, 62–3, 66, 70, 72, 89, 101, 124–5, 151, 213, 217, 225

veto rights 81
violence 10, 30–1, 35, 37, 42, 49, 60, 67, 71–3, 212
   2004 riots 59

Weber, Max 28, 30–1, 73–5, 208
Western Balkans 24, 33, 57, 207, 215, 219, 226, 240, 245

Yugoslavia 10, 41, 70–1, 78, 81, 119, 124, 127, 147–8, 151, 213, 236, 239